THE CHALET GIRLS GROW UP

BY THE SAME AUTHOR

Preface to Hardy
Women in the English Novel, 1800-1900
Margaret Oliphant: A Critical Biography
Six Women Novelists
Selected Poems of Federico Garcia Lorca (translations)
Wilfred Owen
Clare and Effie (for children)
The Sun's Yellow Eye (poems)
The Latin Master's Story (poems)
Jane Austen's *The Watsons* (completed)

THE CHALET GIRLS GROW UP

a sequel to the Chalet School series

Merryn Williams

Plas Gwyn Books

For Diana, who wrote the best bit

Plas Gwyn Books
c/o 19 The Paddox,
Oxford OX2 7PN

copyright © Merryn Williams 1998
revised edition 2005

ISBN 0 9533952 0 0

All rights reserved. No part of this publication may be reproduced, stored in a retrieval system, or transmitted at any time or by any means electronic, mechanical, photocopying, recording or otherwise, without the prior permission of the publisher.

Cover illustration by Liz Silk.

British Library Cataloguing-in-Publication Data
A catalogue record for this book is available from the British Library.

CONTENTS

PROLOGUE, *January 1990.*   7

THE NINETEEN SIXTIES

1 Miss Annersley Receives an Old Girl   9
2 Len   14
3 Con   22
4 Betty Comes Up Trumps   29
5 Enter Mary-Lou   36
6 Felicity's Wedding   42
7 Roger Richardson to the Rescue   53
8 Con Falls in Love   60
9 The Third Generation   68
10 Margot   76

THE NINETEEN SEVENTIES

11 Crisis for the Chalet School   85
12 Sybil Pulls the Plug   92
13 Jack Maynard Has Enough   97
14 Con Contemplates Alternatives   107
15 Plas Gwyn   114
16 Exile   121
17 A Day in the Life of a Single Mother   128
18 Disaster Unlimited   139
19 Out of Africa   151
20 Con in Crisis   161
21 The Triplets are Reunited   167
22 A Wedding at the End of an Era   174

THE NINETEEN EIGHTIES

23 Into the Eighties	184
24 Margot goes to Greenham	191
25 Re-enter Mary-Lou	199
26 Sisters Keeping Secrets	205
27 Maggs	213
28 The Fourth Generation	221
29 The Nun's Story	227
30 Frances	237
31 Summer of '87	246
32 Con Steps Sideways	255
33 Johnno	262
34 'They shall mount up with wings like eagles'	269
35 The Triplets' Fiftieth Birthday	276

EPILOGUE, *January - March 1990.*

36 New Year's Day	287
37 Miss Annersley Turns Ninety	291
38 'Like Hearing the Grass Grow and the Squirrel's Heart Beat'	297

AUTHOR'S NOTE

Elinor M. Brent-Dyer was notoriously vague about dates. However, it is clear that the Maynard triplets were born on 5th November 1939, in Guernsey shortly before the Nazis invaded. So I have made them leave school in summer 1958 and age at the normal rate thereafter.

PROLOGUE

January 1990

The three women got off the train at Lauterbrunnen and asked Axel, the cab driver, for the Chalet Hotel. He swung their luggage into the boot and began to drive up the new fast road to the Gornetz Platz. As they climbed, they saw some magnificent views. The great Alps, not more than twenty miles away, the pine forests, the white slopes gleaming brilliantly in the winter sun, all much as they would have looked to the tired eyes of TB patients, at the beginning of the century.

They were sisters, that was clear, and, he thought, English - they were talking quietly in that language, although when they spoke to him it was in good German. He couldn't tell whether any of them were married because all wore thick gloves. Still, when women of that age were travelling together, it usually meant that they were without a man.

The red-haired lady in the shabby green coat was the one he liked best; she reminded him of his Mum, in fact. She asked him whether he'd lived here all his life and how he liked his job. Axel told her he often brought tourists here for the skiing. The middle sister was dark, very nice-looking and dressed with unobtrusive good taste. He'd noticed when he picked up her case that it was real leather, with a famous brand-name.

And the third - well, Axel thought she was weird. Her hair, which might once have been reddish-gold, was cropped short and she had made not the slightest effort to look attractive; she wore jeans and an old anorak with two badges he couldn't decipher. She stared out of the window, taking little part in the conversation.

'Are you ladies sisters?' he asked when they were about halfway there.

'Not just sisters', the red-haired lady smiled, 'we're triplets. I'm sure you haven't met any triplets before'.

Axel was impressed. He had thought the dark one years younger than the other two, but that would be expensive clothes and beauty treatments, no doubt.

'We used to be at school on the Gornetz Platz - oh, about a hundred years ago. Our father was the head of a big TB sanatorium; that was closed, probably before you were born'.

'TB, yes, it is all over', Axel agreed.

'Not in the Third World', the third sister said.

They stopped outside the Chalet Hotel, a seven-storey glass and concrete monster, and the dark lady paid the fare. He noticed that they didn't go in straight away but stood outside the front door staring at the splendid panorama of mountains; he could have sworn that they all seemed a little upset.

'It's funny', Margot said in a shaky voice, 'but I sort of thought that the hotel itself was the old Chalet School'.

Helena was waving to the driver. Her smile faded as she said, 'No, I've seen the brochure, I knew it was only a name. But I somehow didn't expect that the school and Freudesheim would have been - just swept away'.

They stared across the snow, which was dotted with brightly-clothed skiers. On the slope, two hundred yards away, was a pleasant modern block of flats. Little evergreens in pots grew outside.

'It *is* a shock', Con said. 'Still, what did you expect? You two are sentimental'.

'There was a lot of emotion tied up in that place'.

They went on staring, feeling the cold breeze sting their cheeks.

'How long is it since we left?' asked Helena. 'The summer of 1958 - oh, heavens above, thirty-one years ago!'

'And we were going to send our daughters here, and the Chalet School was going to go on for ever. I remember it as if it was yesterday', said Con. 'You were handing over to the next head girl - everyone said she wasn't a patch on you - and you'd just got engaged. You and I were going to Oxford, and Margot to Edinburgh, and Mother thought that at least two of us were settled for life. Do you remember?'

THE NINETEEN SIXTIES

Chapter 1

Miss Annersley Receives an Old Girl

Miss Annersley, headmistress of the Chalet School for the last thirty years, looked up from her desk and out of the study window at the impressive mountains with their peaks still white with snow. It was July, 1966, and beginning to feel very hot at eleven a.m. This weekend, the last long break of the summer term, most of the girls would be going off somewhere, and she would try to get a good walk above Lake Thun with her friend Nell Wilson and photograph some of the rarer mountain flowers. But on Monday morning she would be back at her desk, energetic as always. She loved her job, could think of nothing more worthwhile than encouraging each girl to make her contribution and stretch her talents to the full.

In the courtyard she could see Miss Wilmot, the deputy head, and her great friend Miss Ferrars, getting into their little car to spend the weekend in Berne. There were rumours about those two but the headmistress did not believe them. Born at the turn of the century, she had been a young girl when the Great War ended and slowly realised, as she grew up, that most of the men she might have married had been killed in that terrible bloodletting. Her own headmistress had been a suffragette and worn a small badge to show she had been forcibly fed. Miss Annersley had always known that women who did not have a private income had to choose between marriage and a career, and for many, like herself, there had been no choice at all. She had sometimes thought, years ago, that she would have liked to marry, but she also believed that a woman was a poor creature if she could not manage on her own.

Rosalie, her secretary, put her head round the door.

'Mrs Sheppard's outside, Hilda, with her little boy. Can you see her?'

'Grizel?' Miss Annersley roused herself from her

abstraction. 'Yes, of course send her in'.

Grizel Cochrane had been one of the Chalet School's very first pupils when it opened in the Austrian Tyrol, half a lifetime ago. Later she had returned to teach music and more recently, at the age of forty, had married Dr Neil Sheppard who worked at the sanatorium. They had all rejoiced at her wedding and at the birth of her only child. Yet the Head had long thought that she wasn't really the best type of Chalet girl. That was one woman who had eaten her heart out during her years as a spinster and who, when she finally got her wish, had made it obvious that she felt superior to Miss Annersley herself and the other unmarried teachers. So she prepared to greet her more warmly than she felt.

'Grizel!' She rose smilingly as a little sharp-faced woman came in, followed by a cross-looking small boy. 'How good to see you, my dear. Rosalie, fetch us some *Kaffee*, please, and a glass of mineral water for the child. I've got Advanced Latin with the Sixth in half an hour, but we can have a good talk first. What's your news?'

Grizel threw herself into the best chair and mopped her forehead. The child fidgeted, but he knew better than to misbehave in front of his Aunt Hilda and contented himself with wolfing his biscuit.

'Gosh, it's hot! You're so full of energy, Hilda. Going climbing this weekend, are you? I don't know how you do it, at your age'.

'I'm sixty-six', Miss Annersley said briskly. 'That's not particularly old, and I've never been in the habit of coddling myself. I did think about retiring this year. Nancy Wilmot will be an excellent Head when it's her turn. But, as you know, it wasn't the right time to make changes'.

'No, of course not'.

They were both silent, thinking of the tragedy three months earlier. Lady Russell, who had founded the first Chalet School before the war, had died, still only in her fifties, under anaesthetic after what was supposed to be a routine operation. Her husband and family had been devastated and the school was only just getting over the shock. It had not been the right time.

'And that reminds me', Grizel said, after Rosalie had brought them coffee in attractive blue and white cups and then gone away again, 'I've been meaning to talk to you about Jo. Don't you think there's been something - well, distinctly *peculiar* about her, since Madge died?'

Miss Annersley sat up very straight. She was not sure that she liked this way of referring to Jo Maynard, Lady Russell's sister and the Chalet School's most famous ex-pupil.

'My dear girl, she was naturally deeply upset -'

'Oh, I know', Grizel cut in, 'but it's more than that. Jo's always been a bit mad, of course' - Miss Annersley winced - 'but as long as her sister was alive, it was kept in check. Now she seems to have gone back to behaving like a teenager, which is all very well if you *are* a teenager but absurd for a middle-aged person. Don't you think, Hilda, that a woman in her forties, with an enormous family, really ought to have stopped hanging around her old school? She's up here morning, noon and night, scrounging *Kaffee und Kuchen* from the staff and having long heart-to-hearts with the prefects about their petty little problems. Don't tell me that it isn't happening. You know it is'.

Miss Annersley was speechless. She naturally felt offended that Grizel should refer to her beloved school in this offhand way, but the fact was that she too had sometimes thought Jo Maynard was behaving strangely. The school liked to keep in touch with its old girls, of course. Often they would send a Christmas card or pass on news of an engagement or marriage, but for most of them, when they left, that was it. Jo was the only one who had never lost touch, who had always insisted on living round the corner, who often said, with peals of laughter, that she would still be a Chalet girl when she was a great-grandmother of ninety.

'She still has two daughters at the school', she said defensively. 'Cecil and little Philippa'.

'It's more than that', Grizel repeated. 'Neil says that Jack Maynard's going around looking hunted. That poor man frequently comes home to find his house in a mess, no supper and Jo lounging about with a bunch of schoolgirls, all shrieking their heads off about the latest scandals in the Upper Fourth! I can't understand any woman treating her husband like that, and he's such a nice man. Or else she's forgotten all about him because she's writing one of her silly novels - I don't know why they get published at all. Neil says -'

'Grizel', Miss Annersley said sternly, 'I can't hear any more of this. I wouldn't wish to hurry you, but the Upper Sixth -'.

'And another thing', Grizel said, taking not the slightest notice. 'I'm worried about Len, too'.

This made the headmistress pause, as she was in the act of rising. Jo had married Dr Jack Maynard just after they had all escaped from Austria in 1938. And she had given birth to triplets, the first Miss Annersley had ever seen, in Guernsey two months after the declaration of war. Nobody who had been there at the time would ever forget those three tiny babies, a symbol of new life among so much destruction. Helena, Constance, Margaret. She'd watched those girls grow up, known them intimately till they left home and was almost as fond of them as if they'd been the daughters she had never had. They were twenty-six now, and all doing well. Con was based in London, working for a women's magazine - not married yet but it was bound to happen soon, as she was a very pretty girl. And Margot, one of the most difficult girls ever to pass through the school, had taken them all by surprise when she announced that she meant to be a medical missionary, working among the poorest people in the Third World. She was a qualified doctor now, had joined the Order of Blue Nuns and was in South Africa. Her parents and the school were all very proud of Margot.

But it was Len, the firstborn, who was secretly Miss Annersley's favourite. A friendly, affectionate, straightforward girl, always ready to help with the younger pupils, she had been one of the most popular Head Girls they ever had. They had been so pleased when she married Dr Reg Entwistle and settled down in a pretty chalet, Die Kiefern, half a mile away. Some of the younger mistresses had said it was a mistake to get married when she had just got a good degree and could have done anything, but the Head had argued strongly that she had the right to put her private life first. And now this wretched woman was hinting that Len was in trouble.

'Oh, yes', Grizel went on smugly, 'there's something very wrong with that marriage. I was there the other day, when Reg was at home, and the atmosphere - ! Neil says that that's a very disruptive young man. Of course, it didn't help that the twins were howling their heads off. Four children in five years; no wonder Len looks so stressed. Personally I'm very happy to have only one child - stop fidgeting, Nigel - and I would have been prepared to have one more if I could. But Len - I wonder if she means to go on, like her mother, till she's got *eleven*. None of those Maynards seem to have heard of the world population crisis. If the Pope had to look after all those children himself, he'd take a very different line'.

'You can't criticise a person's religion', Miss Annersley said mechanically.

But she went to her Advanced Latin class very worried, and with Grizel's last words ringing in her ears, 'There's going to be a big explosion there one day, Hilda. Just wait and see!'

Chapter 2

Len

Len stood at the chalet window looking across at the mountains.

They were twenty miles from the Gornetz Platz, although on a blue summer afternoon like this it seemed quite a short walk. She'd climbed those mountains several times as a schoolgirl, and then as a student home for the holidays; she'd daydreamed about becoming a member of the Alpine Club, but that was years ago. Children were like leg irons; they forced you to move at a much slower pace.

The house was unusually quiet. The little boys were at a birthday party and the twins, Margaret and Teresa, named after the first two heads of the Chalet School and now almost a year old, were asleep. As usual when Reg was due back, everything was in its place. She had tidied away the toys, prepared him a good supper, seen that the water was hot and found time to brush her hair and change her blouse, mindful that it wasn't wise to let yourself go after you had had a baby. And she had never done that; she'd glanced in the mirror on her way downstairs and thought she looked presentable, certainly not a great beauty but her waist and hips were still slim and few people would have guessed that she was the mother of four children.

She could see a little group of Chalet girls, walking briskly along the mountain road in their gentian blue uniforms. It was eight years now since she had left school to study modern languages at Oxford. Five years since she had come home to marry Reg in the Catholic chapel, Our Lady of the Snows. They had been engaged throughout the time she was a student and she had known, ever since she was fifteen, that he wanted her. Something had warned her not to go too fast; she'd been happy in those days, going round in a large friendly group of girls, with their brothers and cousins coming out from England in the school holidays. She had had so many friends, all scattered now, and above all her beloved sisters, Con and Margot.

She missed them. There were eight younger ones at home but she, Con and Margot had been together almost all their lives until they left school. Born on the same day, in the first autumn of the war, and she didn't think anything could really separate them. It was a long time now since they had been under one roof, but their letters went to and fro, from the Gornetz Platz to London, from London to South Africa, and each of them knew that she could trust the other two in any emergency.

Should she tell them?

It was no good talking to her mother, never had been. She mentally went through all the young married women she knew; her cousins, Peggy, Bride, Sybil, Josette. But none of them had been brought up as Catholics, so they would not understand her difficulty. On the other hand, her sisters weren't married, but Margot was a doctor, and Con had worked on the problem page of her magazine and must have seen a good deal of life. Or things might improve, and then she need not tell anyone.

Reg was late. She went into the neat kitchen and confirmed that everything was in order; the red-checked cloth on the table, his beer cooling in the refrigerator, the brown rolls and green salad ready to be eaten. A lot of people were sorry for her because she had all those tiny children, but they didn't understand that she was perfectly happy, looking after her husband and home. She liked children; she had had a lot of experience as the eldest of a large family and the school had taught her to be a well-organised person. It was Reg who wasn't happy.

The telephone rang.

'Len, darling!' It was her mother's unmistakable tones. 'How are my precious babies?'

'They're fine, Mother, thank you'.

'Me a granny!' Jo gurgled with laughter. 'It's ridiculous - everyone says I look young enough to be your sister - but listen, ducky, I mustn't run on; I have a favour to ask. I just this minute got a call from Mary-Lou'.

Mary-Lou Trelawney had been Head Girl of the Chalet School, two years before Len. She'd known her for most of her life, since the time they'd lived at Plas Gwyn, in the Golden Valley, and Mary-Lou and her mother had lived nextdoor at Carn Beg. Truth to tell, she had always been a bit frightened of her - she was one of those people who is called a natural leader and had bossed the young Maynards unmercifully - but Jo had taken a great fancy to her and kept in close touch with her ever since she left school.

'She's going to America soon, but before that she'd like to come to the Gornetz Platz for a little holiday and to see her old friends. I would have put her up but it's just the wrong time - the boys are all coming from England for the summer, and Frieda and her brood are also here for a long weekend. So I literally haven't got a spare bed, but I said she could stay with you. She can, can't she?'

'Yes, of course, Mamma'.

It seemed she was to be given no choice.

'Lovely. She can have her meals with us. We're very lucky to have had that girl in the school, Len; she was such a good influence on you younger ones and we can't let her go off to the States without saying goodbye. So that's settled. She'll be here on Tuesday'.

'Mamma, I'm very sorry but I must go. Reg is just coming'.

She'd heard his car draw up, and it was better not to keep him waiting. But it was a few minutes before she could get rid of her mother, and by that time he had come in.

Reg was a stocky, dark but quite good-looking man, at thirty-six several years older than his wife. He still spoke with a trace of the north-country accent he'd had as a boy in Yorkshire, where the Maynards had met him towards the end of the war. He had been very discontented in those days; the aunt he lived with had refused to pay for him to go to grammar school and he'd been too clever to take satisfaction in anything else. Dr Maynard had persuaded her to let him have his chance and eventually, much later than his contemporaries, he'd taken his MB and come out to work at the sanatorium. Len had the deepest respect for the way he had struggled.

She went over to hug him. It was all right; she'd seen in the first moment that he was not in a bad mood.

'What did your Ma want?'

'She's asked me to give Mary-Lou a bed, next week'.

'That bossy girl? I can't say she ever appealed to me'.

'Well, Reg, you won't have to see much of her. I'm sure she'll be round at Mother's nearly all the time'.

'What's she doing now?' asked Reg as he accepted the cold beer she poured him.

'She's an archaeologist; she's been all over the Middle East'.

'Not married yet?'

'No. She'd be about twenty-eight, but I haven't heard of anyone special'.

'Not surprising, really'.

Len put out his supper; schnitzel, buttered potatoes, and salad followed by a slice of lemon *torte*. Reg was always hungry at the end of the day. She took a smaller portion for herself and sat down next to him at the kitchen table, thinking that it was almost like the first months after they were married. Johnno and Richard wouldn't be back for a while, and it was as if there were only the two of them in the house.

Reg commented on it, too, when he had finished eating.

'Quiet, isn't it, without the little bleeders?'

'The babies are asleep upstairs. Do you want to see them?'

'Oh, yes'. Reg wasn't too interested in the babies. 'Put on the coffee, Len. Since it *is* quiet for a change, we'll talk'.

Len did as she was asked.

'Fact is, I had a word with your Dad today and told him what I've been thinking. I like the sound of the Boston job. I'll take it if I can get it, but whatever, it wouldn't do to stay in this place for many more years'.

Len kept her face away from him, preparing coffee; she'd known that this would have to come one day but her heart sank. She had lived in the Oberland since she was ten and loved it; her family was here and she'd dreamed of her little girls going to the same school as herself. But things were changing. TB, which had killed so many generations of people right up to her own childhood, had been almost wiped out and the hospital was becoming redundant. Each year it had to close down more wards and let more of the staff go. It still specialised in diseases of the chest and lungs, and looked after the health of the Chalet girls, the few people who lived on the Gornetz Platz and the many tourists, but it was obvious that it had lost its former importance. Even her father had talked about taking early retirement. You couldn't expect a young man like Reg to stay there all his life.

'Yes, I see that', she said slowly, 'but does it have to be America?'

'Why, where else?'

'I was wondering if we couldn't go home'.

She was thinking of Plas Gwyn, the white house in Howells village on the Welsh border where she had spent most of her early years. It was let now, but the family still occasionally went there for holidays and she'd never lost her affection for that part of the world. She thought of Reg practising medicine somewhere in Herefordshire, good country air for the children and a mild British climate instead of the extremes of heat and cold you got here. And suddenly, she felt desperately homesick.

'Christ, woman, I don't want to go back to England. It's crawling with snobs. They hear my accent, they think I'm a low class of person. Anyway, don't you know what doctors earn in the States? That's the main reason I'm interested. They're some of the best-paid men around'.

Len bit her lip. She thought, Reg isn't mercenary, it's necessary to think about these things, with four children.

The next thought took her by surprise; he isn't asking me, just telling me what's going to happen.

She poured the coffee and sat down; neither of them spoke for a while but she could feel the atmosphere had changed. Any moment now, if she said the wrong thing, or even if she said nothing, there might be an eruption of that frightening temper which, these days, was breaking out more and more often. She wasn't sure when it had started, probably during her third pregnancy which had annoyed Reg very much. It had always been understood that they wanted children, and he liked the two little boys. But when the twins were born, doubling their family at a stroke, he had not been pleased. He would hardly look at the babies and last night, when they were teething and very disturbed, he'd shouted, 'Whatever happens, I'm not having any more children. You get pregnant one more time, I'll be out of that door like a flash'.

Difficult to believe, now, that he'd pushed and pushed her to marry him, while she was still at school and telling everyone that she meant to be a language teacher. She closed her eyes; she felt dreadfully tired, having been on the go since six that morning. The great words swam round in her mind; love, honour and obey. I will love, honour and obey my husband. It was obviously her job to keep Reg happy, protect the children, present a smiling face to her parents and the rest of the world. That seemed terribly important. Only she felt sure that if one of her sisters was in the same room, she would blurt out the truth.

'Get my cigs, will you?' Reg said.

She got up. At the same moment there was a knock on the front door and the two little boys appeared, each clutching a balloon and piece of sticky cake, wreathed in smiles. Len thanked the neighbour who had brought them and ushered them into the kitchen.

'Daddy, Daddy!' Richard shouted, and rushed over to clasp his leg.

'Daddy' was one of the few words that Richard could say. A fair, rosy, solid little boy, he was very much slower than Johnno, who at just four could hold quite a sophisticated conversation. His official name was John Reginald after his father and Maynard grandfather, but he had been known as Johnno since birth. He was small, skinny, with dark hair and intense brown eyes, and everyone who met him said in awed tones, did they know that they'd got a highly intelligent child? Perhaps it was all the attention he got from his young uncles and aunts, or the fact that his mother had made a special effort in the eighteen months between him and Richard, but he already knew his alphabet, could read several words and would play quietly with his educational toys however much chaos was going on round him. He perched on a high stool and turned his serious gaze on his father.

'Daddy, we went both to Gretchen's birthday party', he announced. 'Gretchen had a cake with three candles because she's three years old. And we speaked in German. I can speak German *fluently*'. Reg, who spoke it only with difficulty, grunted. 'And what do you think we did next?'

Richard was smearing cream cake over his face and his father gave him a disgusted look.

'What did you do, Johnno?' Len asked.

Johnno's eyes blazed with excitement. 'We played musical statues, and then Gretchen's Mum played the Beatles. I thought a beetle was a little insect, but this was pop music. And after that we danced and singed and - Daddy, what's the matter?'

'I said get my cigs', Reg repeated rather querulously.

She started looking in the obvious places. As she did so one of the babies, upstairs, began to cry and her sister joined in. She prayed it wouldn't get any worse. Reg said violently, 'Bloody kids!'

'I'll see to them -', Len began, and at that moment she finally caught sight of Reg's Woodbines. Richard had tipped them from the packet and been quietly pulling them to bits in the last couple of minutes, dropping the pieces in his mug of milk. Reg saw this at the same time as herself and exploded.

'You bloody stupid woman - I work my hide off to support you and those kids and you can't even make them behave when I come home - you spoil them - I'm worn out and can't even have a smoke - '.

'Reg, please'. Her eyes were filling with tears and she fought desperately to keep her voice under control. 'Calm down and I'll get -'.

It was unfortunate that Johnno was so sharp.

His little face turned crimson, his eyes gushed and, while Richard babbled placidly on the floor, he shrieked, 'I hate you, Daddy! I truly hate you! What for are you making my Mummy cry?'

'You little -!' Reg said, and brought his arm round as if he meant to knock him off the stool. Len snatched him out of reach just in time.

'Don't hit him!'

Johnno was screaming hysterically now and even Richard looked frightened. The two babies were also screaming, upstairs. Reg swore, threw a soiled plate against the wall where it smashed, and walked out.

He came back, of course. There was nowhere else for him to go. It was after midnight, the big hotel down the road where he'd been drinking had closed and she was trying to sleep. He flung himself on the bed and told her as he thrust himself violently into her body that she was frigid, that she'd ruined his life by having too many kids and that if he had his time over again he wouldn't do it for anything. She kept silent; it would wake the children if she cried out. When he'd finished, her mouth was bleeding where he'd bitten her and she felt, not for the first time, that she had been raped.

Chapter 3

Con

Con woke up to the sunlight of a perfect July day in London. Friday, and she wasn't due at the office and need go nowhere and do nothing until the buffet lunch at the riverside hotel which *Sixties Woman* put on every year. But it was nearly nine, high time she got going. She climbed into her dressing-gown, switched on the percolator and then padded into the little hall to pick up the *Guardian* and her post.

She often compared this civilised morning routine with break of day at the Chalet School. Up at crack of dawn, with a prefect to hound you out of bed if you lingered, then queue for a cold bath, say your prayers, tidy your cubicle (Matron would soon drag you back if it was less than perfect), and then downstairs for lessons, violent physical exercise and more prayers. Con acknowledged that the school had turned her out able to fend for herself and fluent in three languages, and her sisters - Len especially - still remembered it with affection. But she herself was delighted to be grown up, earning good money, resident in another country - well away from her family and the school - and free to do as she chose.

Con lived in her own flat in Camden Town. She'd tried sharing, but it hadn't worked; she disliked having other people's dirty saucepans or dripping tights in her kitchen or bathroom and she'd found that, if she was going to write, she needed large blocks of time to herself. So a year ago she had taken this granny flat on the ground floor of a Victorian terrace house and turned it into a place she enjoyed living in. She'd painted it white, and put geraniums and Paul Klee prints in the miniature kitchen, and bought the best modern furniture she could afford. There was only one sizeable room, which doubled as bedroom and study, but it had a good olive-green carpet, comfortable blue armchairs and blue-flowered curtains she'd run up herself. They'd made her learn to sew at school. A solid desk with blue anglepoise lamp, her typewriter, books neatly arranged against the wall. There was also a shower-room and a tiny entrance hall with a phone, which was expensive but necessary in her job.

No post, except a letter from her mother. She read it as she sipped her coffee and spread a roll with butter and Swiss apricot jam. It mentioned that Felicity, her little sister, had a boy friend and 'it looked very serious'. Len was 'gloriously happy'; the grandchildren were sweet. And would she, Con, be coming to the Oberland for her summer holidays? Not a chance, Con thought. She'd put in an appearance at Christmas and that was quite soon enough; she'd had difficulty getting out of her aunt's funeral three months ago. But she wouldn't be unpleasant about it; that wasn't Con's way. She would just say politely that she was very sorry, but she'd promised to go with friends to the Edinburgh Festival and was committed.

Two hours to go till the party. Should she linger over the *Guardian* or wander out to the delicatessen where you could get all sorts of exotic foods that she'd never sampled before coming to London? Discipline, Con said firmly, and, still in her blue pyjamas, sat down at the desk and reached for her manuscript. If she was ever going to get this novel published, she must seize every chance to work.

She wrote and corrected for two hours. Then she had a shower, brushed her dark hair till it shone and dressed in a white silk blouse and deep blue skirt, suitable for a burning summer's day. She got out her little car - it had been bought with a legacy from her godmother, Con Mackenzie, who had died rather young - and drove out joyfully into the heavy traffic. Brilliant colours on the fruit barrows, in the window boxes, on the extraordinary clothes of the young men and girls strolling arm in arm along the pavements; London in the summer of 1966.

Something was nagging at the back of her mind, though, and as she drove southwards towards the river, she tried to place it. Of course - Felicity's boy friend. It was absurd, because Felicity was not yet seventeen, but what bugged Con was that her mother would certainly be wondering why there was no obvious man in *her* life, and when she was going to settle down. Her parents' generation would never understand that she actually liked working.

Con had had just one serious romance. When she and Len arrived at Oxford in '58, straight from school, the sisters had been separated for the first time in their lives. Len had been at St Hilda's studying modern languages, Con half a mile away at Somerville studying English. They'd seen each other often, of course, but it wasn't the same. And while Len had worked very hard and been faithful to Reg, only going out with her friends once or twice a week, Con had thrown herself into all the pleasures of university life and got an indifferent degree. In her second year she'd met Clive, and been convinced she was going to marry him. She'd moved to London and got that job with *Sixties Woman* just to be in the same city. But it had ended painfully when he went to Singapore to work for the British Council, and made it clear that he wasn't asking her to come too. That was two years ago, and it had taken Con all that time to get over him. Today she thought light-heartedly, how absurd to take it so seriously! She was quite ready, now, to fall in love with someone else.

Not because she craved for children. Her mother and Len assumed that every woman did but, as the second daughter in a family of eleven, she'd seen enough babies to make her hesitate for a long time before having one. She hadn't totally ruled it out, but she was in no hurry. No, she thought as she parked, I'd just like to meet an interesting, worthwhile man, and get married in a year or two, and go on working for at least another five years. I might even meet him at this party. Who knows?

There were big banners outside the hotel for the *Sixties Woman* annual jamboree. Con felt happy that she'd landed this job, very proud to be part of the team. She was careful to explain to those who didn't know that this wasn't an old-style magazine, all recipes and knitting patterns, but a journal for modern women. There were good film and theatre pages, there were serials by well-known novelists (Con meant to be one herself some day), there were travel articles and serious studies of 'sixties marriage. She did a little bit of everything, mostly book reviews, although she sometimes helped out on the agony page. The editor knew that she was reliable and could write fluently on any subject, and she was steadily working her way up.

The French windows were open, on a terrace and some green gardens sloping down to the river, and most of the guests had already arrived. There were bowls of carnations everywhere and white-coated waiters pouring drinks. Con took a plate of vol-au-vents and a glass of Yugoslav riesling and plunged into the crowd. It didn't take her long to decide that there were few people she wished to talk to - most of them were much older than herself - but she exchanged some pleasant words with those she knew and then wandered out into the garden. She stayed there for a while, looking at the roses and mulling over the latest problem in her novel, then noticed that the crowds were thinning out and decided she might as well leave. As she came back through the window into the long room she noticed a young man with his back to her and immediately recognised someone she hadn't seen for years. Tony Barras.

Tony and his elder sister Clem had originally been friends of Mary-Lou and stayed with her at Carn Beg, next to the Maynards' old home in Herefordshire. Their father, Adrian, had been a well-known landscape painter in the 1940s and their mother also dabbled, so the children had been left to do much as they liked and become, to quote Mary-Lou's Gran, a pair of wild young imps. After a particularly outrageous prank they'd been sent away, Mary-Lou and Clem to the Chalet School and Tony to prep school. But they often met up in the holidays, either in Wales or, after the school migrated, in Switzerland. There had been a large group of young people whose parents knew each other and who went climbing or skiing together when they met, although they had gone their separate ways years ago. Tony had had an acne problem then, and been very silent. She remembered him constantly taking photographs and being interested in little else.

'Hello!' she said, walking up with a smile.

'Con!' Tony said, amazed. 'I haven't seen you since nineteen fifty-something!'

'How are you?'

'Just going to grab some coffee. What about you?'

Con went with him gladly enough. She had taken very little notice of him when they were teenagers but now, she thought him distinctly attractive. His spots had cleared up to reveal a rather nice-looking young man with fair hair, badly in need of cutting, a snub nose and unexpectedly dark brown eyes. He was in jeans and looked not quite smart enough for this event.

'How are the other triplets?' he asked. 'Len and Margot?'

'Well, Margot became a nun, as you know - '.

Tony winced.

'That's a shame, a good-looking girl walling herself up in a convent. I'd have thought Margot was the last person - oh, sorry, Con, am I abusing your religion?'

'Not at all', Con assured him. 'I only go to church at home to keep my parents happy. And Margot isn't walled up. In fact she's seen more of the world than I have. She's in South Africa, running a township clinic. And Len is up to her eyebrows in babies, of course'.

Tony looked gloomier than ever.

'So how did you get here? I didn't know you were connected with *Sixties Woman*'.

'Oh', Tony said, seeming to come back from a long way off, 'I took the Hebrides photos for Queenie's article'.

Con was impressed, and said so. Queenie Black's travel writing was widely admired.

'My parents used to live in the Western Isles', Tony explained, 'so I know the landscape quite well. I'm a freelance photographer. Mostly empty beaches and interesting old ruins, but I'll snap anything'.

'You don't paint, like your father?'

'Well, no; the old man has a certain reputation and I wouldn't want people comparing us'. Con suddenly remembered that Tony's father used to beat him quite unmercifully. 'Do *you* tell everyone that your mother is Josephine Bettany?'

'Not usually', Con smiled, 'but - '.

She was about to tell him that, just the same, she intended to be taken seriously as a writer, when someone touched her arm. After a moment she recognised a little woman called Beatrice Schreiber who was a director of the magazine. Con had passed her in the corridors and she had smiled graciously, but she was hardly ever in.

'Miss Maynard, I think the party's almost over. Would you be very kind and give me a lift back to the office? - I presume you're going. My own car is out of order and I do so hate taking the Tube'.

Nothing to do but say yes, and she was due back at the office anyway. Con said 'Nice to see you, Tony' - when she was younger, she'd have asked him to keep in touch, but now she knew better - and followed Mrs Schreiber out, pausing while she said goodbye to various important people. The last she saw of Tony he was talking animatedly to a very pretty girl.

'That's a nice young man', Mrs Schreiber said as they squashed into Con's car.

'Yes', Con agreed.

They started moving through the traffic and Mrs Schreiber began in a practised way to make conversation. She was about forty, dark and very well-groomed, and with the cutglass accent you still heard occasionally in black-and-white films.

'Do you like your job, Miss Maynard? Do you mean to stay in the magazine world?'

'I love it', Con said, as this was obviously the right answer.

'Not going to give it up, then, when you get married?'

Con laughed.

'No. I like writing too much'.

'And what things do you prefer to write?'

'I wrote a lot of poetry when I was at school', Con said, 'but I don't like what's being published now -'.

'I know. It doesn't rhyme and has no capital letters'.

'So I'm concentrating on fiction'. Con was warming to her subject; the woman wasn't a bad old stick. 'I've had a few short stories in student papers, and I'm working on a serious novel. Of course', she added hastily, 'it doesn't interfere with my job, but I spend evenings and weekends writing'.

'Goodness', Mrs Schreiber said, 'how very dedicated'.

'I suppose it's in my blood', Con said. Afterwards she thought she must really have drunk enough riesling to make her light-headed, because she went on, 'My mother writes school stories'.

'Really? I used to love school stories when I was younger. What's her name, may I ask?'

'She's Josephine M. Bettany'.

Mrs Schreiber gasped.

Con looked round, concerned, to see that her passenger had gone quite white, but she only said, 'Then you must be one of the triplets?'

'Yes. I'm Con'.

'Of course. I knew you and your sisters when you were toddlers'.

'Are you an old Chalet girl? My mother will be awfully interested. I'll tell her I met you, shall I?'

Mrs Schreiber still looked badly shocked. She said, 'No - better not - I was at the Chalet School during the war but I had to leave'.

Suddenly everything came together; certain old photographs, Mrs Schreiber's obvious embarrassment, stories she had heard from her mother and Miss Annersley about the early days of the school. Before she knew what she was doing she blurted out, 'You're Betty Wynne-Davies!'

Chapter 4

Betty Comes Up Trumps

Con had often been told, when at school, that she had no tact. During the last eight years she'd worked on that and she honestly believed, now, that she was a polite and considerate person. But it was obvious that she still hadn't learned to hold her tongue between her teeth at the right times.

Betty Wynne-Davies was one of only two girls ever to have been expelled from the Chalet School. Mrs Maynard was vague about what she'd done, but Con had grown up thinking of her as a disgraceful and exciting character who was much wickeder than any girl she was likely to meet in the flesh. She had the impression that Miss Annersley was reluctant to expel anyone these days, because that particular case had upset her. And now she had the heroine of that episode in her own car and would dearly like to know what had happened. But she couldn't ask, because Mrs Schreiber was looking as if she'd been beaten up.

'I'm awfully sorry', she stammered.

'It's all right'. They had drawn up outside the *Sixties Woman* building, and she mopped her face with a handkerchief. 'Come up to my office, won't you?'

Con followed her. They went into Mrs Schreiber's sanctum, which she'd never seen, and the older woman immediately helped herself to a small glass of gin from a cabinet. When she'd taken a few sips - Con refused to join her - she seemed calmer.

'Well, Miss Maynard, you've uncovered the skeleton in my cupboard. It's strange, I haven't talked about it for years'.

'I never meant to', said Con. 'Honestly, Mrs Schreiber, it's nothing to worry about. I know two people who were expelled from Cheltenham Ladies' College for smoking pot'.

'And nobody mentions me at the Chalet School?'

'No, indeed. It's just that my mother and the Head were once looking through some old photos, and they mentioned that you and a friend of yours were the two wickedest girls in the school'.

'Yes. Elizabeth Arnett is my friend. You'll have seen her name on the honours board, because she reformed and became head girl. She's also in the publishing business - in fact, she's the managing director of Briar Rose'.

Con had once read a Briar Rose novel on a train journey. She nodded, but didn't see what she could say.

'And that brings me back to what you were telling me. If you want to go in for novel-writing as a career, I'm sure Liz could give you some helpful advice. This is her card - and may I give her your private number, too?'

After this, matters moved much faster than Con had expected. The next morning, Saturday, while she was reading in bed, her phone rang and a clipped voice addressed her in much the same way as the prefects at school.

'Miss Maynard? This is Liz Arnett of Briar Rose. My friend, Betty Schreiber, told me about you. Will you please come to my office after work on Monday, let's say at five, and bring your c.v. I'm thinking of expanding my list and looking for promising young writers. So please bring a few examples of your work as well. Thank you, goodbye'.

It was quite a shock. Con was used to having her work sent back, not solicited. But she believed in being well prepared, so later that morning she walked over to the library and got out a stack of Briar Rose paperbacks. As she'd thought, it was cheap romantic fiction and totally predictable. Stories about doctors and nurses, talented young singers who fell in love with famous musicians, brides whose husbands left them on their wedding night and dark-browed, granite-jawed men with a mysterious past. She read the whole pile that weekend - her own novel didn't get touched - and found them quite relaxing. Even though she felt a bit jaded after finishing the last one, like when you'd eaten too many sweets in one go.

Promptly at five on Monday, she kept her appointment. Miss Arnett was tall, wore stylish heavy glasses and looked rather formidable, but Con was used to dealing with older women and remained outwardly calm.

A pot of lemon tea was served. Miss Arnett asked, 'How is your mother, Miss Maynard? Is she still writing her school stories?'

'Oh, yes', Con said, 'two a year'.

'Even though I understand she has quite a large family?'

'Yes, there are eleven of us. I don't know how she does it'.

'And you also want to be a novelist, Betty tells me. Have you thought of writing school stories too?'

'Help, no', Con said. 'I'm a completely different person from my mother, and I'd hate that. I want to write' - she had been going to say 'serious', but that word seemed inappropriate - 'adult fiction'.

'I see. Well, as I said, we have openings for young writers, though obviously we don't take everyone who asks. You have an English degree from Oxford and you work for *Sixties Woman*, so that ensures a minimum level of competence. What about the story you published?'

Con meekly handed over a copy of the student paper *Isis*.

'Hm. This would be a little above the head of our average reader. I see you've used the word 'lust', which is absolutely banned by Briar Rose. Still, leave it behind, with your other things, and I'll look it over. Have you read any of our books?'

'Yes', Con said. 'I enjoyed them very much'.

'We've more or less captured the women's market. Housewives, older ladies with time on their hands, young girls looking for romance. Not university women like you or me, perhaps, but we're a minority. I'm very proud of what we've achieved, Miss Maynard, and I expect my writers to give us of their best. I feel sure we could find a place for you, if you're interested, and if you're as good as you seem to be. But', Miss Arnett went on, speaking quite fiercely, 'I *insist* that you keep to yourself what you've just learned about Betty. She's a very old and dear friend, and I won't have her upset'.

Con sat quite still. It was as she had guessed; the two women thought she was some sort of blackmailer.

'She was a young girl of seventeen at the time. She slipped out of school to meet a man, just as you might have done' - Con hadn't, but she kept quiet - 'and, although he spoke perfect English, he turned out to be a Nazi agent and threatened her in a disgraceful way. Of course she should have gone straight to the Head, but Annersley can be quite frightening, as you know, and she didn't dare. All that Betty ever did was leave a window open, because this man had some idea of finding secret documents inside the school. He didn't, of course - it was obviously a ridiculous idea and she knew it, but it was enough to get her expelled. And ever since, she's lived in terror of people finding out. Not that anyone cares about the expulsion itself, of course, but they don't like the word Nazi, even now'.

'Yes, I see'.

'I wonder if you really do. Betty was so terrified that she never even told her husband - that marriage didn't last, by the way. And on official forms she always gives her maiden name as Beatrice Davies. After all, she was disgraced in front of several hundred people, and you never know where you might meet a Chalet School girl'.

Con decided this had gone on long enough.

'Miss Arnett, I don't know what sort of person you think I am. Okay, you've never met me before, and there's no reason why you should believe it, but I would just like to say that I don't gossip. I have far more interesting things to do with my time. And as a matter of fact, my mother and Miss Annersley don't gossip either. I knew Betty - Mrs Schreiber - had been expelled, but I thought it was for general bad behaviour. No one ever mentioned the word Nazi, and I'm sure the school is anxious to keep it quiet, too'.

'So, in fact', Miss Arnett said, 'I've just told you something you didn't know?'

'Yes, you have'.

'Well, I accept your assurance that it won't go further. Your mother was never spiteful, I remember that'. She was silent for a moment and then went on briskly, 'This is the leaflet we give to all our aspiring writers. You'll find everything you need to know there. As well as our main list, we have one about doctors and nurses, and we're about to start a new historical romance series -

Tudor Rose. You know the rules. No sex before marriage, or indeed after marriage - you can leave that to the imagination. Happy endings. Exotic settings - you know Switzerland and the Tyrol, so that should be no problem. Don't write above readers' heads. When you've written something, send it to me personally, and I'll see what I can do'.

Having spent the evening at a film with friends, Con came home rather late. The telephone was ringing as she got in, and she made a dive for it.

'Con Maynard speaking'.

'Con!' It was her sister's voice, sounding - and this was extraordinary - close to tears. 'I'm so glad - I've been trying all evening - '.

'What's up? Are you all right, Len?'

Len said quietly, 'You're the only person I can talk to'.

'Is Reg there?'

'He's been called out, and the children are asleep - that's why I'm ringing. Oh, and Mary-Lou is coming to stay tomorrow; I don't know how much time I'll have after that'.

'Mary-Lou?' Con harboured unpleasant memories of the bossy head girl who had never hesitated to comment on her manners and morals. 'Well, rather you than me. Cheer up, Len. We can talk quite privately. What is it?'

'Do you think that birth control is ever justified?'

This was such an unexpected question that Con, who for the last seven years had been living among sophisticated people, was struck speechless. All she could find to say, after a stunned silence, was, 'Does that mean you're thinking of going on the pill?'

'Reg wants me to'.

'Okay'. Con had never greatly liked her brother-in-law. 'But, look, Reg is a doctor. He can surely see to all that himself, if it worries you?'

Len didn't answer.

'Anyway, since you ask, yes, I think it's a good idea. You've got four children, that's a large family'.

'That's what everybody says', said Len, the note of strain still in her voice. 'But I don't mind; I like looking after children. After all, Mamma had eleven, and she still writes two novels a year'.

'Yes, I had a woman asking me about that today. Everyone wants to know how she does it, and the answer is, most of the work is done by other people. She has Anna, and Rosli, and you and I and Margot had to do all sorts of things for the younger ones while we were living at home. And we were all sent away to boarding school at the earliest opportunity. Anyway, Len, you know things get chaotic when she's upstairs writing'.

She didn't add that the stuff her mother wrote was trash, but, just the same, that was what she thought.

'I don't like to hear you talk about Mamma like that'.

'Never mind Mamma. I presume you haven't told her about this idea of going on the pill?'

'Of course not; she'd be horrified. I was afraid you would be'.

Con had not been on the pill for two years, since Clive left England; it seemed too cold-blooded to take one every day just in case. She wondered how her sister, who was the same age as herself, could be so innocent. Probably because she still lived round the corner from Mamma and Miss Annersley and had only ever been exposed to their values. Well, it was a good thing she'd worked on the agony page of *Sixties Woman*. She began to explain patiently.

'Len, you're not a teenage girl who wants to take the pill in order to sleep around; you're a married woman. I know you cope with the children very well, but four is a lot, and from what you say, Reg is feeling the strain. Whether you stay together or not, I think - '.

'What do you mean, *whether we stay together or not*? We're married!'

'Sorry. I'm just saying I think it would be good for your marriage if you did what he suggests'. Rotten selfish male, she thought privately. 'You wouldn't be murdering anyone, or harming anyone, or doing anything that most people would find shocking. You can't really believe it's wicked, to swallow a little white pill'.

Len sighed. 'Oh, it's not wicked. It's just that I would feel a hypocrite every time I walked into a Catholic church if I was breaking the rules. You see, I don't think it's particularly honest to pick and choose, taking advantage of the bits you like and ignoring the hard ones. Can you understand that?'

Con could; it was one reason she had quietly detached herself from the church years ago. 'Well, Len, if that's a problem, I can tell you it's very likely that the Pope is going to come round. Everyone in the media thinks so. And Margot said the same, in her last letter'.

'You really think that?'

'Certainly. He's got a commission working on it'.

'Yes, I heard'.

'So wouldn't it be crazy to quarrel with Reg, and perhaps have another child you couldn't cope with, all because of a rule which is going to change very soon anyway?'

Silence. She thought she could hear her sister struggling with tears.

'Len, how *are* things between you and Reg?'

'Awful'.

'Tell me. It'll do you good to talk'.

They talked, but only for a few minutes more; then Len said hastily, 'I've just heard his car - sorry, Con - I must go'. Con went to bed. But, although she was trying to concentrate on all that had happened that day and the chance she'd been offered, she kept hearing instead her sister's words, 'I can't get through to him any more. I've done everything I can think of, and he just doesn't seem to like me'.

Chapter 5

Enter Mary-Lou

Reg Entwistle drove the mile back from San, windows open to admit a breath of air at the end of the hot afternoon. The views were wonderful, as always. The towering Alpine peaks, where the snow never melted, the meadows which at this time of year were a riot of colour: orchids and marigolds, gentians and moon-daisies. When he'd first come here about ten years ago he'd been amazed; to a boy from a poor home in the North of England it had been a magic place. Speaking no German then, he had seen a lot of Dr Maynard's family. The triplets were at their boarding school, but that was next door to their home and they ran in and out. It was always Len that he'd got on with. Con was usually in some dream-world of her own, and Margot had a funny temper. But Len at fifteen had been delightful, friendly to him and to everyone, always ready to tell him a German word or explain the strange customs of the place. She'd been so pretty, too, with her shining greyish-violet eyes and auburn hair worn in a ponytail. He'd noticed how responsible she was, looking after the younger children without complaint, cooking and sewing expertly, and it had struck him even at that age that she'd make a perfect wife one day.

At first, he sensed her resistance. She liked him but she thought of him as one of the adults, and it infuriated him that she was always off with a crowd of giggling kids, playing tennis or building snowmen, when she wasn't helping her mother or in school. Dr and Mrs Maynard had thought he was an ideal husband for their daughter but pointed out that she was very young. So they had backed him up, but he'd had to wait, first until she finished school and then for three years while she went to Oxford to get her degree. He'd seen her in the holidays and it was always frustrating. Why did she want a degree when she was going to be his wife, he'd asked, and why, when they were in love, was no sex permitted? Her mother, scatty though she seemed, had been very much on the ball in that respect, and Len herself had been upset when he tried to push it. There were times when he was on the verge of walking out, but he'd hung on grimly and got her in the end.

And now, he wondered, had it been worth it? He'd waited for six years and now he had got her he was no longer sure he wanted her. Just as he would have given his eye-teeth when he was a schoolboy to be a doctor in a great Swiss sanatorium, and now he couldn't wait to go somewhere else. He suspected that he might have spoiled his life and her life. If only he'd been allowed to get her out of his system when she was a teenager, he could have moved on. Of course he couldn't tell her this; she believed marriage was for life. He had a wife who had no idea what was going on in his mind and four children, but he couldn't dwell on that. It was simply too painful to think about the children.

Getting out of his car, he walked around a little, not wanting to go inside the chalet just yet. Those mountains. He felt they were shutting him in. Then a taxi drew up, and a young woman got out.

She was tall, smartly-dressed, with short, fair, gleaming hair and vivid blue eyes. As she paid off the taxi he remembered that his wife had said something about Mary-Lou, but this surely couldn't be that irritating girl. Then she turned to him, hand stretched out and beaming.

'Reg! How lovely to see you!'

It *was* Mary-Lou.

'Well, you've certainly changed a bit', he said lamely.

'I've grown up, that's all. It's awfully kind of you to put me up; I'll try not to be in the way. Shall we go in?'

Len had been bathing the babies. She quickly lifted them out, wrapped them in towels and dashed downstairs; Johnno and his little satellite, Richard, trailing after her.

'Hello, Mary-Lou. I'm sorry I'm not quite finished. Reg, why don't you sit down and have a drink? Come upstairs and see your room'.

She helped her carry her cases to the small spare bedroom, which had a fine view of the Jungfrau.

'It's lovely', Mary-Lou said serenely.

'Bathroom's there. I'll finish putting the twins to bed - oh, dear!' One of the babies had begun to crawl downstairs, stark naked, and was in imminent danger of either having a fall or disturbing Reg, which would be even worse. 'Just get on with whatever you want to do, Mary-Lou. I'll see to the children, and if I'm held up, you and Reg can finish your drinks, or start supper. There's a cold salad and fruit soup. Is that all right?'

Mary-Lou assured her it was. She took five minutes to freshen up, and then went downstairs. She was a little surprised to find the house in such good order; Len must be a better housewife than she had expected. She'd always talked of becoming a language teacher when they were at school.

Reg was sipping his beer morosely in the pleasant sitting-room. He jumped up and offered her a glass.

'Just sherry, please', Mary-Lou said.

A child's shriek came faintly from upstairs.

'How are you getting on, Reg?' Mary-Lou sat down and gazed out at the mountains. 'I do envy you, living in this lovely part of the world'.

'All right for holidays', Reg said bluntly. 'I won't be here much longer'.

'Really? Where are you going?'

'Boston, if I can get in, and I think I can. The San's dying on its feet, as you know'. Mary-Lou nodded sympathetically. 'America's the place to be, if you want to get on'.

'You're right there'.

Reg looked surreptitiously at the striking young woman opposite, noting her perfectly-shaped legs and imperturbable expression. He knew her father had been some sort of hero who had been killed in the Amazon jungle, and that her mother had also died years ago. It was a fine thing, he suddenly thought, for a woman to have no family. The Maynards were a nuisance - well, the old man was all right, but Len's mother was getting more peculiar by the day, and there was that vast tribe of younger children. A good job they'd be away from the whole bunch soon.

'As a matter of fact', Mary-Lou continued, 'I'm going there myself in a few months'.

'Boston?'

'New York, actually, but it's no distance by plane. As you say, one must go there to get funding'.

'What do you do exactly?'

'I'm an archaeologist. I've already been several times to the Middle East, but my next project is to go to South America in the footsteps of the Murray-Cameron expedition and see the Amazon. I'm looking forward to that'.

'Good lord!' said Reg. 'I mean, it seems strange, burying yourself in the jungle - at your age - '.

It had just struck him that she was a year or two older than Len.

'Oh, you mean marriage and children', Mary-Lou said with that devastating frankness for which she had been famous at school. 'That's no problem. I'm happy as I am'.

'Don't you like men?' Reg asked.

Mary-Lou smiled. 'I certainly don't dislike them. I have several very good friends in London and America. But children - they're another matter'.

'You don't want children?'

Reg was incredulous. He'd always assumed that all women wanted children and a husband (apart from Margot, his wife's sister, who was mad). Those who couldn't get them became dried-up old maids like the so-called mistresses at the Chalet School. Not much chance of them ever being any man's mistress, he thought. Yet here was this attractive young woman taking an extremely relaxed view.

'I don't see them fitting into my life. Can I get you another drink, Reg?'

'Sorry. I should be doing that'.

'You see', Mary-Lou continued, when they were settled, 'I believe if you're going to do something, you should do it properly. Verity, my stepsister, is up to her elbows in nappies and housework. A shame, because she could have been a professional singer, but everyone must do what they want.

That's why Len is so good at running a home - she doesn't even try to do anything else'.

Reg grunted.

'So if I'm going to be any good at my job, it's unlikely that I can spare the time to have a family. Apart from anything else, it wouldn't be fair to the child'.

'And what about a man?' Reg demanded. He wondered if he'd drunk too much, to be talking like this.

'Well', Mary-Lou smiled, 'he would have to be someone special'.

Len came in at this point, with Johnno and Richard in their pea-green pyjamas, and she and Mary-Lou began an animated conversation about old friends. The little boys climbed on Reg's knee and tried to tell him about their day, but he could hardly listen. Then the three adults sat down to supper while the children played in the next room. They had finished, and were drinking some excellent coffee, when one of the babies upstairs began to cry.

'Oh, dear', said Len, 'I'll go'.

Mary-Lou said, 'I was thinking of strolling over to Freudesheim to see your mother. She's expecting me, I know. I'll just give you a hand with the washing-up, Len'.

'No, don't bother'.

Reg could just see Mary-Lou and his mother-in-law, sitting up until all hours and shrieking with laughter over the Middles' dormitory party. How her husband stood it, he'd never know. But somehow he found himself getting to his feet and saying, 'I'll come over with you. I could do with a stroll'.

'Will you stay?'

'No, just see that Mary-Lou gets there safely'.

Mary-Lou smiled, as if she had not been looking after herself for years in various remote parts of the world. They went out together. Len was left to cope with the dishes and the crying baby, but she didn't mind; she was used to that.

The evening was pleasantly warm. As they climbed the mountain road, there was hardly any traffic; they could hear the distant sound of bells as cows grazed in the summer meadows and a small wind lifted the long grass.

'So you're going to the Amazon?' Reg jerked out.

He'd read something about the Amazons, female warriors who fought men on equal terms. This girl, with her tall figure and long stride, looked as if she could have been one.

'Not yet', said Mary-Lou composedly. 'I'll be in the States all winter, as I told you, but now I'm just going to enjoy the next two weeks'.

'Do you miss the Oberland?'

'Not really. I had a very good time at school, but one moves on'.

Reg found himself telling her how his wife's mother had never moved on since her schooldays, how she got on his nerves, how she treated Len like a child. Mary-Lou nodded sympathetically. Then he told her how there was no future for him at the San and that he was determined to get out. They walked more and more slowly, as the light faded, and then came to a rise where the road snaked between thick plantations of pines.

'Look at the sunset', Mary-Lou said.

They looked out over the valley. The sinking sun was deep plum-red, throwing lights in the sky and on the distant snow. A blue mist was rising.

Reg groped for her hand.

'You could do anything you wanted, Reg', Mary-Lou said after a moment.

It was quickly growing dark. They stood there for a while, and then walked on, but not for long. The odd car passed them, headlights gleaming. They went into the pine forest together.

Chapter 6

Felicity's Wedding

Con spent the next week considering Liz Arnett's offer. Sometimes she told herself that it was ridiculous; she was a serious writer and of course could have nothing to do with Briar Rose. But other times she thought that, after all, this could finance the serious work; she was very conscious of the need to support herself and there were certain luxuries she would enjoy. If she made enough money, she might be able to give up office work, concentrate on writing and have a lot more free time. And it was also a challenge. After all, she hoped she could write much better romantic fiction than the majority of the female hacks employed by Briar Rose. Eventually she decided that, since it was too embarrassing to tell her friends, she would use a pen name. At work, she'd continue to be Con Maynard, but the book - or books, there could well be more - would appear under the name of Constance Maine.

The novel itself was easy. It was sensible to set it in a place you knew well but which would seem exotic to most people. The Bernese Oberland was the obvious choice, so she called it *The Snows of the Jungfrau*. And once that was settled the characters fell into place. A young Englishwoman, going out to Switzerland to look after a little girl whose parents lived in a lonely *schloss*. Her employer, a dark, saturnine man of thirty-five who was outrageously rude to her (personally Con hated that sort of man, but women readers seemed to like him) and his shallow, selfish wife. She worked on it every evening when she didn't go out and on Sundays, and found she was enjoying it much more than she'd expected. By Christmas she had reached the bit where the hero's wife was killed with her lover in a hotel fire, and was almost ready to wind up.

By Christmas, though, various other things had happened.

She had been extremely worried about Len after their telephone conversation, and had written to her urging her to go on the pill. Her sister's letters had been very brief but, in

October, she'd said that Reg had left for the United States and she and the children would follow him when it was convenient. Con hated to think of Len, the main reason why she went on visiting the Oberland, going so far away. There was no chance of seeing Margot for years, either, and the idea of the three of them being in three different continents was deeply depressing. Apart from twelve months when Margot had been in Canada, the triplets had done everything together for the first eighteen years of their lives.

Then there was an extraordinary piece of news about the fourth Maynard daughter, Felicity. Fizz, as she was known because of her bubbly temperament, had left school last year with no qualifications whatever and gone to Zurich, where she was staying with an old friend of her mother's, to take a secretarial course. And now she'd met a young Englishman called Greg Furbank who was working there temporarily and in the autumn Con got a letter to say they were engaged. The wedding would be in the Oberland at Christmas so that all the Maynards, except Margot, could be there.

Con did a calculation, and realised that Felicity had only just turned seventeen. At first this shocked her so much that she considered writing to her mother, begging her to make the young couple wait at least a year. But in the end she decided that it wasn't her business. Her parents had presumably thought of that, and she was tired of people commenting on her tactlessness. You were more popular, she'd found, if you smiled and kept quiet. So she got on with *The Snows of the Jungfrau* instead.

With London getting set to celebrate, she packed her presents and flew out the week before Christmas. By the time she reached Interlaken, it was already dark, though little coloured lights were everywhere. Her father met her at the station.

Jack Maynard was a tall, fair man, looking younger than his fifty-four years, although Con thought that just now he looked a little tired and worn. They hugged affectionately.

'How are things, Dad?'

'Chaotic. Climb in, Con; we've got a long drive'.

He began to guide the car carefully up the mountain road.

'Well, Con, how's life in London - not working too hard, are you?'

Con knew what he was thinking but would not say; that here was Felicity getting married, and her younger brother, Stephen, was engaged, while she, Con, had had her twenty-seventh birthday last month, and there was still no sign of a man.

'I'm having a marvellous time'.

Jack grunted and concentrated on the driving for a few minutes.

'I've arranged to stay the night at home, but tomorrow I'm moving in with Len to help with the children. How is she?'

'Looking pale. She says she's fine, but I'm sure she misses Reg. Have you heard from Margot?'

He knew that the triplets had always written to each other, more regularly than they wrote home.

'She tells me a lot about apartheid. I must say, Dad, it sounds very nasty'.

'Yes, it does', Jack agreed. 'Just as well the Church can't get involved in politics, or I can see Margot getting quite cross about that. She's doing a great work, converting the Africans. We can be very proud of her now'.

Only 'now'. Con remembered that her father probably thought she was still a practising Catholic, and she was too fond of him to tell him the real situation. He had always taken his religion seriously; her mother had converted when they got married. They'd both been very concerned about Margot's behaviour when she was a teenager, and extremely pleased when she reformed and became a nun. Con sighed. She remembered a line someone had spoken to Audrey Hepburn in *The Nun's Story* - 'I can see you poor, I can see you chaste, but I can never see you obedient'. Had Margot really changed that much? It was so long since the three of them had been in the same room and talked.

'But the boys - !' Jack said. He sighed. 'Sometimes I think I'm out of touch with the younger generation'.

'Come on, Dad, it's just that you have an easier time with daughters'.

Her brothers were all expected home for Christmas. Stephen had always been sensible, and seemed quite content in his job as an engineer in the Midlands. And Charles, though very silent, had been through Cambridge and won a First. Con said, 'You mean - '.

'Mike's been thrown out of Dartmouth'.

'Oh, dear!'

'Yes. It was bad enough to have all those problems with various young ladies, but just when I thought he was off my hands, the Navy have decided they don't want him, and he doesn't want them. He actually told me that he wasn't prepared to take orders from anyone. I ask you', Jack said hotly, 'how can you get anything done in life, with an attitude like that?'

Con wasn't very surprised. Mike had always been trouble.

'And Felix - ! Well, he just lies about, listening to Rolling Stone records, and the other day I caught him smoking some strange-smelling stuff. I'm so afraid of him setting a bad example to the little ones. Geoff, too. I sometimes think that boy is wanting'.

'What about Felicity, Dad? She's awfully young to be getting married'.

Jack sighed again.

'Yes, I thought of that. But your mother says it's normal to get married young on the Continent. And Fizz is never going to be an intellectual, so she may as well settle down while she can. He's a Catholic and a nice young chap'.

They drew up outside the family house, Freudesheim ('happy home', it meant in English), and carried Con's cases indoors. A wave of sound hit them - Bruno, the dog, barking, Anna the Tyrolese maid clattering dishes in the kitchen, the children playing *Help* very loudly and her mother on the telephone to one of her many friends. She waved at her animatedly but did not stop talking. Jack pushed open the living-room door.

'Can you turn that thing off?'

Felix, his fourth son, who had been leaping about the floor with the eleven-year-old twins, gestured disgustedly.

'Honestly, Dad, you're so square!'

Jack turned off the record player.

'Can't you see your sister is here?'

'Oh, hi, Con. Dad, can I have the car this evening?'

'Have you got a present for me, Con?' shrieked little Philippa. Her twin, Geoff, merely stood and blinked.

'And, Felix, get your hair cut, please. It's ridiculous and unmanly'.

The children ignored him and made a concerted rush out of the room, probably to raid Anna's biscuit tin or watch TV. Con glanced towards her mother, but she was still chatting. Spurts of laughter, references to 'those awful Middles'. Jo Maynard was tall and dark, forty-eight now but looking much younger because she had kept her slim figure and you never saw her face in repose. She had been so much fun when the triplets were younger, always playing games with them, always on the go. What had happened, so that they couldn't talk now? Was it that the young women of her generation were different, as everybody was saying, or simply that she had grown up and her mother had not? She didn't like to think about it too deeply.

There was a whole shelf of her mother's books in the sitting-room - over thirty of them, from *Cecily Holds the Fort* through *Patrol Leader Nancy* to *Diana Wins Through*, published only last month. The first one had appeared soon after she left school and despite a very large family and an active social life she'd been writing them ever since. They had paid the boys' school fees and who knew how many other bills? The latest had a brightly-coloured jacket which showed a cheerful young woman with black curly hair, waving a hockey stick enthusiastically. Con shuddered, wondering if she would be expected to read it. As there was still no sign of Jo coming off the phone she took her luggage upstairs to the bedroom she had shared with the other triplets. But even this would not be hers for long - all sorts of people were sleeping here for the wedding - so she retreated to the one quiet room in the house and had a long bath. When she came down, Anna had made one of her excellent stews and followed it with *apfelstrudel* and a bowl of whipped cream. Con sank into her place, hoping for some adult conversation. The younger children had already been fed and sent off.

There were several familiar faces round the long table. Felicity, the bride, was in the house, but Con hadn't seen her yet as she was doing things to herself in the second bathroom. Her brother Steve was there with his fiancée, Sue, a very ordinary-looking girl who stared at her silently out of round blue eyes. So was an old friend, Roger Richardson, who was one of three children the Maynards had fostered in the 1950s. The other two were far away this Christmas (Roddy in New Zealand and Ruey in Devonshire with her husband and new baby), but Roger, the eldest, had always kept in touch and, although he was now working in the north of England, turned up at Freudesheim each winter to ski. He gave her a friendly grin as she dropped down beside him.

'Well, darling', her mother said warmly, 'isn't this thrilling? My little Felicity getting married; it seems too good to be true! And Greg is *very* handsome. I've been racing to finish my new book; it's called *Girls of the Blue Dormitory*. Mind you get it in your local library, Con, when it comes out. And are *you* writing anything?'

Con had no intention of telling her what she was writing. She smiled and said something about being fully stretched on the magazine.

'You ought to do something creative, darling. I've always said you were the one who inherited my talent'.

'Jolly good, Mrs Maynard', Roger said.

The telephone rang and Anna's head popped round the door.

'Frieda!' Jo shrieked and, abandoning her meal, rushed off to have another long conversation with another old friend. The rest of the evening was much the same; too many people around and too much going on to settle to anything. Con helped Anna wash up - she considered her shamefully overworked - and retreated to bed. But even there she wasn't to be left alone for long, because at half past ten Sue came in.

'Oh, hello, Con. Not asleep yet?'

Con reluctantly put aside *Dr Zhivago*.

'No'.

Sue began to brush out her mousy hair.

'Is it true your mother has *eleven* children?'

'That's right'.

'And your sister Len has *four*?'

Con knew she was being pressured to give an opinion, but she wasn't prepared to criticise her family to outsiders. So she merely smiled imperturbably. 'Yes'.

'That's incredible', Sue said. 'I've told Steve I'm not going to have more than two - a boy and then a girl, I hope. And I'm going to go on working for at least three years to get everything nice. Are you coming to our wedding? It's in September, in my own church - I insisted on that. We've got four little bridesmaids. I hope you don't mind being left out, Con, but you're a bit mature. How old are you exactly, if you don't mind my asking?'

'Twenty-seven', Con said between gritted teeth.

'Oh. Well, they're wearing gold and salmon-pink, and I'm wearing a veil, of course - one of my friends got married in a white hat, but I wouldn't feel properly married - '.

It went on until Con in self-defence pretended to have fallen asleep. She was moving out to Len in the morning, and she could hardly wait, but horrid dreams of little salmon wearing long white veils tormented her all night.

'I don't believe it!'

'You're the only person I've told', said Len, 'but other people probably know'.

Con's father had just dropped her at the chalet - her bed at home was wanted - and they were sitting at the kitchen table, with mugs of steaming coffee in front of them, each giving one dark-haired baby her bottle. Richard was asleep on his cushion while Johnno played with his coloured plastic letters on the floor. In sharp contrast to Freudesheim, everything was in perfect order. The windows shone; the Christmas cactus on the sill spilled its bright pink flowers against a background of Alpine snow. Con thought furiously, Reg never had anything to complain about. I'm damned if I'd take as much trouble as that for any man.

'*Who* knows?'

'I'm not sure. Mary-Lou wrote last week that "all our friends" think I'm selfish for not having agreed to a divorce. So, presumably, she's also been writing to half the Chalet School'.

Tears of sheer rage filled Con's eyes. She still couldn't take in the fact that Mary-Lou, the priggish and upright Head Girl she remembered, was having an affair with her sister's husband; it was rather like hearing that Miss Annersley had been picked up drunk. But obviously the permissive society had reached even this remote corner of Europe. It was strange that she was so angry and Len, apparently, so calm; although now she looked closely she could see that she was very pale and had deep shadows under her eyes.

'What else did Mary-Lou say?'

'Oh, she was very civilised. Just that she hoped we could be friends, and it was best to get out of an unhappy relationship, and I'd be happier if I moved on. Only', Len added, 'it isn't so simple to move on, with four children'.

'I should think not!'

Nothing was simple any more. After what Con had learned, she would have strongly advised her sister to cut her losses and get out, if it hadn't been for all those children. What was Len's future likely to be as a single mother? In fact if there was any chance that Reg might come back, it was clearly best that she should swallow her pride and take him. In that case, Con thought, they would all go to live in the States, and even when they met there would be an emotional barrier, because she would feel hatred every time she mentioned Reg or he came in the room. There was nothing to separate sisters and friends like getting mixed up with men.

'Do you think anyone - our family - suspects what's happening?'

'Mother doesn't'. There was a moment's silence; they both knew their mother liked to close her mind to anything unpleasant. 'Dad might - I'm not sure. Reg left in October and I thought at the time that we would follow when I'd got everything sorted out. Now he hardly ever writes. He hasn't asked me for a divorce; just ignores us. It's becoming embarrassing, but I've told people that I'm staying on for Felicity's wedding and we'll get that over first'.

The church was crowded. Practically all the extended Maynard clan was here, and assorted friends and well-wishers; Con thought that the last twenty-four hours at Freudesheim must have been hell. She had looked in briefly and met her awful Aunt Mollie who had demanded to know why her younger sister was getting married first and then tormented Len with questions about Reg. Now they were sitting near the front with the two little boys between them. The babies had been left behind but Johnno was thrilled to bits and asking questions non-stop.

Apart from Margot, everyone who mattered was there. Miss Annersley, very dignified in grey silk (she had greeted both the triplets with great affection), and their mother, tall and striking in leaf-green. The church was decorated with fir branches and Christmas roses. Her brothers, wearing suits and with angelic faces, showed the visitors to their seats. Then the anthem began.

Felicity swept up the aisle on her father's arm looking absolutely breathtaking. She was the fairest of the Maynards, with baby-blonde hair, eyes of forget-me-not blue and a delicate complexion. All in white, and carrying a bouquet of irises, she was so beautiful that people in the congregation caught their breath. She was followed by her younger sisters, in gentian blue - Cecil, a very pretty dark-haired girl of fourteen, and little Phil. At the altar she was met by Greg, whom Con had said hello to briefly. He had the dark striking looks of a film star and appeared to be madly in love.

As the splendid ritual of the nuptial mass rolled forward Con glanced at her sister, who was looking straight past the happy couple and towards the altar. Len must be thinking about her own wedding in this same church only five years ago. Then her thoughts wandered; was it going to be her turn next and what sort of man would she choose? Not one like Reg, that was certain, and not like the boy Greg either. And definitely she would not let her family vet him. She would be far away from here next week and then she would begin to look seriously.

Len was hoping she could get through the service. Richard was becoming bored and had started to climb all over her; she held him tightly and tried to ignore the waves of nausea. She had been sick once already that morning and, although she had eaten almost no breakfast, it seemed to be happening again. There could no longer be much doubt about it; she was pregnant. Had her sisters chosen the better way, Con the career woman and Margot the nun? Then your body needn't be invaded by men and you could concentrate on the things of the mind, which were more lasting. When she had been standing in Felicity's place, five years ago, she had been fresh from Oxford with a good degree and all sorts of interesting jobs open to her if she wanted them. She glanced down at the two little heads below her; Richard sucking his favourite bit of cloth and Johnno watching everything that was going on with wide eyes, storing up questions for afterwards. No, she could never imagine being or want to be without her children.

But she was feeling increasingly sick. Nobody to blame but herself, for there was no saying that she hadn't been warned this time. After a lot of agonising she had taken Con's advice and got herself to a clinic in Zurich where she'd sat for hours, desperately embarrassed and afraid of bumping into someone she knew. And after all that, they had said that the Pill was not suitable for her. So when Reg began groping her, two nights before he left, she had lain there miserably, feeling she had no choice but to submit. She was supposed to be a Catholic; she couldn't tell him to do what he obviously didn't want to do and take precautions himself. Whether or not their marriage survived, he wasn't going to like it. Thinking back, she had little doubt that his affair with Mary-Lou had started during the summer; they'd often been out of the house at the same time and afterwards there had been some mysterious phone calls late at night. Reg had got her pregnant when he was already deeply involved with Mary-Lou.

The service was coming to a climax. The white and black figures of Felicity and Greg stood at the altar rail, hands entwined. Len knew that she couldn't hold out much longer. She passed Richard into Con's arms and said under her breath, 'Look after them'. Then she was hurrying down the aisle, past all the people in their wedding clothes looking at her in amazement, until at last she was outside in the bracing air. It was fine but bitterly cold. She got as far away from the church as possible and then was sick in the snow.

Chapter 7

Roger Richardson to the Rescue

The day after the wedding was Christmas Eve.

Woken very early by the children, Len and Con got the house in order and then walked over in mid-morning to have coffee at Freudesheim. It was something they couldn't get out of, but Con would have preferred they had been left alone to talk, for her sister had just told her, in one of the few quiet moments of their day, that she believed she was pregnant.

The trip was just under a mile. They got the children into the big pram and wheeled them along the slushy road, the twins in their matching yellow woollies and Richard wrapped up like a little parcel with his legs dangling over the edge. It was a grey day, with wreaths of mist over the distant mountains and pine woods. Johnno ran alongside the pram and came back every so often to talk learnedly about what he had seen.

'I don't like abortion', Con said soberly, 'but in your case, if you could get one -'.

Len said, 'No'.

'But, if Reg doesn't come back, it could ruin your life!'

Her sister didn't answer but bent over to speak to Johnno who had rushed back to inform them that he had 'just seed a big black raven'. He was always coming up with unusual words. Con felt a wave of anger, although she had no intention of showing it. Wasn't her life already ruined? Unless Reg changed his mind and decided he truly loved her, like the heroes of Briar Rose novels, she was going to be bringing up those children on her own for the next twenty years. Len was the nicest of all the Maynards, much nicer than Margot who was supposed to be the saintly one, and she didn't deserve to be kicked in the teeth by Reg Entwistle. He had been a man of thirty when they married, quite old enough to know what he was doing, and Len had been so unsophisticated that she had never envisaged this. Only that morning, as they prepared to go out, she had caught a glimpse of them both in the mirror and thought she looked bruised, years older than herself.

'Don't push me, Con. I know what I can do and can't do. And I suppose there's always the chance that when he hears about this baby, he'll think again'.

'You're not hoping for that?'

Len sighed. 'Not very much'. They had entered the snowy garden of their old home. 'Anyway, don't forget, while we're here, that they know nothing about this'.

'When are you going to tell them?'

'I won't spoil their Christmas'.

Their mother's house was in its usual state of controlled frenzy. There was a huge Christmas tree, wreathed in coloured tinsel and with piles of presents, and the children were lying about the floor eating muesli or doing whatever else they liked best. Mrs Maynard - Anna the housekeeper told them - was writing her daily chapter upstairs and was not to be disturbed. The babies' coats were taken off and they were put down to play. Steve and Sue - Con was glad to find - had gone off for the day to visit friends, but Roger Richardson was still there. Like Steve, he was an engineer and he'd always pulled her leg about her ignorance of science. He was a big, powerfully-built man of twenty-eight, with red cheeks and ginger bristly hair.

After half an hour their mother appeared and, over coffee and Anna's excellent scones, they discussed the wedding. The happy couple had spent last night in Geneva and were flying to the Canaries for their honeymoon. Dr Maynard turned up later, from the hospital where he'd been working for most of the night. The post arrived - piles and piles of Christmas cards - and Jo threw herself on them with cries of joy.

'Nearly all for me! Grizel - my publishers - Miss Slater, our old maths mistress - I haven't heard from her for *years*, Jack! Isn't it good to have so many friends?'

Con went into the kitchen to fetch some more milk and unexpectedly found Roger at her elbow.

'Hello, Con! Haven't had a chance to talk yet. How's life in the book world?'

Con smiled and said that she was enjoying it.

'I read a book once', Roger said proudly.

'Did you? What was that?'

'*Lady Chatterley's Lover*. A chap told me it was quite good, so I got it. The heroine had the same name as you, by the way. Connie'.

'Nobody calls me Connie now. What did you think of it?'

'Well, I was a bit surprised', Roger said. 'Hot stuff and all that; I didn't think it was allowed. Well, of course it *wasn't* allowed until after that trial. I admit I read the spicy bits first but I did skim through the rest of it'.

'Don't say that in front of my mother', Con warned as they headed back to the sitting-room. 'She wouldn't like it'.

'What do you think I am?' Roger said, shocked. 'I say, Con, shall we go skiing later, if it clears up?'

'Yes, let's'.

Mrs Maynard was still working through her post and gaily waved a letter at them. 'This one came with a card from Clem Barras'.

Con wondered why Tony's sister should keep in touch.

'Clem Hodges, I should say. She's running a little art gallery with her husband and - *what's* this? Jack, have a look!'

Before the doctor, who looked grey-faced with exhaustion, could comment, Jo had snatched it from under his nose again and was reading aloud:

' "I was so sorry to hear about your trouble" - what trouble? - "I'm absolutely disgusted with Mary-Lou and have told her so - please give my love to Len - these things blow over". She must be out of her mind!'

Con and Helena exchanged a look but, without giving either of them a chance to speak, Jo went on stormily:

'Attacking Mary-Lou, one of the best girls the Chalet School ever had! People get very bitter and jealous when someone else does outstandingly well; I've noticed it in my own case. Mary-Lou is getting to be quite well-known in her subject and that must be the reason. And I thought she and Clem were such old friends!'

Jack Maynard was looking at his eldest daughter.

'Len?' No answer. 'Len, what does she mean by referring to you?'

'I think you'll have to tell them', said Con.

Len said steadily, 'Reg is having an affair with Mary-Lou, and she wants to marry him. I don't know if he wants to marry her, because he hasn't made contact for weeks. They're seeing each other regularly in the States. I haven't told you about it because I didn't want to upset you'.

The next two hours were indescribable.

When Jo was convinced that it was true - which took some time - she abruptly turned against Mary-Lou, who had been her close friend and favourite for the best part of twenty years. The younger Maynards slunk out of the room one after the other as she worked herself up into a rage.

'To think that girl should turn out like that - I could never have believed it - and to do it to *this* family! If she really had to go off with someone else's husband she could have left my daughter alone, at least. I did everything for her. I had her in this house for weeks'.

'Yes, you did', Jack Maynard said.

'And when her mother died, I went to Howells, leaving my own children behind, to help clear up because I was sorry for her! No wonder she hasn't written to me for ages; she ought to hang her head in shame. She's behaving like the lowest type of woman. She deserves to be smacked - no, flogged!'

'Oh, I say, Mrs Maynard', Roger protested, but Jo ignored him. With her black eyes flashing, and her colour up, she looked every inch as formidable as when she had been the strict disciplinarian head girl of the Chalet School, thirty years ago.

'Jack, *say* something!'

'All right', the doctor said, with the air of a man driven to the last ditch. 'You won't like it. If you hadn't encouraged that girl to move in on us, this might never have happened'.

'Jack!'

'It's true. *I* never cared for Mary-Lou, from the first time I set eyes on her, but that didn't matter, because she was *so* good for the Chalet School, wasn't she? You've had her here, and plenty of other silly women, chattering morning, noon and night about things which are none of your business and ignoring your own children. Or else you were running over to the school, or running after Mary-Lou, leaving your family to cope. It's an obsession. Sending your daughters to a decent school is one thing, making the school the centre of your life is quite another'.

'You're mad', Jo said with conviction.

'When Mary-Lou rang up, you should have told her yes or no, not sent her into Len's home to make trouble. Reg was a decent boy until he started getting work worries. I'm not defending him, but it's mainly her fault. Men run after other women but they go back to their wives eventually. Oh, yes, they do; you're too sheltered to know about these things'. The doctor pushed back his chair and got up, still looking haggard. 'I can't stand much more of this; I've been up half the night. Len, I'm sorry about this. If Mary-Lou -'.

Johnno had crept in and had been listening round-eyed. He piped up, 'I don't like Mary-Lou very much. Con says she's a complete bitch'.

Len silently picked him up and carried him out of the room. Con looked at her mother.

'Do you have to make a scene in front of her?'

'You expect me to take *this* quietly?' Jo's eyes were snapping. 'We *helped* Reg, brought him out here and treated him as a son. And now he's ruined my daughter's life - '.

'Don't say that when she can hear you, for heaven's sake, Mother! She needs to talk calmly and get some good advice'.

'Oh, shut up', Jack said to his wife.

They were clearly determined to carry on rowing. Con picked up the two babies, who had been playing on the floor but were showing signs of distress, and took them out. The fight continued for the next few hours, ebbing and flowing, even stopping for a short time when Anna brought in soup and sandwiches, but taking no account at all of other people. Len grew paler and paler, and concentrated on keeping her children out of the way. It was obvious to Con that her father had been storing up resentment of her mother's lifestyle for some time, and now it was all coming out.

Roger had been looking as embarrassed as she was. Early in the afternoon he said:

'Sun's out. What about some skiing, Con?'

Con agreed joyfully. She wrapped up, rooted out her old skis from the garage and joined Roger who was waiting for her with Felix and the little twins, Geoff and Phil. All of them looked depressed.

'They're just not with it', Felix said, jerking his head back at the house to indicate his parents.

'I'm sure it'll work out', Con said more confidently than she felt. 'Come on, let's blow the cobwebs away'.

They left the garden, passed the Chalet School, now closed for Christmas, and soon got to the crest of the slopes. There were about two hours of light left, and the snow gleamed brilliantly. Con put on her sunglasses, checked that the children had done the same, and then gave herself up to sheer enjoyment. She had learned to ski in Canada when she was a child and Roger, after years of visiting the Oberland, was also good at it. For such a solidly-built man, he was very light on his feet. He spun and raced like an expert, conspicuous against the snow in his red costume, and helped her up, laughing, when she had a tumble. Con thought he clung to her for a moment longer than was necessary.

At last it began to grow dark. They turned back and began to trudge towards the lights of Freudesheim, visible for a long way in the dusk, although there were no lights in the school buildings nextdoor. Inside, Con thought, there would be nothing but unhappiness; her conscience pricked her for leaving Len and she thought that she would ask her father to drive them home. However, she could not bring herself to hurry.

The sky was pale mauve, with one or two brilliant stars. The snow had the blue look which it always had on winter evenings, and which she loved. Most of it was untrodden, only broken by the dark lines of pine wood. She and Roger walked more and more slowly. The children went in through the garden gate, and she felt her arm brush his; then suddenly they had stopped under the group of silver birches and moved together. Without any words at all, they began kissing passionately.

Chapter 8

Con Falls in Love

'I didn't think nice girls did this', Roger said blissfully.

They were lying in the single bed in his Pontefract flat on a Sunday in March, three months after the fateful ski trip. One of the minus points in their relationship was that he lived so far north and hadn't a car, but they did manage to meet at his place or hers most weekends. On this occasion, Con had left her car behind, and for some reason she couldn't get her mind off the boring train journey ahead of her, and the things she would have to do at the office next day.

'Does that mean I'm not nice?' she asked smiling.

'No, silly, you know perfectly well what I mean. Of course the pill makes a difference'. He sat up. 'Shall I have the bathroom first, or will you?'

'You go'.

Left alone, Con snuggled under Roger's tatty eiderdown and tried to keep warm. It was a cheerless sort of place (he was no good at housework, like most men), and she felt she'd spent far too many hours looking at his ceiling; moreover, they had to share the kitchen with the family downstairs and this embarrassed her because they knew perfectly well that she stayed overnight. Next time, she thought, he can jolly well come to me. Perhaps not for a fortnight, as she really needed a weekend by herself to work hard on her book. Briar Rose had accepted *The Snows of the Jungfrau*, on very satisfactory terms, and she was working on a new title for their historical series, *Gunfire off Guernsey*, a tale of the Napoleonic wars. Roger was one of the few people who knew about her unofficial earnings. She would not have wanted to tell her parents or more high-minded literary friends, but he thought it a great joke.

While they were having breakfast she ran over the things she might do before she left. Clean and smarten up the flat - that would be a kindness to Roger, but she wasn't sure she felt strong enough. Go for a walk - but it was raining, and she'd already seen most of what there was in this unexciting northern town. She'd tried bringing a book, but that made him restless as he didn't care for reading. He had once taken her to a football match, something she had no wish to experience ever again. They would just have to get the Sunday papers and glance over them together, then a pub lunch and then she would go. It surely couldn't be the case that she was looking forward to it.

'I'm tired of all this commuting', Roger said unexpectedly.

'So am I', said Con.

'So that just proves, it's high time you moved here. Yes, I know what you're going to say, Con, and I'd move to London like a shot if I could, but that's impossible. So really, we ought to do some planning'.

'I can't leave my job yet'.

'Couldn't you get another job?'

'Not the sort I'm trained for'. And she was determined not to teach.

'But, look, Con, there's no reason why you should have to work at all. A man's earnings are meant to support his family. And I thought you wanted more time for your writing, and you can do that anywhere. We could always find a little house where there's more space'.

Con looked at Roger's nice, straightforward face, on the other side of the cornflake packet, and was silent. She had no intention of giving up her comfortable flat, or her interesting social life, or her job which she might indeed relinquish when it suited her but which was bringing in a good income meanwhile. Pontefract struck her as one of the dreariest places on earth and moving into a little redbrick house of their own would not change that.

'And then', Roger went on, 'I could go to work each day and you could write. Well, until the babies arrive, but you can start again once they're at school'.

Con shied away as she always did from the mention of babies.

'Roger, the truth is I'm a little frightened of getting married. You'll have to give me time. When I think about Len – '. No need to say any more; Len who was five months pregnant, Len whose husband was now demanding a divorce.

'I know', Roger said, outraged, 'I think that Entwistle chap is a complete skunk. Poor old Len. I say, Con, you don't think *I'd* behave like that, do you? Children need a proper home life; I should know. I'd quite like playing with the little blighters'.

Con sighed.

'You're coming to London for Easter, aren't you?'

'I certainly am'.

'Well, I'll show you the sights, and you'll see why I'm not keen to move. We're quite happy as we are'.

'But, Con, I miss you awfully during the week!'

There was no answer to that.

Roger hugged her warmly on the platform, and Con experienced an obscure sense of shame. He was the last person she would willingly hurt and yet, she felt, she was somehow doing it. Now she had to survive the interminable Sunday train journey. She took out her paperback and realised it was one she'd already read. Nothing to do but watch the vast cooling towers of Pontefract moving further away, and think.

She had got involved with Roger for a variety of reasons - Felicity's wedding, Helena's situation, the fact that for two years she'd done no more than exchange a goodnight kiss with a very few men. That night in the snow and darkness it had seemed absolutely the right thing, and for a while she had been extremely happy. But perhaps that was because she'd never spent long periods of time alone with him. The last two weekends, they'd been running out of things to say.

She had not been brought up to have affairs with men she didn't mean to marry, and certainly, at first, that had been in her mind. But now that Roger was talking seriously about marriage, she was beginning to panic. Oh, damn, Con thought, watching the grey landscape sliding slowly past, I feel really cheap. There was Len, who was on her own and needed a nice, supportive man, but Roger was in love with her, Con, and Len was religious and didn't believe in the validity of divorce. Everything was a mess.

Next morning, addressed to her care of *Sixties Woman*, she found a party invitation from 'Tony, Malc and Kermit', in North Finchley. She tried to work out who it had come from, and decided that it could only be Tony Barras. That was nice; she'd rather regretted being dragged away from him. Accepting by return of post, she spent an unusually long time deciding what to wear. As yet she hadn't quite dared to try a miniskirt, but eventually she visited her favourite boutique and got a skimpy gold and orange dress which flattered her dark complexion, and came well above the knee. It was a Friday night, and Roger couldn't get away until Saturday, so there was no question of bringing him. In fact, there seemed no particular reason to mention Roger at all.

There was a real sense of spring in the air. Pink and white and yellow froth on the trees and bushes round Hyde Park, little patches of bright colour in the town gardens. Con bought a bunch of daffodils and a bottle of wine and drove herself to the address as early as she decently could. I do hope I can spend some time with him, she thought. I would so like to talk about the old days.

Tony lived in a small terrace house in London brick, the sort of base you'd expect for a struggling young photographer. The front door was open and the haunting strains of 'Eleanor Rigby' drifted out into the street. Not many people had arrived yet. A very short boy, who introduced himself as Kermit, welcomed Con and bore her into the kitchen where there was a huge bowl of punch. She accepted a glass and then set out down the corridor hoping to find Tony.

But as she turned into the front room her eye was caught by an enormous photograph of herself and the other triplets, aged about sixteen. She looked up at it in disbelief; she couldn't remember it having been taken at all. Well, yes, there had been a summer at Plas Gwyn when Tony had been staying at Carn Beg, and he had always been snapping things. And as she went closer she recognised the old plum tree in their garden and a corner of the white house. It was rare to get two people looking good in one photograph, let alone three, but somehow this one had achieved it. No wonder Tony thought it worth having on his wall.

They all looked so innocent. Schoolgirls in their time off, wearing what had probably been blue-and-white check dresses or handed-down blouses. Len with her ponytail tied back, looking happy and confident. Herself looking dreamy, probably thinking about some story she was writing, dark eyes ignoring the camera. Margot holding a white cat. She'd always been the bad one of the three in those days and it showed in her slightly naughty smile. Heavens above, Con thought; it was more than ten years ago.

'Do you like it?'

Tony was standing just behind her and Con summed him up with a quick flick of her eyelashes. He was interesting-looking rather than handsome, tall and a bit thin, with very light brown hair burned gold by being out a lot in the sun. He wore a blue and grey fisherman's jersey and was smiling as if he was seriously glad to see her.

'I wondered if you'd got my card'.

'Yes, thank you for asking me. Tony, that's a brilliant photo'.

'I was lucky', Tony said. 'That was the first one I ever took where everything came right'.

'Is that unusual? Sorry, I'm very ignorant'.

'Well, usually you get about ten fairly average pictures, and two or three disasters, for one that's any good'.

Con thought, he's obsessive about photography, like I am about writing; I can see him snapping away until he gets just what he wants. That's why he's so damn good at it.

'You should have sent us a copy'.

'I'll do that now if you like. How are you all? I haven't seen your sisters for ages'.

'I don't see them very often myself', said Con. 'The three of us haven't been in the same room since Margot became a nun'.

She felt a wave of nostalgia. All those summers when

they'd been teenagers and practically lived out of doors, making themselves sick on green apples from the Carn Beg orchard, or climbing, camping, pony-trekking in the Black Mountains not far away. Clem and Tony had frequently been there when their parents were on painting tours and it had always been a wrench when they went back. She remembered that Tony had not seemed too happy in those days. A bad-tempered father, a philistine boarding school. How had they lost touch?

The silence had gone on longer than was comfortable. 'I hear Clem had a row with Mary-Lou'.

'Yes. I'm afraid I know all about that'.

'Oh, it's no secret. My mother still pretends that Reg has gone on ahead of his family for work reasons, but everybody else knows the real situation. I never liked him anyway. It was Mary-Lou's behaviour that really surprised me'.

'I wasn't a bit surprised', said Tony.

'But Mary-Lou was always so frightfully goody-goody! The Head used to hold her up as an inspiring example!'

'She was goody-goody because that was the way to get on in your old school. Now we're out in the world, the rules are different, and Mary-Lou has only ever been interested in Mary-Lou. She's a bossy, selfish, go-getting woman, and I'm very glad', Tony said, 'that she and Clem have stopped speaking, because I'm not sure I could trust myself to be polite to her. Help! Am I losing my poise?'

Con laughed.

'Well, Tony, it may turn out all right'. She ought not to be feeling so happy, when they were talking about her sister, but she could hardly help it at this moment. 'Len is very forgiving - actually she doesn't believe in divorce - and she thinks Reg might come back, after the baby's born'.

'There's a baby?'

'Oh, yes. Due in July'.

A laughing group swept into the room, and the moment was shattered.

'You must meet some people', Tony said. 'This is Christine, and this is my flatmate Malc, and this is - oh, help, I must go!'

Someone had dragged him off saying he was wanted on the phone, and Con was surrounded by strangers. The girl called Christine asked her what she did, but after a moment she detached herself and wandered back to the kitchen under the pretext of getting more drink. The little house was filling up, 'Eleanor Rigby' was on again and all sorts of strange people were sitting intertwined on the stairs. She edged past them, looking at the enlarged black and white photographs which had been put up at intervals. Apart from the one she had just seen, none were portraits; she remembered Tony preferred working out of doors. Sailing boats, a ruined cottage, probably in the Highlands, a sky with black clouds, a seascape with rocks and gulls. He was definitely the most attractive man she'd met in years, and a superb photographer. Suddenly she knew that whatever happened, she could not go on with Roger Richardson.

But why should nothing good happen? She went back down the stairs, deep in thought but managing to chat to Kermit, who was wearing something that resembled a patchwork quilt, and seemed to like her. She could give a party of her own, or an intimate little supper, anything so long as it wasn't obvious. She and Tony had so much shared background, that had to be a good start for a relationship.

'Ladies and gentlemen, your attention, please!'

It was Malc, now standing on a chair. Christine, the pretty fair-haired girl whom she'd met briefly, was being pushed forward to the centre of the crowd, and Tony was also somewhere in sight. The Beatles were turned off in mid-phrase - *'Eleanor Rigby, wearing a face that she keeps in a jar by the door'* - and then nothing.

'I have an important announcement to make'. Malc's beard sprouted all over his chest and was really hideous, Con thought; her father would have called it degenerate. 'As you know, Tony, Kermit, and I have always said we were the three musketeers and were never going to get married but go round breaking women's hearts instead'. The girls in the audience hissed. 'Kermit and I are still of the same mind, but I'm afraid that Tony - '.

Con felt suddenly sick. Fortunately no one was looking.

'Well, Tony met Christine at - where was it, the love-in at Hyde Park?'

'No, you filthy-minded freak', Tony said.

'OK, anyway, they met, and there's no doubt whatever that Tony is a lucky chap, but I don't know what Christine sees in him, when she could have had me. She's a great girl'. Absolutely commonplace, Con thought furiously. 'Despite everything we tried to do, they're now engaged, and we'll have an even better party when they get married. Please raise your glasses to the happy pair!'

Con raised hers automatically. *Eleanor Rigby, picks up the rice in a church where a wedding has been*; her brain crawled round and round the words. Tony had his arm round Christine and they both looked sickeningly happy. The toast was drunk.

Next week, Tony sent her the photograph, and she wrote to thank him. But he didn't send an invitation to the wedding, which took place three months later, and if he had, she most certainly wouldn't have gone.

Chapter 9

The Third Generation

Helena woke up in the early hours, with the dragging pain at the base of her stomach becoming more frequent. The fourth time she had gone into labour, and she knew more or less what to expect. She got up, put on her bedside lamp and pulled back the curtains; the stars were fading and she could just see the outline of the Jungfrau against the greyish sky. Catching sight of herself in the full-length mirror, as she moved about cautiously to avoid waking the children, she didn't much like what she saw. Not only her hugely swollen womb, but her skin was muddy, her loose hair dull reddish brown, her whole posture that of the downtrodden housewife which, she supposed, she was. There'd been a time when she could have afforded nice clothes and a good haircut, but that was years ago. She was still only twenty-seven, but she seemed to have lived through so much.

She remembered how at Oxford she'd seen a student production of *The Scarlet Letter*. A young woman with a brand on her forehead, capital A for adulteress. Sometimes Len felt like that, only in her case it was a capital D for divorcee. D for deserted wife, D for discarded, dumped, disgraceful. Everyone in this conservative little community knew exactly what had happened and she could feel their eyes on her every time she took the children out. The first divorce in her family, that was another mark against her. Her Aunt Madge, the foundress of the Chalet School, had lived happily all her life with her husband and family. Her father was devoted to her mother, although they sometimes quarrelled, and her mother's friends had all married at about the same time as her and seemed blissfully happy. If any of the husbands strayed, the secret was well-kept. She knew that some wives had a lot to put up with and she knew that they were supposed to bear it, but her own situation was worse again.

She hadn't much doubt now that it was starting. She put on a loose dressing-gown to hide the bulge, went downstairs and made a cup of tea. Then she walked around, trying to take her mind off the discomfort; she could just see the furniture through the strengthening light.

Some of Reg's clothes were still hanging in their wardrobe. At first, she had kept one of his old jackets near her and held it against her face when she felt most depressed, trying to remember the feel and smell of him, willing him to contact her. It was some months since she had done that and now, as the pains grew more insistent, she thought, this is my last child, he'll never come back. Not after all this time, when he's had a taste of freedom. She'd spoken to her husband on the telephone just three times this year. He'd been very reluctant to make contact, but she had persevered, since he obviously had to be told about the baby. He was furious of course, said that it was her fault and then, 'You mustn't have it'.

'Reg, does it concern you, if you've already left me?'

'Of course it does; I'll have to pay for it, won't I? Listen, I *know* a man in Zurich who can get it done'.

She had refused. There were two more calls, this time initiated by him, raving at her to 'do something about it'. Then silence.

And, last month, another letter from Mary-Lou. It had said that she was quite wrong if she thought the child would make any difference to Reg, and that if she filed for divorce now she, Mary-Lou, would make sure she got a reasonable settlement. She couldn't believe that it was part of her religion to make other people unhappy. Len hadn't replied. She couldn't see any urgency, since Mary-Lou had made it clear that she didn't want children of her own, and she'd already got Reg. Her instincts told her that it was best to deal with one thing at a time, and first she wanted this baby born safely.

But over the last few days, she had been working on a letter to her husband. It was already addressed and stamped; now she took it out of the envelope and read it over again as she walked up and down. It wasn't particularly good; it certainly wasn't a passionate or loving letter, but she thought the children might never forgive her if she did not try.

Dear Reg, (Not 'dearest' or 'darling' Reg; she couldn't quite manage that). *How are you and what is it like in Boston? Do get in touch and tell me. You must know that, whatever happens, I'm still awfully interested.*

The baby is due any day now. I know how you feel about this, and I'm sorry; I think now that a lot of what went wrong between us was probably my fault. I just sort of assumed when we got married that we would have a large family like my parents, without taking into account that children are an awful lot of work! As you know, I've already agreed not to have any more, and, if you feel that you cannot accept a fifth baby in the family, I will arrange to have him or her adopted straight after the birth. Apparently it's very easy to find good homes.

She had checked on that. Even for Reg she was not going to dump her baby in an orphanage. But as she re-read the letter she was struck by another fear, would he want her to give up the twins too? That was impossible; they were nearly two years old and had never been looked after by anyone but her although they were practically strangers to him. Her words sounded stilted and unreal.

The children have changed so much since you last saw them. Johnno is doing little sums on his abacus and can read about a hundred words - they'll be amazed when he starts school! Richard has finally begun to speak in sentences and is now just like any other three-year-old. They talk about you all the time and are longing to see you again. The twins have changed most of all; they run about all over the place on their fat little legs and chatter to each other in their own funny language. Maggs is the dominant one and Tessa follows wherever she goes. I can tell them apart but no one else can. Even Con, when she was here at Christmas, was perplexed.

Reg, is it absolutely impossible to try again? I'm not asking this for myself. The children need you - boys, in particular, need their father. It can't be good for them to be in a different continent from you, and they love you so much. If you send for us, we'll come out to you as soon as I'm fit to travel. You will not have to see any more of my family, and I will never say a word about the past. *Or if you like to come back for a flying visit we can meet up as a family and talk. I know that five - or four - children are quite a lot, but I will take full responsibility for them; you need do nothing.*

As a matter of fact, she thought rebelliously, Reg never had done anything very much with the children. Overseeing Johnno in his bath when he had time was about as far as he'd got. Again, he'd often complained about broken nights when she was the one who actually got up to feed the baby. But there was no future in thinking like that. Words of love wouldn't come but she had said what she could. *We have known each other for nearly half my life and I think we shouldn't give up too easily. Please let me know how you are getting on. Always yours, Len.*

She sealed the letter and put it prominently on the mantelpiece, to be posted later that day. The pains were definitely getting worse. She went over to the phone and, as arranged, dialled Miss Annersley's private number. Waiting for a reply, she remembered how Reg had never missed a chance to sneer at her old school. Old maids, he had called the mistresses, probably lesbians; a game of rummy after the girls were tucked up in bed was about the greatest thrill they got. He'd said that her mother had never got over being a schoolgirl, which was true, and that neither had she, which wasn't. Why had he been so determined to hurt her over the last two years?

The headmistress's voice came on the line.

'Aunt Hilda, this is Len Maynard'. She seemed to be using her maiden name more and more frequently. 'I think I'm going into labour'.

'All right, my dear; I won't be long'.

'Did I wake you?'

'No, people of my age need very little sleep and I spend most nights reading. I'll be with you very soon'.

This had been agreed between Miss Annersley and herself, ever since the school broke up for the summer holidays. She didn't want to disturb her parents in the middle of the night. Over the last months she'd seen her father growing greyer and more tired, her mother alternately raging that she was going to punish Reg, have him run out of town, and saying brightly that she was sure he would come back once the baby was born. It made her feel deeply guilty.

She went into the children's room. The twins, Maggs and Tessa, occupied the same cot and as usual were lying with their arms round each other, the two dark heads close together. Richard was fast asleep with his short arms flung up, Johnno sucking his penguin, which had gone almost bald over the last few months. She crossed the landing, washed and dressed, then went into the guest room where her sister Cecil was sleeping.

'Cecil? Sorry to wake you, but I'm just leaving. Everything is ready downstairs for the children's breakfast. Don't ring home until it's a reasonable hour'.

Cecil opened her eyes, mumbled 'OK', and immediately went back to sleep. She looked very vulnerable, with her dark curls scattered over her striped nightie, and as Len went downstairs she found herself hoping fiercely that no man would hurt her little sister when she grew up. Even the baby twins would be expected to go through all that in twenty years. She picked up the case she had prepared and went outside to where Miss Annersley was waiting in her car.

'How are you feeling, dear?'

'I'm fine', Len said, and they began to drive down the valley as the sun appeared between the peaks.

Even at this hour in the morning, the headmistress was neatly dressed, her hair arranged in its grey bun as usual. How did she do it, Len wondered? At sixty-seven she was still running the school successfully; it contrasted so starkly with the mess she had made of her own life. Her thoughts were far away when the Head said abruptly, 'You know, Helena, I've always had a great respect for you'.

'I can't think why you should', Len said.

'Oh, yes. Your sisters each have their special gifts, but you were the one we could rely on in an emergency. When I was a girl I saw several young war widows bringing up families alone and making a good job of it. Some of them even married again, but the point is, they were perfectly capable of managing by themselves. I hope Reg will come back, but if he doesn't - '.

'Aunt Hilda, I'm not even sure I want him to come back'.

'You can't mean that, my dear', Miss Annersley said, and stopped at the entrance to the great sanatorium which had more maternity cases than TB patients these days.

The next few hours were a confused nightmare. She should have been used to it by now, but there were the same pains as usual, the smell of gas making her sick, the midwives going in and out and talking over her head while she bit on her tongue, not to scream. And finally a baby girl, very small and with reddish hair, was pulled out spattered with blood and washed roughly before being given to her. The next moment they took her away again, then Len herself was sponged and helped into a clean gown before being wheeled back to the new mothers' ward. On her way she could hear a woman screaming.

Hardly any time later her father, who had been fetched from another part of the hospital, was standing over her smiling.

'Well, Len, you've certainly come up trumps! She's a fine little thing. Did you say you were going to call her Frances?'

Len smiled back dutifully. 'Yes'.

'I've brought my camera', Jack said unnecessarily. 'Let's take the two of you together'.

She sat up and received the sleeping baby in her arms. There were still traces of dried blood on her hair and ears. No one could understand the shock of giving birth until they had experienced it. Jack took a photo. She knew he was going to send it across the Atlantic.

'And now get some sleep, my dear girl'.

It wasn't a proper sleep. Only nightmares, in which her baby was crying but could not be found, and she herself was standing in the pillory with a scarlet letter on her forehead. Len exhausted herself trying to make out if it was A or D. The day must have passed, because she was aware of people talking round the next bed, the clashing of knives and forks. Then she was roused so that the baby could be put to the breast. She sucked strongly. Then it was the evening visiting hour, and she took in that every other woman in the big ward was with her husband, except her.

Her mother came in, followed by a morose Felix, who had driven her to the hospital, and Johnno in a state of high excitement clutching a bunch of marigolds.

Jo looked splendid and much younger than the other grandmothers.

'Well, darling, this *is* a thrill! What a pretty baby! Five children already, Len, you're catching up on me!'

'I want a little brother', Johnno announced. His cheeks were crimson and Len guessed that there would soon be tears.

'But, darling', his grandmother said, 'you can't have one this time; it's a girl!'

Johnno took one look at the baby, then threw his flowers down and said scornfully, 'It looks exactly like an insect'. He then refused to talk and spent the rest of his visit running up and down the corridors, with Felix in reluctant pursuit.

Jo perched on her daughter's bed and talked about how lovely the baby was, and how exciting it had been when she had the triplets, more than twenty-five years ago. She said that all young couples had their little spats and Reg would soon return, or send for his family to come to the States. Len could only smile and make the appropriate responses.

But it was a relief when the visitors were gone, the lights out and the babies taken away to the night nursery. In the darkness she could hear someone else crying and remembered that the waves of grief usually hit you a few hours after the birth. Suddenly her own tears were falling, and she buried her face in the pillow so no one could hear her. Five children, when Reg might have tolerated two, even if he was incapable of being faithful. And now everyone was trying to comfort her by saying he would come back.

She'd been lying for the best part of a year, she thought, pretending that everything in her family was normal when it plainly wasn't. And, to her intimates, she'd said that she was eager to save her marriage. Not that she didn't stand by what she had written in her letter. She would forgive him over Mary-Lou, because she believed in turning the other cheek; she would take him back if he asked because she had made a promise to him before God and because the children would do better with any father than none. But as for how she felt, that was a very different matter.

She hadn't thought that anything could kill her love for Reg, yet he himself had done it. Mary-Lou was not the main issue at all. It was the years of little snubs, the sneers at everything she believed in, the evenings when she'd waited to see if he would or wouldn't come home in a temper, the nights he'd used her to slake his lust and then complained about her lack of response. It was more peaceful without him. She'd felt that increasingly in the last months.

Anyway, whatever her parents hoped, she was sure that this baby would make no difference. The decision was out of her hands; he would never come back.

She was crying now, not for her husband as everyone would have supposed, but for her sisters. She wanted them, she needed the only two people with whom she didn't have to pretend. But it was hopeless of course. Con had her own life in England and when Margot had walked out of the family home, they had known she would never come back. Even in an extreme emergency, she was under orders. God knew when the three of them would meet again. Her shaky self-control broke and she wept into her pillow, 'Con! Margot! Margot!'

Chapter 10

Margot

'WE SHALL FIGHT, WE SHALL WIN! PARIS, MOSCOW, ROME, BERLIN!' It was May 1968 and Margot Maynard was in London, living in a friendly convent and doing a short course at the School of Tropical Medicine. She'd had three years in South Africa, seeing things which she had never heard or dreamed of, and didn't know herself where she'd be sent next. The headlines blared at her.

Student riots in Paris, Socialism with a human face in Czechoslovakia, and, always, the continuing brutal war in Vietnam. Martin Luther King assassinated, Bobby Kennedy assassinated and an election coming up in the U.S. that November. An announcement on birth control was expected from Pope Paul in the summer. Margot hoped that the old man would not blow this one.

Saturday morning and she was sitting in a workmen's cafe opposite the School, spinning out a cup of tea while she waited for her cousin Peggy Winterton, formerly Peggy Bettany, who'd got her address via Con and insisted on a meeting. They hadn't been in touch for years, belonged almost to different generations, and Margot guessed she was only doing it because she wanted to talk to a real-life nun.

Peggy had some difficulty recognising her when she turned up, rather breathless and laden with Harrods bags. The wife of a naval officer, she was in London for a shopping spree before his leave and, as Margot had surmised, was curious to see how her young cousin had turned out. Her idea of a nun was a figure in flowing black or white robes radiating goodness and purity, like Julie Andrews in *The Sound of Music*, so she was more than a little startled when she identified the only other woman in the cafe. A plain dark blue outfit with half-length skirt, nothing on her head, hair brutally cropped, heavy glasses (and she had been such a pretty girl, Peggy thought regretfully). Margot was just Margot.

'Hello! Lovely to see you!' Peggy ordered coffee and eclairs, while Margot stowed away her *Guardian* and theology paperback in her duffel bag and prepared to be bored for half an hour. 'But you *did* give me a shock, old thing. I didn't think nuns were allowed to dress normally'.

Peggy herself looked what she was, a housewife of thirty-six with her two sons at prep school; perm, nails, blue twinset and string of artificial pearls all exactly as they should be. Both women were a total contrast to the young people on the sunny pavement: the girls with long hair and amazingly short skirts, the boys also with long hair, ruffled shirts and the odd string of beads. Outside the dark little cafe there was riotous colour everywhere.

'That's Vatican Two', Margot said. 'Anyway, I could hardly wear a robe in the tropics. I'm a doctor; I need to dress sensibly'.

'Your work must be absolutely fascinating'.

'Hm'.

'And how's your family?'

'Con's okay. She seems to like her job'. Con was getting more than a little materialist, Margot thought, but didn't say. 'And, of course, you know about Len'.

'Yes. So sad. How old is the baby now?'

'Frances? - nearly one, I think. I've never seen her. Len's very efficient, and our parents keep an eye on her. So she's okay too'.

'I expect you'll be popping over to Switzerland to see them all?'

'I can't just pop over to places', Margot said austerely. 'I'm under obedience. It's possible my father and some of the rest might visit England this summer, but I'm here solely to do this course and when it's finished I'll go where I'm sent. Almost certainly outside Europe'.

'But while you're *in* Europe, you've got to see your family!' Peggy sounded horrified.

Margot shrugged. She wondered whether to quote *I have no mother and no brothers*, but this woman wouldn't understand,

and anyway, she really did want to see Len and still hoped that it could be arranged. So she only said, 'I see Con every few days. We get on'.

But Peggy's mind was on something else.

'Tell me, Margot - you won't mind if I ask you something personal -'.

Margot waited. She knew exactly what it would be.

'Don't you *mind* being a nun? - I mean, I'm deeply religious myself, of course, but don't you miss having children and a husband and – well - all that - ?'

'You mean sex', Margot said bluntly. 'No, not really. How could I?' Taking pity on the older woman's puzzled expression she went on, 'I'm a bit curious, perhaps, because it's something I've never experienced, but then I've never seen the pyramids and I can live with that. Given the choice, I'd prefer the pyramids'.

'That's awfully unusual', Peggy said.

'Yes, it's unusual, but it happens to suit me. Look at it this way. I have to go where I'm most needed - it could be the Congo, it could be south-east Asia - anywhere that people need a doctor. I couldn't do that if I was running round after a husband. And as for children, plenty of children in the Third World don't live till five because of measles or polio or other things which are perfectly curable. My father is going to be out of a job soon because Europeans no longer get TB, but it's still a big killer over there. People are too interested in their own families and not enough in the things that matter. I worked very hard for six years to get my MB. I'd be throwing all that away if I had a private life'.

'But haven't you ever *wanted* to get married?'

'It's okay for those who care about it. I don't particularly'.

Peggy nodded, but it was obvious to Margot that she would never understand. A wave of depression swept over her, and she was relieved that she no longer had to spend much time with her family. They had all looked up to Peggy when she was head girl, and now she'd become completely bourgeois and trivial. Always behind her eyes she saw the images which kept her going; the sprawled bodies after Sharpeville, the Vietnamese with a revolver held to his head. And worse, an African baby about the size of a kitten, who had died literally between her hands. The mother had had no milk because her breasts had run dry. People in the affluent West just didn't seem interested.

As they were saying their goodbyes, an American student from her course came into the cafe.

'Hi, Margot, baby!'

'Oh, hi, Wolf'.

Peggy's eyes grew round.

'Joining me for lunch?'

'I don't eat lunch', Margot said.

'Well, stay for coffee anyway'.

Margot's lips twisted slightly as she waved Peggy off. She was just the sort to think that if a man and a woman talked to each other affably, they must be having an affair. There were people with nothing else on their minds, like the mad Professor Marcuse in California who preached that you could have a revolution through sex, but you'd have to be pretty sheltered, Margot thought, really to believe that. And there were also people in the Catholic church who wanted nuns to go around in pairs to avoid temptation, but that made her impatient too. She wasn't tempted; it so happened that she liked tall fair Englishmen, not little men with straggly beards about the same height as herself. The reason she was interested in talking to Wolf was because he had spent two years in Vietnam as a medical officer. What he had seen had drawn him deeply into the anti-war campaign. And she wanted to find out what was going on in the US protest movement now.

'Who's the dame?' Wolf asked as he tucked into a bacon sandwich.

'My cousin. I haven't seen her for years'.

'I don't think she approved of me'.

'I'm sure she didn't'.

'Going to the demo this afternoon?'

'Yes'.

'Well, hang on. We'll go together'.

Margot asked for a glass of water and joined him at the grubby table. Wolf showed her a cartoon from his *Private Eye* and she looked at it without amusement.

'Too frank, huh?'

'No, just not very funny'.

'Margot, can I ask you something - ?'

'Not you too', Margot said. 'Peggy's just been quizzing me about why I'm not married'.

'Oh, it's not that. Hell, *I* don't believe in marriage. No, this is what puzzles me, I always thought the Catholic church was on the far right in politics. Bishops blessing bombs and that. Jeez, you should have seen those padres in Vietnam. So how come you're a radical *and* a nun?'

'Everybody makes that mistake', said Margot.

She took off the glasses which she'd started wearing as a student when her eyes began to give trouble, and Wolf was startled by the difference this made to her face. Hell, this babe could be good-looking if she let her hair grow. It was a nice colour, reddish gold, and she had a neat little figure too. He watched fascinated as she wiped the lenses and turned the full force of her personality on to him.

'The Catholic church became corrupt when it took up with governments. It's like Communism. The Czechs are trying to get back to the original ideas and exactly the same thing is going on inside the church, since Pope John. I despise the bishops who bless bombs as much as you do, but they're not what Christianity is about. It's about justice, non-violence, defending the poor against the powerful. Readiness to be martyred, if necessary. You notice that priests and nuns are in the vanguard over Vietnam'.

'Yeah', said Wolf. 'There was this guy throwing blood at a recruiting office'.

'I want to go to America', Margot said. Her eyes, which were a vivid cornflower blue, blazed at him across a distance of about eighteen inches and he felt quite weak. 'That's where so many things are happening. The civil rights movement, liberation theology. People like Dan Berrigan I'd really like to meet. Even if it was only for a month or two, I wish I could go'.

'I'll take you, baby'.

'You know that's impossible', Margot said. She replaced her glasses and the light went out of her face. 'I can only go where I'm sent'.

'But, look, Margot - '.

'We'll be late if we don't move'.

They left the cafe and started heading, like many other small groups this bright afternoon, for Trafalgar Square. On the way he tried to convince her that she shouldn't obey the Church authorities but do what she herself believed in, and Margot told him it wasn't blind obedience but self-giving service. She enjoyed a good argument, and was quite relaxed by the time they reached the square. Plenty of people were already milling about and there was a marvellous assortment of banners - CND, Socialist Labour League, the Anglican Pacifist Fellowship, the World Federation of Anarchists. Red and black flags, black and white and green lollipops with the international peace symbol; Margot drew a deep breath of happiness.

'See you, Wolf. I'm just going over to talk to my friends'.

She ran over the busy road to South Africa House, where a small group of men and women were standing outside the main door. They had pledged that someone would always be there to bear witness for as long as apartheid went on. Margot stayed with them for about quarter of an hour, while the square filled up behind them and Wolf fidgeted with impatience. When she got back she seemed surprised to find him waiting.

'Oh, are you still here?'

'Sure am. Aren't we going to walk together?'

'Okay', Margot said, but she was not entirely pleased. She had intended to meet some friends and was still looking for their banner as they went deeper into the crowd. Wolf attempted to take her hand but she side-stepped; she couldn't believe he meant to be taken seriously.

'Just wanted to show you that guy up there. The beard. I know him; he's very big in the anti-draft movement'.

'Really?'

'And who's the old guy with white hair? Is it Bertrand Russell?'

'No, he doesn't go anywhere now; that's Michael Foot. Wolf, I'm looking - '.

'Margot?'

'What?'

'How old are you? You must have been a kid when you went behind bars'.

'I'm twenty-eight'.

'Twenty-eight and you've never done it! Wow!' Wolf rolled his eyes in amazement.

Margot was beginning to feel annoyed. Twice in one day, when all she wanted was to get on with her job, she'd had to endure people sniping at her. 'Wolf, I've explained this several times; I've never wanted - '.

'But, baby, how do you know you wouldn't like it if you haven't tried it? I could show you things. I could open out a whole new world to you'.

'No, thanks'.

She'd been trying to walk faster to get away from him, but so many people were pouring into the square that it was nearly impossible to move, and now that they were jammed in the middle of a crowd of Sussex University students she could feel his hand in the small of her back. She removed it, none too gently.

'What's the matter with you?' Wolf asked. 'Are you a lesbian or something?'

God help me bear this, Margot prayed. Aloud she said patiently, 'No, but I've made certain promises and I intend to keep them. I've given you absolutely no reason to think –'.

'Oh, come on, baby - '.

He was actually trying to grope her under cover of the crowd, while the speeches boomed above them; presumably he thought she'd be so confused and embarrassed that she wouldn't know how to stop him, and then passion would sweep her away. She jerked back furiously, cannoning into a couple of bearded young men with a banner, and addressed him in the biting tones she had learned long ago, from Miss Annersley.

'Listen, you squalid little man, since you force me to be frank, I don't like you. Actually, I find you repulsive. Morally *and* physically. I'm a doctor, remember; I've seen more male bodies than you've had hot dinners, and if I wanted to go against my principles and sleep with someone it most certainly wouldn't be you. I'd rather go to bed with - with LBJ. I talked to you out of common courtesy and because I wanted to hear about Vietnam, not because I have the faintest interest in you as a person. Is that clear? I'm going to join my friends now, and I warn you, don't come after me!'

There was a ragged cheer from the group of students behind them. Wolf gaped at her, completely surprised. Margot looked at her nearest neighbour.

'Please keep this man away from me. Before I wring his neck'.

The crowd parted to let her through. She went on walking towards the edge of the square until she thought she was clear, but tears were misting her spectacles and she felt so upset and shaken that after a while she was forced to sit down on the steps. A voice from the plinth of Nelson's Column was saying 'unarmed women and children'. Why were women always targets? she wondered. She knew she'd just behaved in a highly unsuitable way and that perhaps she had been asking for trouble. Because she dressed in ordinary clothes, went round by herself, invited her fellow-students to call her 'Margot' instead of 'sister', it could be said to be her own fault. She'd thought about how she would react to being raped - that was a real hazard in some of the places where she might be sent - but she had not expected to have to deal with a common sex pest. You tried to talk to an acquaintance, who happened to be a man, about the things that interested you, and all the time he was planning to boast to his friends how he'd made it with a nun. Exactly the sort of stuff she had hoped to put behind her for ever. And she would have to face him in lectures on Monday. Oh, damn!

The crowd was moving. They were marching towards Grosvenor Square and the United States Embassy. Margot fell into step with them, trying desperately to look calm. She wiped her eyes, hoped that no one was looking at her, and then came up against the Pax Christi banner and a group of people she knew.

'Margot, how nice to see you!' It was Bernard, a Dominican from Oxford, with a nun, Pauline, who'd accompanied her on marches and vigils before. They were smiling down at her. The relief of being with people who didn't think she was mad was enormous.

'We shall overcome, we shall overcome. We shall overcome some day'. The crowd was singing, and Margot joined in. Traffic roared past them, rocking ancient statues, and the multicoloured banners waved bravely overhead. She walked forward, into a world that needed changing.

THE END OF THE NINETEEN SIXTIES

THE NINETEEN SEVENTIES

Chapter 11

Crisis for the Chalet School

It was March 1971.

Outside her study windows, Miss Annersley could see the snow melting rapidly. It had been too slushy for winter sports this last week and now there were patches of bare earth and some starved-looking grass in the school garden. But the sky was grey, the chilly wind unpleasant and it had been too foggy to see the mountains for several days.

Well, the crisis meeting would be held tomorrow and she was going to do her very best to save her beloved school. And afterwards, whichever way the decision went, she would have to think about her future. She was seventy - would be seventy-one in three weeks - and she knew that most people of her age had retired years ago. The plan had always been that she and Miss Wilson would retire together and do all the things that they'd never had time for, basing themselves at her friend's cottage on Dartmoor and doing as much globe-trotting as they could afford. But Miss Wilson had died in 1969, two days after a stroke, the second tragedy to hit the school in less than three years. She hadn't had the heart to leave straight after that, although Nancy Wilmot had been dropping hints about old ladies who didn't know when they'd outstayed their welcome. Miss Annersley was well aware of these remarks and they hurt her, but she felt in her bones that she had got to stay and see the school through its problems. Nancy was too young and inexperienced to deal with the appalling crisis which was now upon them. If the Chalet School survived, Nancy could take over, and she herself would go quietly.

People said the sixties had been a decade of revolution, and looking back, Miss Annersley thought that she hadn't enjoyed them. They had taken some of her dearest friends and brought in several changes which she could not approve. Girls with long straggly hair and mini-skirts (not permitted in her school), revolting students, young people who listened to loud strange music and said it was all right to have sexual relations outside marriage so long as the girls didn't get pregnant (although frequently, of course, they did). Not that Miss Annersley disagreed with the young rebels all the time. She was appalled by what she heard about the war in Vietnam. And she had no strong feeling against the Beatles or Rolling Stones; it was natural for each generation to prefer its own music. But there were other things going on which worried her deeply.

Perhaps the rot had started when a girl came back after the summer break sporting a tattoo on one finger which, she said, she'd had done at the Reading Festival. Miss Annersley had scolded her and pointed out that she would be stuck with it for the rest of her life. Then a sixth-former was found to be pregnant. It hadn't happened at school, of course, but in London over Christmas; however her parents had blamed the staff for not having discovered it earlier. Straws in the wind, but they couldn't have happened in the great days of the Chalet School. She was always having to confiscate silly magazines or Briar Rose novels from the girls' lockers, or reprove them for getting too friendly with the younger workmen. And then there had been the dreadful business of the drugs, last year.

A fifteen-year-old had been caught smoking marijuana. Miss Annersley now knew exactly what the famous weed smelled like. She had excused her, but made it clear to the whole school that anyone caught with illegal substances in future would be expelled. Nothing happened for a month, then three girls were found giggling and incapable in Miss Ferrars' geography lesson and one, it turned out, had been making a nice little profit selling 'joints'. All three had had to go, although it brought back distressing memories to the Head, from the time of Betty Wynne-Davies.

Miss Wilmot had said sourly then that it wasn't very sensible to throw people out when their rolls were already falling. For by the end of the 1960s, there had been a sharp drop in the numbers of girls. It was partly to do with the decline of the sanatorium;

the school no longer got girls whose parents were receiving treatment or who were delicate and needed to live in the Alps. And partly it was because people no longer wanted their daughters to go abroad to be 'finished'; they sent them somewhere nearer home or even to ordinary non-feepaying schools. There was a feeling, too, that the Chalet School was somewhat old-fashioned. And that was what was causing so much trouble now.

The school was owned by a company, Chalet School Ltd., founded by the late Lady Russell and her husband. Sir James had died last year and his shares had passed to his six children. Miss Annersley had just had a sharp letter from their accountant, Herr Braun, pointing out that the school was in the red and something would have to be done quickly. There was a crisis meeting scheduled for tomorrow. Two of Lady Russell's daughters, Sybil and Josette, were in Switzerland and would be attending. Their brothers took no interest in the school and had agreed they should do what seemed best.

The Head got up, feeling the pain of arthritis in her back; her timetable would wait for no one. She was dreading that meeting. The accountant would only care about profits, of course, and she was not certain she could rely on the two Russells. Josette had always been a sensible, warm-hearted girl, who surely wouldn't want to destroy her own old school. But Sybil!

Sybil, Lady Stornoway, got out of her taxi and wrapped herself more closely in her silver fox fur as the chauffeur carried her baggage up the snowy path to Die Kiefern. It was years since she'd been back to this place; the thought of schooldays made her shudder and when she went skiing, it was to more fashionable resorts like Klosters. And it must be an age, she thought, since she'd seen poor old Len.

Sybil had been a problem since early childhood. The Chalet School had seemed to improve her somewhat but she had never been thought worthy to be Head Girl, a job which most members of her extended family had taken on as of right. A very glamorous young woman, she'd got married in Australia at twenty-one but that marriage had ended in circumstances (thought to be connected with a Sydney stockbroker) which her mother could not bear to speak about. A year later she was back home and had opened a little boutique in Chelsea. Then her name began to appear on the society pages with those of various men, in particular Archie Stornoway, whose wife had failed, after ten years, to give him any children. The columnists knew that Archie was unhappy at the thought of his title becoming extinct. There was a messy divorce, Archie and Sybil were married and she'd immediately produced a bouncing son. That had been seven years ago, but she was still, at thirty-four, considered one of the most beautiful women in London; London meaning the small group of people Sybil knew. She was staying at Die Kiefern because her sister, Josette, was staying at Freudesheim and Jo Maynard had said she wouldn't have that wretched girl in the house.

The door was flung open by a crowd of children and Len, who greeted Sybil with more affection than she had expected, seeing that they had never had much to do with each other or a lot in common. But Len rarely got the chance to talk properly to anyone of her own age, and was delighted to have her cousin under her roof. When you'd known someone a long time, hardly anything else mattered, although she knew that Sybil's name was mud in some sections of her family. It was almost as good as having Margot or Con.

Johnno, the eight-year-old, scampered up with her to the guest room, asking questions all the time. What was the difference between Lady and Mrs, he wanted to know, and did she live in Stornoway? He'd looked it up and found it was the capital of the Hebrides. Sybil explained that she never wished to set foot in the place, and her home was in London, which surprised him a lot. Then he helped her arrange her bottles and jars on the dressing-table, still chattering, and led her proudly downstairs.

'Mum, Sybil's very kindly brought us some presents!'

Sybil produced a box of Swiss chocolates and some Elizabeth Arden perfume.

'Sybil!' Len contemplated the brand-name in awe. 'How kind - but you shouldn't have bothered'.

'No bother. I haven't seen you for years'.

Sybil had been unobtrusively looking over her cousin, the way she always did when she met another woman. There were several years between them but, she thought with satisfaction, no one would guess. Len was wearing slacks and an old blue jersey, suitable for this chilly weather, and her reddish hair, once so abundant, had been cut short. The children all had colds; she must have a boring life with them. As a teenager she had been quite pretty, but now the most you could call her was pleasant-looking. Reasonable features, still slim, but absolutely no glamour. Poor Len.

'I was hoping you might bring your little boy. He's almost the same age as Johnno'.

'Binkie? Oh dear, no; he's in school'.

Len knew that many people dumped their sons in prep school at the earliest opportunity. Her own parents had done it, but she herself believed it was cruel to send a child away from his home. The very idea of doing without Johnno, who was so much fun and so full of extraordinary questions, appalled her, but obviously not every woman felt as she did. Margot, for instance; the one time she had met the children, on a flying visit in '68, she'd hardly looked at them. And Con, though perfectly friendly, clearly wasn't all that interested. She would never understand it.

Sybil had plenty of time to sort out the children's names when they gathered round the kitchen table for a meal of soup, brown bread and gruyere cheese. Johnno, with his intense black eyes, was easy to remember; his little brother Richard was fairer and squarer, and obviously not half so bright. She couldn't tell the twins apart, both rosy little girls with dark hair. And Frances, now three, was a pretty little thing whom they all made a great fuss of.

After the children had been bathed, said their prayers and gone to bed (Sybil re-read *Vogue* while this was going on) they sat by the fire with mugs of cocoa and talked.

'Are Reg and Mary-Lou actually married?'

Len sighed. 'Oh, yes'.

'I thought you didn't believe in divorce'.

'I don't believe in it for myself. So long as Reg is alive, I obviously can't get married again' - neither of them pointed out that this was unlikely anyway - 'but I agreed to the divorce. To be honest, Sybil, I got very tired of Mary-Lou telling everyone that I was being selfish'.

Sybil remembered how Archie's wife had cried and struggled. 'I hope you got a good settlement?'

'The cheques come every so often. We're all right'.

'Do you get any social life?'

'Well, I see other mothers at kindergarten, and I help out at the school when I can. Sybil, about the school - '.

'But, Len, that's no kind of life for a woman your age!' Sybil knew people thought she was selfish, and perhaps they were right, but suddenly she felt very sorry for her younger cousin. '*How* old are you now?'

'Thirty-one'.

'That's nothing. Look' - Sybil decided she was going to do the thing properly - 'why don't you park the children with Aunt Jo, come back with me to Knightsbridge and I'll give you a month in London. I'll take you to my hairdresser and round the shops, my treat. You never know, you might pick up a man'.

'Really, Sybil, I'm not sure that they're worth picking up. And seriously - '.

'Okay, if you don't want to have an affair you can still have a holiday. You need a break from kids; everybody does'.

Len looked impressed.

'It's very, very kind of you, Sybil. I'll never forget it. Apart from anything else, I would love to see Con'. Yes, Con, thought Sybil, why didn't she do anything for her sister? 'But there isn't anywhere to leave the children. My mother wouldn't be suitable at all'.

'Why, what's wrong? She's used to looking after children, surely!'

'There are only Geoff and Phil now, and they're sixteen.

But over the last few years - '. Len hesitated, but after all she could tell Sybil, who was a family member. 'Well, she's become rather - strange'.

'How?'

'Little things; they sound trivial by themselves. For instance, she's told several people that Reg has died. Of course, divorce was a terrible scandal when she was a girl. And in other ways, she simply isn't coping. Poor Anna does what she can, but she's fifty now, and it's a big strain for her, and for Dad. So you see, I can't expect her to help me. I have to help her'.

Sybil gave up. She'd done what she could.

'Incidentally, this business about the school is worrying her a lot. You know how she feels about it. Is there any hope that it can be saved, do you think?'

'I'm not sure', Sybil said. Her own mind was made up, but she wasn't going to admit it yet. 'We'll have to see how the sums work out'.

Chapter 12

Sybil Pulls the Plug

There were five people at the meeting: Miss Annersley, her deputy Nancy Wilmot, Sybil, her younger sister Josette, and the accountant, Herr Braun. His letters had already made an unpleasant impression on the Head and, as she showed him around, making polite conversation, she kept thinking of the phrase 'gnomes of Zurich'. Herr Braun did look a little like a gnome, being very short, squat, and with a long nose and deep red complexion. He seemed to communicate mainly in grunts.

Jo Maynard, the person who cared most passionately about the fate of the Chalet School, was not there. Her husband had told her firmly to keep away, as she had no official standing, but she had made sure that everyone concerned knew exactly how she felt.

Miss Annersley escorted them round the new gym, the two chapels which the school had financed itself (Herr Braun made a snorting noise), the pleasantly furnished reception rooms. She showed them the many awards the school had won, the long roll of university graduates, the photograph of their star pupil, Nina Rutherford, meeting the Queen at the Royal Festival Hall. Then she told them about the school's achievements over the forty years since it started in the Tyrol, how the Nazis had failed to suppress it, how it had straightened out several difficult girls. She spoke of its many gifts to charity, its policy of teaching in three languages so that all girls became fluent linguists, its emphasis on religion, scholarship, and good behaviour. Herr Braun listened to all this without a word. Sybil didn't say much, either, only yawned from time to time, so Miss Annersley directed most of her remarks at Josette. Tall, dark and eager, the younger woman listened politely and kept some sort of conversation going. Josette had married an Australian and picked up a slight accent over the fifteen years she had lived in Melbourne. She and her family were in Europe for a year, but were returning soon, and she mentioned that she was going to teach aborigine children now her youngest was at school.

'Very good, my dear', Miss Annersley approved.

She had high hopes that Josette would be on her side.

When they had gone back to the Head's sitting-room and been given coffee the meeting proper began. Through the windows they could see a number of Middle School girls playing netball, and hear their cheerful voices.

'The matter is perfectly simple', Herr Braun announced, as soon as he had got out his folder. 'The school is, how do you say, up shit creek'.

'Do you prefer to speak in German, Herr Braun?'

'As you please'.

'He's right, you know', said Sybil, who had been studying her face in her powder compact. 'I've looked at the figures, and they're quite horrendous'.

'But, my dear Sybil, you were a prefect at this school and it was founded by your mother. I can't believe that you would wish to see it disappear'.

Sybil just yawned.

'There's no need to give up so soon', Miss Wilmot said stormily. 'If the school had a second chance, with a younger woman - '.

'I'm afraid not, Nancy'.

It was obvious to everyone in the room that Lady Russell's eldest daughter had absolutely no feeling on the subject. Miss Annersley knew very little about the lives of the rich but she remembered the story about a millionaire outside the Savoy Hotel, bending down to pick up a coin from the gutter. Sybil would grab every financial advantage and refuse any sacrifice.

She turned to Josette.

'How do you feel, my dear? You were Head Girl back in 1955, and I would like to think that the Chalet School still means something to you'.

Josette was looking uncomfortable.

'Aunt Hilda, it's not the money'. There was a slight movement from Sybil. 'Well, that isn't the prime consideration for me. I did enjoy my time here, and I agree my mother did a splendid thing, starting the school in the Tyrol before the war. It was quite an achievement for a young woman in those days - '.

'That is ancient history', Herr Braun said rudely.

Josette turned to face him.

'You're right, we *have* moved on since then. I appreciate what the school did for me, I think it's very good of its kind, but I'm afraid, in spite of all that, it's elitist'.

'I beg your pardon?' Miss Annersley had never encountered that word.

'I mean it only serves a few people. Just think, Aunt Hilda, what it costs to ship out rich girls from England or whatever country they live in and educate them here, cutting them off from their families and their natural origins. I could only agree to propping the school up if it was a community school, open to every child on the Gornetz Platz'.

'But, Josette - '. Miss Annersley had picked up on the word 'rich', and thought she knew what the young woman was getting at. 'We can't solve all the problems of the world, but we've never cared about a girl's background, and we do have one or two scholarships, in fact, for the less well off. You must know that we aren't some sort of finishing school, as you imply. We've always tried to give our pupils a good sound education and turn them into responsible women. I don't believe that anyone of your age can have any idea what it was like for girls when I was young. A little embroidery, a little tinkling on the piano, that's all they were offered. My dear mother made sure I went to one of the few good schools that existed in those days so that I would be able to support myself, whatever happened. And that's what I've tried to pass on to my own girls'.

'Middle-class girls, Aunt Hilda. There's no way an ordinary working person could afford to send their daughter to the Chalet School'.

'But you have daughters of your own!' Miss Annersley felt she was floundering.

'Yes, I have two daughters and a son, and all of them are doing very well at the school in our own street. I wouldn't dream of sending them away from home, and I wouldn't segregate my daughters from boys, either'.

'But, Josette!' Miss Annersley really thought the young woman's brain must have been addled by her long stay in the New World. 'You can't go along with this absurd idea that girls and boys should be educated under one roof! It's surely obvious that if you throw young people together, some of the girls - the sillier ones - will get into serious trouble!'

'Not necessarily, not if they're sensibly brought up. And what's the alternative? Would you prefer them to leave school knowing absolutely nothing about men?'

Josette's dark eyes were glowing and she looked disturbingly like her aunt Jo Maynard, who would have been appalled by what she was saying. She went on, 'My idea of a good school - '.

'All this is very interesting', Sybil cut in, 'but I think the decision's been taken'.

Miss Wilmot burst into tears and stumbled from the room.

'Well', Miss Annersley said, after a long silence, 'I see that none of you agree with me. If you've all made up your minds to kill the Chalet School, you will do so. But please don't think it has anything to do with the fine ideas you've been explaining, Josette. I'm afraid it comes down to one thing - money'.

Later in the day Len phoned the school to ask the Head how she was coping. Josette had looked in to say goodbye, visibly upset. Someone was crying in the background but she was fairly sure that it was not Miss Annersley.

'So kind of you to ring, Helena. How is your mother taking it?'

'Badly. Aunt Hilda, is it absolutely certain?'

'Yes. The basic decision was taken this morning and we've spent the rest of the day trying to salvage what we could. Herr Braun wanted to send the girls home straight away, without even finding out if there's anybody there, but after a lot of argument we agreed that they should leave at the end of term, in two weeks, as arranged. I shall write to their parents and hold a final assembly before they go. And the girls who are taking public exams will come back next term and be coached by a skeleton staff. It took me a long time to convince Sybil that we couldn't let them down'.

'Sybil and Josette – '. Len could find no words.

'Yes. Your Aunt Madge built up the school from nothing, and now her daughters have killed it. I wonder what she'd say if she could see us now'.

'Aunt Hilda, what are you going to do?'

'Me personally? Oh, I shall survive. Nell Wilson left me her little cottage, as you may know, and I mean to go there and collect my old age pension. I have plenty of friends and interests and I'm sure I shall enjoy having more free time'.

'I'll miss you', Helena said, almost in tears.

'My dear, if I were you I should start planning to come to England. Your parents will do so, I'm sure. There'll be nothing left on the Gornetz Platz without the School'.

Chapter 13

Jack Maynard Has Enough

Dr Maynard decided to walk home.

It was over a mile, but lately he'd grown reluctant to come back too soon after work, especially since the awful crisis, three weeks ago. His wife had been almost impossible to live with since the death sentence had been passed on her beloved school. Wearily he thought, the worst thing of all hasn't even sunk in.

For the end of the Chalet School would almost certainly mean the end of the hospital in its present form. He'd seen this coming for many years, and perhaps he ought to have got out. But the right offer hadn't come up, and he was not keen to go from being head of the Gornetz Platz sanatorium to a subordinate position somewhere else. And Jo had fiercely resisted any suggestion that they should move away from the school and her friends. So, weakly, he'd always said to himself that it would last his time. The younger doctors had moved on, Grizel Sheppard's husband had died and she had gone weeping back to England, but he had stayed, watching the work shrink every year. Now that the four hundred girls and staff had been removed, there was hardly enough work to keep one doctor going. The Platz would of course try to build up a tourist trade, but that would take time.

The setting sun gleamed on the wet pools by the roadside. He went over his assets, and thought that, like his patients, they were shrinking fast. Their summer home in the Tyrol had had to be sold years ago to pay school fees. There remained Plas Gwyn, the family house in the Golden Valley, where three of the boys had been born. It had been rented out, and was in a poor state of repair, but they could go back there while they decided what to do. Then there were Jo's earnings from her silly books. They would help, and a doctor could always find work.

But the children - ! He sighed; most of them were independent now but there were still those five little things at Die Kiefern. How they were to be educated he had no idea, if Reg didn't pay up more generously than he was doing. Jack still felt very bad about having encouraged his eldest daughter to get married. He'd known Reg as a boy; he had been aware of his bad temper but had believed he'd improved. It made him feel worse, somehow, that Len did not complain in his hearing and was managing so well. If she'd waited a little longer - If she'd met more young men. It was too painful to think about for long.

At least Con was not trapped in Len's awful situation. But thinking of Con set off a new train of worries; why was a pretty and attractive young woman, thirty-one last year, still unattached? If she had any boy friends she did not mention them to her parents. He couldn't understand it.

And Margot? Well, Margot at least was settled, thank God. The family hadn't seen her since she went back to South Africa in 1968. Her letters were very short and all about 'the struggle'.

His sons were all in England. Steve was married to Sue and they had a little boy. None of the Maynards liked her, but they seemed to suit each other well enough. Charles at twenty-seven was a lecturer at Durham University, which was the next best thing to Oxbridge, he believed. Apparently he knew more about some obscure seventeenth-century German poet than anyone else in the world. So far, good, but it was almost impossible to talk to him; he never phoned his parents and sounded embarrassed when they phoned him. Charles was very strange.

Mike was still a problem, as he had been all his life. He loved messing about in boats, and the original idea had been that he should go into the Navy, but he'd been thrown out, around the time of Felicity's wedding, because he couldn't take the discipline and said he didn't want to be killed, anyway. Jack had pointed out in vain that there was most unlikely to be another war. So Mike had become an estate agent in a small south coast resort which had a boatyard where he spent every weekend. Ever since he was sixteen there'd been a procession of girls and Jack had had to take time off to sort out his private life, only a few months ago. Rosemary, the current girl friend, was pregnant and she and her parents were distraught. Jack had flown to England and told him sternly to face up to his responsibilities, and between them the three adults had got the young man into his penguin suit and down the aisle. Neither his mother nor any of his sisters, except Con, had been there. The girl seemed a nice little thing and her baby was expected very soon.

Felix had taken a degree in something called drama studies and was now hanging around London, doing odd jobs in the theatre. Jack couldn't help thinking that it wasn't a real profession. So far as girls were concerned, he was behaving exactly like Mike. And Felicity, his twin, was based in Surrey but racketing all over the world with Greg. She was having a marvellous time and didn't mean to have a baby for ages, she said.

That left Cecil, his fifth daughter, now at a teacher training college in London, and the twins, Geoff and Phil. The boy was still at his boarding school in Suffolk until they could sort out what to do with him, and Phil was at home. It was likely that they'd have to lower their standards and send both of them to state schools.

He passed the school just before he got to his own house and thought how desolate it looked, with no one in the garden and the dying sun gleaming on windows from which most of the curtains had been taken down. Only a handful of girls would come back to be coached in the summer term, and then it would all end.

Jo was nowhere in sight when he let himself into Freudesheim, although he could hear her voice haranguing somebody upstairs. With a guilty feeling of relief he helped himself to a whisky and slunk into the little den just off the sitting-room where he dealt with his personal mail. There he looked over the post, which he'd been refusing to think about for the last few days. All bills, bills, bills.

The only sensible thing to do was look round for a job in Wales or England, preferably one which would enable them to live at Plas Gwyn. Then they could try to sell this house, which was now much too big for them. It had been a hotel once and could become one again. He would have to take what he could get, and, after all, his wife could do her writing anywhere. It kept her happy.

And Len perhaps could come with them. There would be nothing left for her on the Gornetz Platz, and they could help her settle back into life in her own country, perhaps all living under one roof. He worried about those little boys growing up without a father. Johnno was very bright. It would be splendid to have him around all the time.

He thought with sudden longing about opening up Plas Gwyn, himself perhaps working part-time and going walking with the dog in the Black Mountains, Jo earning an income for the reduced family with her children's stories. He'd have to persuade her that there was no chance of the Chalet School reopening. It seemed difficult for her to take that in.

He had reached this point when the telephone on his desk rang and he picked it up to be connected with his daughter, Cecil. They hadn't seen the child for six months as she'd declined to come home for Christmas, saying that it was too far and she was staying with friends. It was quite unusual for her to ring instead of sending postcards.

'I'm engaged', her cool voice said.

Jack wasn't very surprised. Cecil had the sort of porcelain good looks - small, dark, composed - which appealed to a lot of men, and they had been buzzing round her for two or three years now.

'My dear girl! Tell me about him'.

'He's called Hywel Davies. I met him at the London Welsh club the first week I came here. He's a music teacher, he's twenty-five, and I've stayed several times with his parents in Cardiff. They're lovely'.

Somewhere at the back of his mind Jack registered that his daughter had had a boy friend for over six months and said nothing about him, and that she had preferred to spend Christmas away from home.

'And before you ask, Dad, they go to chapel, but he's agreed to bring up the children as Catholics. Not that we're going to have any for a while; I want to get my diploma and do a few years' teaching'.

Jack could never get used to the way these young people

ignored what the Pope had clearly said in *Humanae Vitae*. Clearing his throat he said, 'Splendid. I look forward to meeting him. Now, I'll get your mother, and we'll start to plan the wedding'.

'Oh, help, no', Cecil said, sounding shocked. 'Honestly, the last thing I want is a big wedding like Fizz's. We'll do it very quietly in London next month. You'll come over, won't you?'

'Of course, but - Cecil, are you quite sure you're doing the right thing? It's a big decision. You're only nineteen, and we wouldn't want you to make the same mistake as Len - '.

'I know him really well, Dad, and it's okay. We both like the same things - ballet, and Gilbert and Sullivan, and his family and all our friends think it's great'. The pips went and she added rapidly, 'I won't ring back. 'Bye!'

Jack put down the telephone and wondered why he was worrying instead of rejoicing. Cecil was young but she had always been sensible. It crossed his mind that they hadn't said a word about the closure of the school, which had been the main topic of conversation in their home for three weeks. Sighing a little, he went out into the sitting-room to find his wife and almost bumped into her and their youngest child, Philippa, a sulky-looking girl of sixteen with a ragged mane of dark hair. Jo's colour was high and she was waving a typed letter.

'Jack, where *have* you been? Look at this! It's an outrage!'

'I've just been talking to Cecil. She's engaged'.

'Oh, good. Now read this! I haven't been so insulted in thirty years!'

Jack took the piece of paper. It carried the familiar letterhead of his wife's London publishers:

Dear Miss Bettany,

I have now read your novel, **Sylvia, Games Prefect**, *and am sorry to say that we are unable to publish it. We feel that children in the 1970s need a different type of story, one that deals with boys as well as girls and, preferably, characters from a wide mix of social and racial backgrounds. I am afraid your work now seems a little old-fashioned and would* be unlikely to appeal to present-day readers.

    We have unfortunately been confirmed in our suspicions by the sales figures from your previous books, which have been falling for the last seven years. Consequently we will not be reissuing the **Girls of St Faith's** *series, and do not feel we can take any new titles, as they would be unlikely to sell in sufficient numbers.*

    I know that this will not be welcome to you, but we have been forced to make many hard decisions in the present economic climate.

    I am returning your manuscript with regret, and hope that you will be successful in placing it with another publisher.
Yours very sincerely,
Caroline Pemberton-Walsh.

    'What *is* she on about?' Jo demanded as soon as her husband had finished reading. 'My work "old-fashioned"! I suppose she wants stories about fifteen-year-olds who get pregnant by coloured men. The kind of sordid stuff that gets in print these days is unbelievable! And who is this Caroline woman anyway? Violet can't have seen my book herself. I'll ring her'.

    'You've forgotten', Jack said patiently. 'Violet retired last year'.

    'Oh, *that's* it! They've probably put in some young girl straight from Oxford who doesn't know the first thing about books. I'll ring every other publisher in London, if need be. They'll take it'.

    She whirled out of the room.

    'They won't', Philippa said as soon as her mother was out of earshot. 'No one reads that stuff nowadays'.

    'Phil!' Jack said warningly.

    'Oh, don't worry, I won't say it in front of Ma. Dad, where am I going to go to school next?'

    Jack sighed.

    'That's a problem, Phil. It depends on where we're going to live and I rather think that you and Geoff may have to go to ordinary state schools. That is, if any school will have him without being paid for it'. It was well known that most of the brains which the twins had between them belonged to Phil. 'Just do as much reading as you can and get ahead'.

'Anna says that, if we move, she won't come'.

This was an unpleasant surprise. Anna had been the person who kept the house going while her mistress was writing or having babies, and the family had been heavily dependent on her for the last thirty years. Jo claimed she was so devoted that she had even turned down an offer of marriage to stay with them, although Jack had never quite believed that story.

'Are you sure?'

'Yes. She says she wants to go back to the Tyrol'.

Anna confirmed this when he ran her down in the kitchen.

'I am sorry, Herr Doctor, but I'm over fifty now, and the children are nearly grown up. I did not want to leave them in *this* house -' she sighed and rolled her eyes upwards - 'when they were little. But I will *not* go to England again - I was most unhappy there during the war - and my sister in the Tyrol is offering me a home now her husband is dead'.

'Well, Anna', Jack said, 'you must do what seems best, of course'.

Jo wasn't going to like this, not one bit.

Anna was still glowering as she served supper to the three of them who were the only family members left round the vast table. Jack tried again to turn the talk to Cecil's marriage but it hardly seemed to register with Jo. All through the meal she kept fuming, about her treatment by her publishers, about her new book which she would now not be able to place, about the dreadful behaviour of her nieces, Sybil and Josette. As he listened - there was never any call for him to speak - Jack grew more and more depressed. She had always had this obsession with her old school, this need to keep in almost daily touch which would have been natural in an unmarried headmistress but was bizarre in a woman with her own family. What was she going to do, now that it had been taken away?

She had been so full of life when he first met her, in the

1930s when he was a young doctor doing his first job in the Austrian Tyrol and she was a tall dark girl in her mid-teens. He remembered her picking moon-daisies in a summer field, wearing a big shady hat and talking earnestly about Napoleon. She spoke three or four languages, she was friendly with everyone, she was so bright and outgoing that she made other young girls seem insipid. He had fallen heavily for her almost straight away and after all these years he still loved her, even when she most exasperated him. Where had it all gone wrong?

Not in the first few years. They had adored each other right through the early crises, the birth of the triplets, their brief reunions during the war, that terrible time when he was missing believed killed. But at some stage they seemed to have stopped talking to each other; he had an exhausting job and she was getting more and more preoccupied with her children, her books and the school. And all those friends of hers who swarmed into the house and prevented them ever being alone together. At some point he'd realised that they meant more to her than he did, perhaps it was the day she had woken him, after he'd been up all night, from the first hours of a deep sleep so that he could drive to the school and collect Matron. That damned school. Always he was being dragged there, to the sales of work, to the Christmas plays, to little conferences in the staff room. He'd put up with it, he supposed, because he was crazy about her still.

And how did she feel about him, after all this time? Oh, she liked being Mrs Maynard, the doctor's wife, she liked having a tribe of his children, she would tell anyone who cared to listen that they were the ideal couple. But would it matter to her, in fact, if he disappeared? When her mind had been absorbed for so long in so many other things?

He could hardly bear to listen. When the meal was over he got up, saying he had to do some more work in his study. The dog, Bruno, tried to follow him, but he was getting very old and feeble and Jack told him to lie down again on his rug. That was going to be another problem if they returned to England. Bruno would never survive six months' quarantine.

He locked the door, not wanting to be disturbed. Then he

opened his desk, which was also kept locked, because he'd hung on to his service revolver after the war and it could not be left lying around where children might get at it. There were a number of papers which he had promised himself to go over when he had a free evening. A letter from his son Geoff's school, saying it was quite impossible to keep the boy. Well, that was the least of his problems; the twins would just have to go to the free schools which he had been brought up to think were strictly for working-class children. As he looked over the heap of bills, which were heavier than he had thought, he became convinced of it. Money was going to be very tight for the next few years - well, perhaps for all the years he had left. Without the income from Jo's books, and the rent from Plas Gwyn, there wouldn't be much.

Then there were the job advertisements in the *Lancet*. He read through them, and could see that all were much more suitable for a younger man. At fifty-eight, and with no connections left in England, who would employ him? It was probably true that a doctor could always find something but for the respected head of a Swiss sanatorium to scrabble round, looking for part-time work on part-time pay - that was hard. Probably he'd end up as the assistant to some young GP in whatever part of England they would have him, some place where he and Jo had no roots. The twins would eventually leave home and they would look at each other, knowing that there was no longer anything to say.

But no, the twins were not yet launched. And Len would have to come with them and there would be her five children to think about, and the knowledge that she wouldn't be in this situation, if he and Jo had not encouraged her to marry Reg.

At least the older ones had jobs. But that brought another humiliating thought, would he be reduced to depending on his own children?

He heard his wife's voice on the other side of the door. What could it be this time? She surely wasn't going to break in here, when he was trying to think? He heard her saying, 'Jack, do you know what that unspeakable woman -?'

If he had had time to think, he would not have done it, but there was no way out of the little room and for the moment the only thing that seemed to matter was being left alone. He picked up the revolver, which had been lying in front of him all this time, and shot himself.

Chapter 14

Con Contemplates Alternatives

Con never regretted not marrying Roger Richardson (who got married, to a girl called June, less than a year later), but she did regret not having tried harder to cultivate Tony Barras. Looking back she could see that, when he was an ugly duckling of a teenager, he'd probably been too shy to get anywhere with girls, and she hadn't had time for him. And now that he was grown up and extremely attractive, it seemed he had no time for her. She heard of him occasionally, having his work displayed with that of other young photographers in the Whitechapel Gallery. Once she glimpsed him at the Henry Moore exhibition, with Christine, and stepped quickly behind a sculpture. Kermit, whom she sometimes saw, had mentioned that they had a baby. It was a hopeless situation.

There had been one other man in her life since that disastrous party. Alan was an economics lecturer with political ambitions, and for a while everything had been fine, but after he won a seat, in the election of June 1970, it had all gone sour. He'd wanted her to live in the north-east, for heaven's sake, and be a good constituency wife. Like Roger, he thought that she should fit in round his career and could do her writing anywhere. Men didn't seem to realise that she might have a life-plan of her own.

She was no longer living in the tiny flat in Camden Town. Mike, her estate agent brother, had advised her to buy the best place she could get before prices shot up, and after careful searching she had found a much larger flat in West Hampstead where she thought she'd be happy to stay for the rest of her life. It was on the top floor of a Victorian house and she had her own entrance; the couple who lived on the other two floors, and with whom Con was on excellent terms, looked after the delightful spacious garden where she could read, sunbathe and give barbecues for her friends. Her front window looked down into the cedars and chestnuts which had been growing there since the nineteenth century. She had a big sitting-room, which was also her work room, a modern kitchen-diner, a bath with claw feet, a comfortable-sized bedroom and one more little room for visitors. It was all furnished in restful green and gold and she had treated herself to some luxuries, like a small colour TV. She was thinking of a freezer so that she could cut down on shopping and have more time to write.

She was still doing a lot of work for *Sixties Woman*, now known as *Seventies Style*. As Con Maynard, she edited the books page and wrote heavyweight articles about the divorce wave or the effect of unemployment on relationships. As Con Maynard, too, she had published some short stories, mostly in respectable, low-circulation magazines which paid only with a few free copies. Her serious novel was doing the rounds of London publishers; every so often she made changes and tried again. And as Constance Maine, she churned out one or two not so serious novels every year under the imprint of Briar Rose.

On the day after her father committed suicide Con was sitting at her desk, working spasmodically on her new book for the Tudor Rose series, *Wife In Name Only*. She did all her real work in the early morning when she was feeling fresh, and this was hardly work at all, just writing up some notes on her electric typewriter:

Sir Miles's fine-cut features were pale with anger.

'As you wish, madam. I know not what freak this may be. But rest assured that I would never stoop - nay, have never needed to stoop - to force myself on any reluctant female. Wife or no'.

Penelope trembled before the scorn in his blazing blue eyes, but stood her ground.

'And though you may have no need of me', her husband continued, 'Sir Francis Drake has. Mayhap ere long the Spaniard shall rid you of an undesired encumbrance, leaving you free to enjoy the gold and lands for which you basely sold

yourself'.

Sir Miles spun on his heel and left her standing alone in the great tapestried chamber.

'Tapestried'? No. Yes. 'Opulence, lots of opulence', Liz Arnett's guidelines had said. Why on earth did modern women read Briar Rose books at all? What did they have in common with Lady Penelope, forced into marriage to please her greedy relatives and still without a sex life? Their situation was more likely to be the exact opposite, hanging around hoping their live-in boy friends would agree to marry them. Con knew two women who had been hanging around for seven years. Her mind wandered; all the men of the right age seemed to be married, or as good as. And having seen what her sister had suffered, she really didn't like the idea of getting mixed up with married men.

It was no use trying to work. For one thing, she was bored; for another, the pips were already sounding for the one o' clock news and she had an appointment at two. Liz Arnett had written personally to all Briar Rose authors, asking them to attend a meeting where she would be making an important statement. Con nibbled an avocado salad and went out, first reconnecting the phone which she had unplugged after breakfast. She didn't expect to find it interesting, but she was careful to keep on good terms with Briar Rose, because it was Briar Rose who had paid the mortgage on this flat.

The room was the largest in the building and, even so, it was crowded. Women of all ages and dress styles sat on the rows of orange plastic chairs and waited for the meeting to begin. Con didn't know many of them but she recognised Dame Maud Harcourt, the well-known romantic novelist and television personality, looking very striking in sapphires and floating blue draperies. And heavens, there were even a couple of men. Liz Arnett, looking exactly like a successful headmistress with her clipped grey hair and sensible suit, stood up to greet them. She was accompanied by a secretary with a stack of smart maroon-coloured files.

'Thanks for coming, and I'm so glad that so many of you are here. You may wonder why I've dragged you to my office on this lovely afternoon, but we're contemplating some very important changes, and I wanted you - and our other authors who are not here - to be the first to know'.

Con stopped day-dreaming and gave the meeting her full attention.

'It's now fifteen years since I founded Briar Rose. During that short time we've become the leading publishers of romantic fiction in this country and America - there are others, but we're unique because we insist on the highest standards and are very careful about who we take on. Literally millions of women read our novels and we're now an important part of their lives'.

'You've done a superb job, Liz', one of the two men said.

'Thank you, Humphrey - but obviously, we must never become complacent. We have to keep on looking at all the ways our books can be improved. Now, women's lives have changed enormously over the last ten years, moral attitudes are changing too, and my colleagues and I feel that what we write should reflect these changes. Jane, give out the files, please'.

The secretary began to pass round the files, which took quite a long time. There was a buzz of conversation, and then the first question.

'Does this mean that Briar Rose heroines are allowed to have sex before marriage?'

'Yes. Provided it's within a serious relationship. Of course it must be done in a tasteful and moral way. If you read the file, you'll see that there are detailed instructions about what we will and will not accept'.

'Can we do without happy endings?' asked a woman in the back row who hadn't received a file yet.

'No, happy endings are a must. The heroine will still end up with the hero, as normal, but a lot more happens to them along the way'.

By this time Con had got her file. It contained an account of Briar Rose's new policy, a list of do's and don'ts, and a sample from a soon-to-be-published book by someone called Yseult

Ash. This was a detailed description of sexual intercourse in the style of *Lady Chatterley's Lover*, but less well written.

Little gusts of laughter went up from all over the room.

'Have you seen this?' muttered the young woman next to Con. 'She calls it his *manhood* - well, I've heard it called a lot of things, but never that one!'

Con rather liked her. She had frizzy hair and looked as if she didn't take herself too seriously.

'Are you going to do it?'

'Not much choice; my husband was made redundant last month and we've got two kids under five. I'm the only breadwinner. I write these things on the kitchen table while they're at playgroup. What about you?'

Con was saved from having to answer by a small commotion in the front row. Dame Maud Harcourt had got up and was protesting vigorously.

'Outrageous!' they heard her say. 'Total lack of artistry - wretched - titillating -contrary to all the finest traditions of Briar Rose!'

'That's another point', Liz Arnett said coolly. 'We've decided that the name Briar Rose is slightly old-fashioned and sends out the wrong message to younger readers. In future the publishing house will be known as Silk Slip'.

'I see', Dame Maud said. 'Formerly it was love, romance and commitment, now it's women's underwear. Well, I for one prefer not to get involved. And I hope, Miss Arnett, that when we see the next crop of broken marriages and illegitimate babies, you will acknowledge your share of the responsibility!'

She swept out. About six other women followed her. Liz said that coffee would be brought in and those still left could ask any questions they liked, and Con continued to study her file. Yseult Ash; she wondered if that could be Yseult Pertwee, a feather-headed girl she had known at school. Damn, Con thought, I should have been given this job. She can't write. Liz was saying that the new policy was purely an experiment, and that those who wished to go on writing romance in the traditional way were free to do so. But she hadn't any doubt that it would become compulsory in a few more years.

Oh, well, she'd spent quite a lot of time writing about innocent virgins. How about something more up-to-date when she'd finished with Sir Miles and Penelope? A professional woman, perhaps a buyer for a fashion chain, who has a passionate affair with a brilliant young photographer? Not that she'd actually had a passionate affair, or any sort of affair, with Tony, but she was a writer, she could make up that bit. And then they quarrel, and she goes to the States, and comes back to find he's married. She scribbled some notes in the margin of her file. It looked promising.

She thought it wise to stay until the end of the meeting, even though she'd already fully grasped the arguments which, for some people, took quite a time to sink in. In the car park she encountered Liz Arnett.

'Well, Con', she asked, 'what did you think?'

Con had her answer ready. 'I think it's a marvellous idea, Liz. I'll look forward to having more freedom'.

'And we'll look forward to your next book. How is your mother?'

'She's fine'. She wasn't, she was furious, but there was no point enlarging on that.

Driving home, Con reflected that Liz was a bit of a mystery woman. No one seemed to know much about her, except that she lived alone and had a little cottage in the Chilterns where she invited a few selected friends for weekends. Probably the simple and unexciting truth was that she meant to get to the top in her profession and had little time for a private life.

As she parked and walked upstairs the opening sentences of the new novel formed themselves promisingly:

Monica's plane circled Heathrow and she looked down at England for the first time in two long years. Two years in New York during which she'd made amazing progress, becoming the highest-paid woman executive the company had ever had. Two years of trying hard to forget Peter Aspern, the man she still loved, the one man she had given herself to, the man she had lost through her own folly.

And now she was back in England, soon to be back in London, the same city as Peter. But Peter was married. That scheming girl, Mary Beth, had caught him on the rebound after their foolish quarrel ....

It sounded good. She thought she would jot it down straight away. As she opened her door, the telephone began to ring.

Chapter 15

Plas Gwyn

Plas Gwyn (the white house, as it was called in English) had originally been a Tudor farmhouse, but had been modernised in the 1930s and had some large new windows put in, overlooking the eastern scarp of the Black Mountains less than ten miles away. It had a twisty staircase, several odd-shaped rooms with low ceilings and an overgrown garden, and stood in Howells village on one of the minor roads running from Hereford through the Golden Valley into mid-Wales. Dr Maynard had brought his family there when the triplets were six months old, having got out of Guernsey just ahead of the Nazis, and they had lived there for most of their first ten years and returned at odd times ever since. Now his widow and the youngest children were coming back to stay.

Con had checked it out, after flying back from what had been a very emotional funeral. The house hadn't been occupied for over a year, and was cold and damp, so she'd had the roof mended and the grass cut, although it was growing again. Her brothers had all said they were too busy to help with the big move, so she and Len had done most of the work. It was late May now, the spring bank holiday, and the fields were white and green with cow-parsley and flowering hawthorn. Len had driven the family car across Europe with her mother and the three little girls, while she, Geoff and Phil (who had been no help whatsoever) and her nephews had followed by train. That trip was enough to convince Con that she had no maternal instincts. Johnno had been very upset, throwing tantrums in full view of the other passengers and inciting Richard to behave equally badly. They'd spent the night squashed into her flat and driven down this afternoon through the holiday traffic with the two boys brawling in the back seat. Geoff, though twice their size, just sat there limply while they punched each other. Con was not hopeful of him ever making anything of himself.

But her heart lifted when they finally came in sight of the big white house and drew up on the short drive under the copper beech tree. She'd been happy here; she intended to come down and see her sister whenever she could. The little boys tumbled out of the car, whooping, as Jo appeared at the front door.

'Darlings! Isn't it marvellous to be all together again?'

Con did not know what to make of her mother. After one terrible scene, when she said that Jack had committed a mortal sin and was in hell, she'd suddenly calmed down and started saying how exciting it was to go back to England and how they were all going to have a wonderful time there. Perhaps Len could explain it; she could not. But Len had appeared behind her now, smiling and wearing the checked blouse and old skirt she used for housework.

'Con - everyone - how lovely to see you!'

'Is there a telly?' Geoff asked, showing his first sign of life.

'Yes, there is, Geoff, in the small room on your right'.

Geoff sloped off into the house. Philippa turned her nose up and followed him.

'Come and have some tea', Len said. 'You must be worn out - and look, the girls are here!'

The twins, hand in hand as usual, were first out and ran up to be cuddled. Little Frances, sucking her pink squirrel, came next and allowed Con to kiss her cheek. They went into the familiar house, which was rather dark, but felt pleasantly cool on this hot day. With her usual efficiency, Len had already done some unpacking and organised tea and Welsh cakes, served on the willow-pattern china they had used as children. They gathered round the huge oak table in the kitchen and relaxed.

'Show me the garden', Con said when they had finished. 'I'd like to look round'.

In reality, she wanted to talk to Len away from their mother - who, though, seemed perfectly happy. Jo had got the two little boys on her knees and was telling them an old Tyrolean legend with great verve. The sisters went out on to the untidy lawn, which stretched as far as a meadow where sheep were grazing. Only the occasional car could be heard; it was still a very quiet village.

'How are you?'

'Fine. Do you know, it's ten years since I've been in England? It's great to be able to talk one's own language. I haven't got used to the money yet, and nor have the people at the shop - everything's gone decimal'.

'Some people are *never* going to get used to that'.

'And I've staked out the garden', Len said. 'There's an orchard, a patch of rhubarb, lots and lots of raspberry canes and even a little herb bed. I can grow most of our own food when we're properly organised. Come and see'.

They wandered round together, noting what had to be done. There was a rambler rose, straggling over most of the elderly wooden fence, and some enormous fruit trees. Con remembered that they had got hundreds of apples and sweet blue plums when they lived here, too many for them to eat so most had had to be given to the school. The herb bed was overgrown - some of the tenants had been poor gardeners - but she could make out parsley, orange mint and a rosemary bush in full flower.

'I'll give you a freezer. Then you can store what you can't eat'.

They had come to the fence now and a short way off she could see Carn Beg, Mary-Lou's old home, although she had sold it years ago. There were more apple trees growing on the slope above it: Worcester pippins, Con remembered the taste. And there was the field with alders and the small pond where Anna had taken them to play, one day when they were all about eight, and Mary-Lou had crawled through a hole in the hedge and marched up to make herself known. If their mothers had not made friends, a lot of things might have turned out differently. Tony had been a little boy then, in the baggy shorts that boys wore just after the war. A wave of nostalgia swept over her. To go back, to have her time over again.

'Con, you've already done too much for me. I'm sure we'll manage'.

'No, listen, I want to talk while we've got the chance. I've spoken to the boys, and we all agree that Mamma should have an allowance for as long as she needs it'. She didn't add that

Steve's awful wife, Sue, had been most reluctant to part with any money. 'And Geoff and Phil are to be supported until they've got through university or have some other qualification. *If* Geoff can get in anywhere, which I rather doubt. It's necessary, because I've looked at Mamma's royalties and they're down to almost nothing. You're different, because you already get child benefit and whatever Reg sends you, but it's understood that the house belongs to us all and you live here rent free. Oh, and Sue says could you sometimes have her child to stay, while she and Steve go on holiday?'

'Of course', Len said cheerfully. 'I don't want to be a burden. When Frances starts school, next year, I'm going to look round for some translation or part-time teaching'.

Con liked the sound of that. She wished that her sister could forget her scruples, go out more and find some nice man who was prepared to take on the children, but there couldn't be many such men, and burying herself in Howells village was hardly the best way to find one. Yet she thought that Len was already looking happier, more energetic, than when she had last seen her only five days ago. At their father's funeral she had seemed ready to collapse.

'You *are* better, aren't you, Len?'

'Oh, yes. I started feeling better as soon as we got to Plas Gwyn. It's going to be so good for the children. Johnno was in a bad state - he's had several nightmares since it happened - but he's interested in finding out about another country. I was getting to hate the Oberland, you know'.

'Because everyone knew about Mary-Lou and Reg?'

'Yes. You can't live in the shadow of your old school for ever. By the way, I've told everybody at this end that my name is Helena Maynard'.

'Well, it's certainly a much better name than Entwistle', Con said.

'I think so. Helena, John, Richard, Margaret, Teresa and Frances Maynard. It sounds good. And I decided it was time to drop my baby name too'.

They were interrupted. The twins rushed up, one of them

clutching a very thin ginger cat with huge green saucer-eyes. Con still had trouble telling them apart, but she had worked out that Maggs was the bossy and pushy one; Tessa, the younger by half an hour, was quieter and more clingy.

'We found him - ', Maggs gasped out.

'And he's almost starving'.

'We gave him some milk and crusts. I'm sure he doesn't belong to anyone, Mummy. He's very thin, you can feel his bones through the fur. Can we keep him? *Please*, Mummy!'

'Perhaps he can have some kittens', said Tessa.

'Not if he's a boy cat', said Maggs.

'He is *not* going to have kittens', Len said firmly. 'But I'm sure we can keep him, if he'll eat our scraps. Cats in the countryside have to pay their way, you know; the farmers won't feed them'.

Jo had wandered down the garden towards them. Like her daughter, she was looking happier, although her dark hair was now deeply streaked with grey.

'Are you all right, Mother?' Helena asked.

'Oh, yes, dear', Jo said briskly, 'but I was looking for Anna. We really ought to get supper going for all these people'.

'Anna went back to the Tyrol, Mother - remember? Don't worry; I've already made a stew'.

'Jack always loved her *Zurchertopf*', Jo remarked vaguely. 'Reg isn't here either, is he? Such a young man. Such a shame'.

She strayed back towards the house, followed by the excited twins.

'Is she often like this?' asked Con.

'Yes, she goes round telling people that I'm a widow'. Len sighed. 'But over the last few weeks, it's got even stranger. A lot of the time she seems to think that Daddy is at the hospital and is coming home in a few hours. But just before we left, I heard her saying to Frieda on the phone that he had an accident with the gun and it wasn't a mortal sin. I wonder -'.

She broke off and Con realised that she was almost crying.

'Len, that's rubbish; you know it is. If you really believe that Daddy, after a lifetime of helping people, is in hell because of one moment's depression, then I should think you wouldn't want anything to do with that sort of God'.

'I know, but - '. Helena brushed her sleeve over her eyes fiercely. 'Con, do you think there's any chance it could really have been an accident?'

They had had this conversation before, many times, but it kept recurring.

'I don't know. There wasn't a note. And a doctor would know better ways of committing suicide'. But, she reflected, perhaps Jack had not wanted his family to believe it was suicide; perhaps he had preferred to leave room for doubt. 'But in the end I keep coming back to the fact that Daddy knew about guns, and wasn't a careless person'.

'That's what I think too'.

They were both silent for a moment.

'There was actually a phone at his elbow', Len said. 'If only he'd rung me, if only I'd had the least idea. But he never told anybody that he was depressed. I can only think that he couldn't face leaving the San after all that time'.

'Yes. He should have got out years ago'.

The younger children had come out again and were running about the garden, Frances picking buttercups and the twins chasing the ginger cat. Children bounced back very quickly, Con thought. Something about the three little girls tugged a memory and she patted her sister's arm.

'Come on, Len. This is getting too depressing. I've brought you a present'.

She went back to the car and then led the way into the drawing-room with her parcel. It was a very long room, with a polished floor and French windows opening on to the back garden. Bits of dark oak cottage furniture from the nineteenth century stood around. There was an old-fashioned white marble fireplace where someone had put a jar of moon-daisies, but the wall above it obviously needed a large picture.

'Look. I think this belongs here'.

It was a blown-up black and white photograph of three young girls in the Plas Gwyn garden. The small plums on the tree were distinctly visible.

'Con! That's amazing. Oh, dear, we all look such babies! When was it taken?'

'The summer of '56, when we were here for Grizel's wedding. Tony Barras took it'.

'Oh, yes, I remember now. Do you ever see him?'

'No'. *I go out of my way to avoid seeing him*, she thought, but did not say. She propped the photo on the mantel, and they looked at it silently for a few minutes. Both of them were thinking about the third triplet, whom they had not seen for three years. And then only fleetingly. Were they ever going to be in the same room at the same time again? each was wondering. What was Margot doing now?

Chapter 16

Exile

Johannesburg, 1975. Dr Margaret Maynard was well known in medical circles and among the few whites who were openly opposed to apartheid, though cut off from everyone she had known before the age of twenty-one. She put in long hours each working day at a Soweto clinic and was also a member of the Black Sash movement. She was thought to have had some family trouble, four years ago, but that had not seriously affected her work. Not that she wanted to sever all contact with her family, as some members of religious orders had been known to do, but it was understood that they could not expect her to help with their problems. After all, these could hardly be as important as those she dealt with on a daily basis here.

That morning a young man had been brought in with knife wounds. She hadn't asked him how he got them, probably a brawl but she occasionally saw bullet wounds which might well have been sustained in a clash with the police. There was also an endless procession through her clinic of babies with gastro-enteritis, women who were too anaemic to look after their children, though they tried, young people with syphilis or the early signs of TB. Then there was kwashiorkor, a disease never seen in the West, which was caused by a lack of protein and affected mainly children. The contrast between her patients and the people of the pleasant Jo'burg suburbs was mind-blowing. Between us and you, Margot thought as she journeyed in and out of the opulent centre, there is a great gulf fixed. She did what she could but it was like sticking elastoplast on a gaping wound.

Black Sash had been started by a group of respectable white housewives. Dressed in white, apart from the diagonal sash, they staged a silent protest whenever leaders of the National Party appeared in public. The ministers hated them and tried to avoid contact, having their cars drive down side streets and leaving meetings by the back door so as not to walk past them. The official line was that they were middle-class ladies who had nothing better to do with their sheltered lives. There was some truth in that, perhaps, but, for obvious reasons, black women could not be asked to join. Margot went on these vigils whenever possible.

She lived with seven other nuns in a modest Dutch-style house in the suburbs. All of them were involved in some sort of work with the black community but none had stuck their necks out quite as far as Margot, and it was accepted that she used the house only as a base. For one thing, she sure as hell was not going to get up at night to pray when she needed all the sleep she could get; nor did she think it necessary to ask anyone's permission before she went to Black Sash. It couldn't have happened ten years earlier but religious life had changed drastically in the years since the second Vatican council. Priests and nuns were leaving in droves, sometimes to get married; those who stayed were flirting with views which sounded, to the older ones, little short of Communism. Mother Agnes, the tough little Scotswoman who ran the convent, had been tolerant. She sensed that if Margot was pushed too hard, she would walk out and might even join the underground. And the work she was doing was valuable; she must be allowed to do it in the way she wished.

This particular afternoon Margot was tired and sweating. The seasons were the wrong way round here; the warmest months were around Christmas and it was a very hot January day. It was her habit, after she'd made the exhausting journey home from the clinic, to wash quickly and then head for the tiny garden where she would sit in the shade of the single avocado tree and unwind. The sisters knew better than to disturb her at these times. She would take a long glass of chilled mineral water, the newspaper and any post, and make them last an hour. Without that quiet time, she didn't think she could have kept going.

This afternoon there were two letters from England. One was from Len, who wrote regularly although she seldom had time to respond; the other turned out to be from Miss Annersley:

Dear Margot,

I write to let you have my new address. Having turned seventy-four last March, I reluctantly decided that the drive into Exeter was getting too much for me and have moved into a pleasant bungalow in the city. I was sorry to leave Nell Wilson's cottage and my little garden, but have found many interesting activities here. Music is a great pleasure, and I have joined the Townswomen's Guild and the Friends of Exeter Cathedral and am trying for an Open University degree. It is most exciting. I expected to be the oldest student in my group but have met another lady who is eighty!

How are you, my dear? I hope you will find time in your busy and worthwhile life to drop me a line, if convenient. You are the only one of my old girls who has become a missionary in Africa. It must be gruelling work, but hopefully Christianity will have some eventual impact on the terrible problems of what we used to call 'the dark continent'.

I have not seen Con for many years, but was pleased to hear one of her short stories on the radio last week. She is a good writer. I saw Len and your mother in 1973, when I visited Hereford with friends for the Three Choirs Festival. They drove in to meet me with the three little girls, who are delightful, and we had a long talk about the past. Len is bringing up her family very well, as I never doubted she would.

Miss Wilmot and Miss Ferrars moved to a girls' grammar school in Sussex, but left when it went comprehensive. I am not sure what they are doing now, but am always interested to get news from anyone who remembers the Chalet School.

I do hope that all is well with you.

With love and best wishes,

Hilda Annersley.

Len's letter was the usual budget of family news. Cecil was having a baby - their mother was living in a world of her own, writing novels and sending them away to publishers, who always sent them back - the children were happy. There was a photograph of the five of them in the garden at Plas Gwyn.

Margot sighed. She liked letters, in a way, but the echoes from her old life were never anything but muted, like that remote buzzing in a shell which was supposed to resemble the sea. Why couldn't people accept that when you left, you left? Probably because the person who had gone was totally absorbed by their new experiences, which those who stayed behind couldn't hope to understand. When her aunt Robin became a nun in 1950 she had stepped off into the blue, flown to Montreal and none of her family and friends had ever seen her again. She did not want such a break for herself, not quite. Some time she might go back for a visit but the only people she would actually be glad to see were her sisters, by which she meant the other triplets. It was bad about Len. Margot still felt upset when she thought of how that marriage had ended (not that she had ever had much time for Reg), but if Len's only problem was being an unsupported mother, there were worse ones. She took off her glasses and rubbed her aching eyes; she hadn't been feeling well for the last week.

'Margot! I'm so glad to find you in!'

A man's voice. She looked up, slightly annoyed at first but her feelings changed at once when she recognised Bernard Martin. She'd met him in England in '68, when they were both in Pax Christi, and in the years between had enjoyed reading his articles in *New Blackfriars* and elsewhere. Still under forty, he had already made his name as an impressive theologian. His main tenet, which had caused some fierce arguments, was that 'other-worldliness' was a sin and the Church ought to get involved in fighting oppression. Earlier that month he'd come to Johannesburg with a friend on a fact-finding mission, disguised as a holiday, and Margot had been very glad when he looked her up. Living as she did with a foot in two camps, it wasn't always easy to find someone she really got on with. For so long now traditional Catholics had thought her weird for being a radical, and radicals had thought her weird for being a nun. Talking to someone as congenial as Bernard was a rare pleasure.

And he was a likeable man in himself, tall, with dark blue eyes, and a way of bending his head to listen which she found very appealing. He was wearing a grey shirt and no dog-collar, so it wasn't obvious to the casual eye that he was a priest. She noticed Esther, the little Cape Coloured novice, growing flushed and conscious as she brought out a tray of iced beer for them. That one wouldn't last very long in this convent, she thought. But Bernard was totally absorbed by Margot.

'I looked in at the clinic, and found you gone, so I drove on here. We've enough material for a good solid report, but I didn't want to leave without saying goodbye. I'm due in Rome on Wednesday'.

'How long do you think the Pope can last?' asked Margot.

'Well, not long, I imagine, as he's nearly eighty. It's sad; he's done a lot for peace and justice, but I'm afraid he'll always be remembered for *Humanae Vitae*. Does that question come up in your work, by the way?'

'There's a birth control clinic round the corner', Margot said. 'I haven't any quarrel with them, but I wonder if they know that the rich have always nagged the poor for having too many children. And keep throwing pills at them but nothing else'.

'Yes, that's true too'. Bernard sighed and ran a hand through his thinning hair. 'I do hope, Margot, that when this Pope goes they'll elect someone reasonable, preferably from Latin America. I'd like to see changes in so many areas. Celibacy, to start with'.

'That worries you?'

'It does rather'.

'Why?' Margot had always been reluctant to think about that, although at this moment her body was reminding her that she was a woman and, indeed, still fertile. She thought that too many people were obsessed with the Church's attitude to sex when the real problem was its attitude to the ruling class. 'The point about celibacy is that it frees you to serve others. I couldn't do this job if I had a husband and children. Still less if I was worrying all the time about tarting myself up for men'.

'Oh, I know, Margot, and I absolutely respect people like you who are working in the front line. I can see that one couldn't bring one's wife to a place like Soweto - '.

'Well, I like that!' Margot said, outraged. 'Why couldn't a priest bring his wife, when women like me are working there permanently? We're not completely helpless'.

'Oh, dear', Bernard said. 'I really have put my foot in it. Sorry, I should have realised it sounded patronising. I meant to say that if I had children, I could hardly bring them to South Africa under present conditions, but - '.

'You'd like to have children?' Margot said, enlightened.

'I would actually. I miss them more as I get older'.

'So why did you become a priest?'

'Well, I went to a conventional public school, run by monks, who pushed the idea very hard, and I didn't want to go into the army or the city, which was where most of my classmates were headed. Besides, I *like* theology. People like me are unusual, of course, but if they don't happen to come from a religious background they call themselves philosophers and have domestic arrangements like everyone else. I take your point about celibacy; if you're going to lead a dangerous life then it obviously makes sense. But I don't see why I can't be allowed to work quietly at my books, which is the one thing I'm good at, and still have a family'.

Margot grinned. 'So you'd go to the library every day, while your wife looked after the children?'

Bernard smiled back. 'We could work out some arrangement'.

It was pleasantly cool in the garden. The shade was spreading, and there was a clinking of dishes from the kitchen as the nuns prepared the evening meal.

'So why did you decide against marriage, Margot? I'm sure it wasn't for lack of opportunities'.

'Oh, well - '. Margot hadn't talked about this for years. 'To start with, I had a religious crisis when I was a teenager'.

'I can imagine. Did you go to a very repressive school?'

'No, it was a good school, but it was very narrow in some ways. The worst crime you could commit was rudeness to a prefect, and the next worst was talking slang. And I was a very difficult, temperamental girl, not the sort who normally takes vows. I didn't do anything particularly wicked, I can see that now, but the school authorities and my parents were worried about me. I thought I was well on the way to being damned and ought to do something about it. Later on I found better reasons for being a missionary, of course'.

'And what about boys?'

Margot remembered the cheerful group of boys and girls who used to meet up at Freudesheim or, in occasional summers, Plas Gwyn. Tony and Clem Barras, the three Richardsons, her cousin David, who was a doctor now, and the Bettany boys. And always somewhere in the background, thoroughly disapproving, that awful Reg who had messed up her sister's life. They had all been so innocent in those days.

'There was one boy who asked me out when I was sixteen. Oh, dear, it wouldn't be fair to tell you his name. We liked each other, but he was at school in England, and it didn't have a chance to develop. And later, in Edinburgh, there was a medical student who wanted to marry me. He was a lovely person but we didn't have much in common; he only really got excited about golf. He was quite happy to tolerate my religion, and my politics, but - well, it's no good when people think that the most important thing in your life is a hobby'.

'I know', Bernard agreed. 'I've had that problem too'.

There was a friendly silence. Margot would have said something more but she was beginning to feel increasingly unwell.

'So you never wanted to have children?'

'I've got several nieces and nephews', Margot said.

She would have liked to go on talking to him but it was now imperative that she should get away. She said faintly, 'Excuse me', got up, and almost ran into the house and along the corridor to her tiny room. There was nothing there but a bed, basin, crucifix and chair. She shut the door on herself with relief. Her underclothes were soaked with blood and, as she stood there, a great jet of it gushed on to the floor.

Chapter 17

A Day in the Life of a Single Mother

'Mum, I've done it again'.

'Oh, no, Johnno!'

Helena woke up to see her eldest, in soaked green pyjamas, standing at the foot of her bed and looking horribly embarrassed. In a way she wasn't very surprised. Johnno had been virtually dry since the age of ten, after a long history of bedwetting brought on, the doctor said, because he was a nervous child and had had various upheavals in his life. He was nearly thirteen now, and had not lapsed for a year, but he'd been doing exams and they had obviously been a strain.

She sat up.

'Okay, have a shower and get dressed. I'll put your sheets in the washing machine'. That had been a gift from Con, and she sometimes thought she'd have cut her wrists without it. 'Then we can have breakfast'.

'I thought I'd put all that behind me', Johnno said in injured tones.

'Don't worry. This is probably the last time'.

Johnno disappeared and she got up, climbed into her ancient blue dressing-gown, and went round the downstairs rooms pulling the curtains. She enjoyed doing that at Plas Gwyn, there were always lovely views of the garden and the Black Mountains, clearly visible on this summer morning. Late June was the very best time to be here. There were foxgloves in the long grass, pale pink dog-roses scattered on the hedge, elderflower blossoming in the meadow where she and her sisters had once gathered around the small pond with Mary-Lou. Then she made coffee and some muesli and buttered rolls for Johnno. Breakfast was always laid the previous night, and the children's school clothes put out, which avoided the worst of the morning rush. You had to be highly organised, she'd discovered, to bring up a family of five on your own.

Philippa was not here at the moment but in Birmingham,

where for the last two years she had been studying sociology. Geoff, her twin, had also drifted to the city and was working in a car factory. She worried about him, though he seemed happy enough in his dim way. There were only herself, the children, and her mother; quite enough to keep her on the go.

Johnno came down in his school uniform and they started a leisurely breakfast. It was still only seven o'clock, no need to call his brother and sisters just yet. And she always enjoyed her conversations with Johnno, when they had time for them; you could never tell what this ferociously intelligent little boy would think up next.

'I'm sorry', he said again. 'I must have had a nightmare'.

'Probably those frightful comics you read', his mother said.

'That reminds me', Johnno said. His huge eyes blazed as they always did when he was excited. 'I've got an idea'.

'Yes?'

'I thought if I could get hold of a deadly laser ray, I could murder Mary-Lou by sending it across the Atlantic, and when she's been *exterminated* - he said this with savage emphasis - 'Dad might come back. What do you think, Mum?'

'That's not a very Christian thing to say, Johnno'.

'I'm not sure if I'm a Christian', Johnno said, diverted. 'Mr Chalmers says there's no scientific proof that God exists'.

Helena refused to get side-tracked.

'What I mean by being a Christian, Johnno, is treating other people as you would like to be treated yourself. Mary-Lou may not be my favourite person but I think it's a waste of time to be angry with her. And even if she dropped dead tomorrow, that wouldn't mean Dad would come back'.

She saw Johnno's face fall and wondered if she had been unnecessarily brutal. But she had got things quite clear long ago in her own mind. Her parents had blamed Mary-Lou for the break-up of her marriage, and Con blamed the Pope, but the fact was that only one person had been responsible for breaking it up and that person was Reg. She didn't talk about him if she could help it, that was too painful, but the other thing she had decided was that she would never abuse him to the children. So she carefully answered any questions they asked.

'I can remember Dad', Johnno said. 'I remember playing football with him in the garden. Richard does too, vaguely, but the girls don't remember him because they were too young'.

Helena wondered if he had got the sequence of events jumbled up in his mind. Did he know that Reg had never even seen his youngest daughter? Or had he registered the fact that he never sent them presents at birthdays or Christmas, indeed had probably forgotten when their birthdays were? Well, the cheques arrived quite regularly; some women were worse off than she was. And she knew how to reach him in emergency.

A thump from upstairs announced that Richard was now awake. Little Frances, her red-gold hair streaming over her Miss Muffet nightie, came downstairs and flung herself into her mother's arms. The twins were pulled out of Tessa's bed where they'd curled up together, warm and sleepy like two little dormice. The beginning of another day.

Somehow in the next hour everybody got fed, dressed and had their hair brushed and teeth scrubbed. The boys got on the bus for Hereford and the three little girls walked off, holding hands, to the village school. Helena went with them to the end of the lane and then started on her jobs.

Hang out Johnno's sheets to dry, sort another giant pile of washing and get it going. Wash the breakfast dishes, tidy the children's rooms and beds. Then she went round the garden with two jugs of water, carefully noting how the lettuces, tomatoes and baby marrows were getting on. The weather had been very hot and dry for several weeks and they needed constant attention. Over the last few years the price of food had shot up in a horrifying way, and although the children got free school dinners she didn't know how she'd have fed them without her garden and the cheap eggs from Rhiannon Jones' farm. The little apples were coming along nicely, so were the blackcurrants and raspberries. She pulled some rhubarb for the evening meal and went back into the house.

Jo was up and sipping a cup of coffee. Helena often thought how young she looked, compared to other people's mothers, and still striking, with her abundant waves of black and grey hair.

'Hello, darling! Isn't it a lovely day! Do you know where the twins are? - no, not yours, *my* twins. Geoff and Phil'.

'They've gone to Birmingham, Mother. Remember?'

'My babies', Jo said reminiscently. 'Jack and I talked about having quads after they were born, but it never happened. Oh, the post has come, dear. Two bills, and a card from Margot - that's the first we've heard for ages. She says something about the end of the war in Vietnam'.

Helena sighed. Yes, it was over, a war that had killed so many people. She looked at Margot's card, but it was only a few scribbled lines.

'Will you need the typewriter, Mother? I thought of getting on with my translation this morning'.

'Yes, you have it, Len. I'm very busy; I'm on the last chapter of *Excitements at St Faith's*, but I always write it out by hand first. There's going to be a thrilling chase over the Alps and I think it'll be one of my best books ever'.

She went upstairs and got the typewriter from Jo's little study, a room at the top of the house with a view of the mountains, which she liked because they reminded her of the Tyrol. The shelves were packed with first editions of her children's stories, although none had been published for five years. Every day she sat down at that desk and wrote for several hours and then, when a book was finished, wrapped it up and sent it to a publisher in London. After it had come back three or four times she would lose interest, because by then she would have completed another one, and would put it away in the oak chest with her other rejects. The manuscripts would be worth quite a lot, she'd say cheerfully, when she was dead.

Helena established herself at the dining-room table with her books and dictionary. She'd long since realised that her only marketable skills were her languages; the school had made her fluent in French and German and she'd also done Spanish at university. An old friend, Carmela Walther, who was now a partner in a publishing house, sent her plenty of work and she sometimes thought that she might earn a living doing this when the children had grown up, although that seemed a long way away. It was no good working when they were at home (she knew, because she'd tried), but now, when her mother had wandered off, she began to concentrate. It was a modern French novel, one of the fashionable sort in which nothing happened. She worked hard on it for nearly two hours. The deep silence of the house enfolded her.

After she'd come back from the Oberland, bruised and bleeding from the series of disasters that had overtaken her family, she had realised straight away that this was where she wanted to be. She remembered nothing before this house; the familiar rooms, the garden and the distant mountains gave her a feeling of peace and calm. At first some of the women in Howells feared she was a dashing divorcee who might come between them and their husbands, but older people could remember Dr and Mrs Maynard and the three little girls and they had gradually come to accept her. She had friends who would help in an emergency and if she got depressed, as she sometimes did, there was always plenty to do. She could honestly say now that, if the children were all right, so was she.

It was such a good place to bring up children. The Maynards, with one or two exceptions, usually came to Plas Gwyn for Christmas and brought their families; this was particularly welcomed by the wives because it was understood that all the housework was done by her. Steve and Sue left their children with her twice a year while they went on holiday abroad; Mike and his wife sometimes did the same and she had just finished looking after Felicity's elder child, a little girl of two, while her mother got over post-natal depression. Sue still said occasionally that Len was on to a good thing, living in that big house, but the rest of them were happy enough for her to be there.

By eleven o'clock her eyes were swimming. She made a cup of coffee, took one to Jo who was writing at a great rate, and then walked down to the shop. When she was a child there had been two banks and a weekly sheep market, but now there was only one bank, a doctor's surgery (very important) and a post office and general stores. Only farmers, and a few commuters to Hereford, lived in the village now, and it was kept alive by tourists. She picked up a few things for the house, being careful not to overspend. If the children had been there they would have been clamouring for sweets.

More translation, and then a bread and cheese lunch with her mother, who announced that she had done enough for the day and was going to watch TV. Helena was tempted to take a break too, but knew it was important to get on with her work while she could. She'd found that if ever life seemed to be going smoothly, and if she was unwise enough to feel complacent, something would go wrong. She didn't count a little thing like Johnno's bed-wetting; what she was afraid of was that a machine would break down, or one of the children would be ill, or she would have to take on some big job. The last few weeks had gone quite well, so it was about time for something awkward to happen.

It did. That very afternoon.

The children came home from school, changed out of their uniforms and had their milk and buns. Johnno and Richard ran around with their arms out shouting, 'Exterminate'. Then there was a knock on the door and she opened it to Gretchen Schmidt, a German woman living down the road with her husband, who was working temporarily in Hereford.

'Oh, hello, Gretchen. Come in'.

She'd had coffee with her a few times and tried to get the boys to befriend her son, Klaus, who was about the same age. Unfortunately he was very plump and spoke almost no English, and it had not been a good idea.

'Something is wrong', Gretchen said.

'Oh, I'm sorry'. She switched to German. 'What's it about?'

'Richard and Johnno, and another boy - somebody Jones - beat up Klaus when they all got off the school bus today. He came home crying, and covered in dirt, and his books had been thrown in the hedge'.

'But that's - '.

She broke off as Johnno appeared at the top of the stairs and saw them. She had never seen guilt written so plainly on anyone's face. Before she could speak, he rushed into the bathroom, followed closely by Richard, and locked the door.

'Johnno', his mother said, going halfway up the stairs, 'come out, please'.

'I'm not coming out while she's there', Johnno shrilled.

Helena went back down.

'I'm sorry, Gretchen, I'll have to speak to them on my own. Don't worry, if they really have beaten up Klaus I shall be extremely angry'.

'I've spoken to the headmaster', Gretchen said.

'Then I'm sure he will too'.

After the other woman had gone she rattled the bathroom door.

'Okay, you can come out'.

Johnno released the bolt. Richard was sitting on the edge of the huge old-fashioned bath and looking sheepish.

'Now, please tell me what's been going on'.

'It's all your fault', Johnno said aggressively. 'You made us be friends with him when we didn't want to, and we got laughed at, because nobody likes him. Everybody at school picks on him and says, who won the war?'

'I suppose you think you won the war, Johnno?'

'And she's already rung up Mr Chalmers', Richard added, 'so we'll get told off *twice*'.

'Serves you right. What exactly did you do?'

Richard said, 'We got off the bus, and Johnno stopped him, and Evan Jones and I caught up, and - well - '.

'You attacked him?'

'We didn't do anything serious, Mum; he's not hurt or anything. We just thumped him a few times, and emptied his bag on the grass, and made him cry'.

'But why did you do it at all?'

'Well, he's fat', said Richard.

'And the Germans started the war', piped up Johnno.

Helena sighed. Later on she'd think about what this meant,

but right now, it was obviously her job to reprove them for their unpleasant behaviour, and she wasn't sure where to begin. Miss Annersley had been known to reduce badly-behaved children to lumps of quivering jelly but she doubted very much whether she'd be any good at it. Besides, Miss Annersley had never had to deal with the male sex. She would simply have to do the best she could.

'You're two disgusting little boys. I asked you to be nice to Klaus because you speak German, and he doesn't speak English, and if we were in a strange country I'd like to think someone would do the same for you. Blaming him for the war is ridiculous. My mother knew a lot of German and Austrian girls while it was actually going on, but she had more sense than to blame them. And it isn't very brave for three people to gang up against one. What do you think Grandad would have thought?' That was below the belt, for Johnno had been very fond of his grandfather. 'Well?'

Johnno dissolved into tears. Between sobs, he said that he knew he was a horrible person, but there was nothing he could do about it, and he might as well go off and kill himself if his own parents didn't like him. Richard said in injured tones that he didn't mind being told off once, but now the school knew about it there would be more trouble tomorrow. Dealing with them took her quite a long time and when she had fed the other children, and seen them into bed, and got things ready for the morning, it was late and she was very tired.

Dropping down in the old rocking-chair in the sitting-room, where she remembered her mother feeding Michael, she thought that she wasn't making a very good job of being a single parent. Johnno had been bullied in the past, because he was small for his age and obviously different, but it had never crossed her mind that he might become a bully himself. It suggested he was more deeply disturbed than she could have imagined. And Richard, she was afraid, would always go with the crowd. It might turn into serious violence later, if it wasn't stopped, and she was not sure she could stop it by herself.

It all came down to the fact that there was no man in their

lives, hadn't been since Jack Maynard died. One-parent families were getting more common, she had heard, but Howells was a fairly traditional community, and they were the only two boys in the village whose father wasn't around. All the experts seemed to think that boys who grew up without a father were more likely to become criminals, would be hostile to women, would have marriages which would fail.

And for the first time in years, she allowed herself to feel anger against Reg. Perhaps she had always been angry but not admitted it. There had been plenty of men at Oxford who wanted to take her out, nice men, some of them, probably happily married long ago. She had turned them all down out of loyalty to Reg. Why had he kept following her around, why had he taken her out of her own age-group, if he wasn't prepared to abide by the consequences? Even if, as she now believed, she was so dreary that no man could be expected to stay with her, he could at least have stayed in touch with his own children.

Children - yes, perhaps it was her fault for having had so many, but nobody could say that the first two had been foisted on him. He had been quite pleased when they were born and very proud that they were boys. He surely owed them something, beyond the cheques which were never quite enough to live on, anyway.

The Maynards' grandfather clock began to strike and she realised it was midnight; she must have sat here for hours worrying. That meant it was early evening on the eastern seaboard. She had never contacted him, apart from a note to tell him they were moving back to England, because she didn't want him or Mary-Lou to think she had any feelings left for him. There had been no word of interest or sympathy, even after her father committed suicide. But she had his phone number, and if she rang him now there was a good chance that he would be in. She thought, damn the expense, I'll do it.

Mary-Lou's unmistakable bell-like tones answered the telephone.

'Hello, Mary-Lou, this is Helena. May I speak to Reg, please?'

'I'm sorry - *who* is that?'

'Len'.

'Oh. Yes, of course, I'll get him'.

A moment's pause, and then Reg came on.

'Hello, Len! How are you?'

She found herself shaking uncontrollably. His voice sounded calm, even friendly, with the north-country accent not at all worn away by years of living in Boston.

'I'm ringing you because the boys - don't worry, we're all quite well - but they're in a bit of trouble'.

'The boys?'

He surely couldn't have forgotten who they were.

'Your sons, Johnno and Richard, have been caught bullying another boy and are going to be reported to the school. More important, I'm afraid they might become delinquents as they get older - I'm seriously worried - '.

'But, Len, that sort of thing happens all the time at school!'

She ignored him and went on, feeling the tears splash down her face and relieved that he couldn't see them, 'Reg, I'm not asking you ever again to have anything to do with me. I'm not even asking you to take any notice of the girls. But I do think you should have some contact with your boys, because they remember you quite well, and it could make all the difference to them. Johnno was talking about you only this morning - he misses you - '.

She found that she couldn't go on; she was crying too much, probably the relief of breaking a lifetime's habit, and making a scene.

'Hey, calm down!' To her surprise, Reg seemed genuinely interested. 'Look, I've always intended to keep in touch with the boys, and you, but you know how it is - I can't just pop over for weekends. But I'm perfectly willing to arrange something'.

'Do you ever come to England?'

'No, but I can have them for the summer holidays, if you like. When does school finish?'

'About the third week of July, but - you don't mean - '.

'Sure I mean it. I'll book two air tickets, you get them on

the plane and I'll keep them until September. I'd like to see the little chaps'.

'What does Mary-Lou think?'

'She won't mind. Don't *worry*, Len. It'll be a great experience for them. Now, I'll write to you in a few days with the tickets, and details, and you can ring me again if there's anything you want to sort out. Okay?'

They talked for a few more minutes, quite amicably, and then, still shaking, she put the phone down. It was almost seven years since she had spoken to Reg, and it had churned up all sorts of feelings she didn't know she still had.

Quarter past midnight.

She dragged herself to bed, knowing that if she didn't sleep she'd be no good in the morning, but tossed and turned and had uneasy dreams for several hours, until little Frances crawled in with her and asked was it time to get up.

Chapter 18

Disaster Unlimited

She didn't really expect to hear again from Reg, after she'd done such an unheard-of thing as to make demands on him. But a few days later two plane tickets arrived, with a note asking her to arrange about injections and visas and all the other things they would need. The little boys were wildly excited to hear that they were flying to America to see their father. As she got them organised, Helena had pictures of them camping under the stars, running along the shore at Cape Cod and all the other things that a man ought to do with his sons. She had to be careful not to let them think it was a reward for bullying Klaus, which, of course, it was.

'Why can't *I* go?' Maggs asked rebelliously.

'I'd rather stay with Mummy', said Tessa.

Maggs was nothing like her younger sisters, who both loved to be cuddled and were shy with strangers. She was sparky, independent, not very patient with those less bright than herself.

'Perhaps another time, darling. We might go to stay with Con and have a look round London'.

But Con was evasive. She didn't know what she was doing, she might be abroad, she'd come down for a weekend later on. Helena realised that, whatever Con was up to, she didn't want them at the moment. Well, the girls would just have to take second place as usual. She promised that they would go fruit-picking, and swimming, and she'd try to find the money for a day's pony-trekking in the Black Mountains. They accepted this happily enough; their father meant nothing to them, after all.

The boys flew out on the first day of the summer holidays, and she suffered agonies until their plane had landed. A week later, Reg quite unexpectedly phoned and said that they wanted to talk.

'They're grand little chaps', he told her.

Their life in the U.S.A. was not exactly what she had envisaged.

'The telly's in colour', Johnno told her excitedly, 'and it's got about twenty different channels. We sit here and watch it when Dad's at work, and Claudette makes our meals'.

'Who's Claudette?'

'She's a black lady who keeps house for Mary-Lou. We haven't seen Mary-Lou because she's in Brazil on an expedition. We're always eating hamburgers, and Coke, and a thing called fudge sundaes'.

'Dad's going to take us up a skyscraper this weekend', Richard said.

Reg came on again.

'Well, Len, you can see they're having a good time. Everything all right with you?'

'We're fine', Helena said rather faintly.

Even some hours after the call had ended, she still felt shaken and disturbed. A few days later, she was asked out for the first time in fifteen years.

There were several campers in the field below Edwin Jones' farm, and now that the summer holidays were under way you often saw them in the shop, or walking or cycling towards the hills. Sometimes they knocked at the door of Plas Gwyn to ask for water. One afternoon, a man turned up carrying an empty oil can while she was clipping the hedge.

'Oh, good afternoon!' He held out his hand. 'Quentin Haines; I'm camping in the field above Carn Beg. I'm so sorry, but I've run out of fuel for my little cooker. Do you think your husband could help?'

'I haven't a husband', Helena told him. 'I'm divorced, but I can probably find you something'.

They went to look in the garage, which was full of the relics of past camping expeditions. As they searched, they talked. He told her that he'd been all over Italy, and the Austrian Tyrol, but never to this part of the country before.

'The Tyrol!' She could feel her own face light up. 'How lovely; I've spent several summers there. In a chalet above the Tiernsee - do you know it?'

'I do indeed. The most beautiful little blue lake'.

He was thirty-fivish, about her own age, with a small brown beard. He taught at a language school in Chelmsford, and usually spent his holidays going round Europe on a shoestring, but this summer was so hot that there was no need to go so far.

'Look', he said when they parted, 'why don't we have a drink in the Green Dragon when it opens? Suppose I settle in and meet you there about half past six?'

She found herself saying that would be very nice.

Going back into the house, it was evident that the family hadn't noticed him. The curtains were drawn and they were watching *Dr Who*, which Jo and the children all loved. Frances was on her grandmother's knee and the twins were cuddled up in one armchair. She made a cold supper, laid it on a trolley, and then brushed her hair and changed into a nicer blouse and skirt. Somehow she felt that she ought to make an effort, although she was only meeting him for a drink, for heaven's sake.

The pub was Elizabethan, with dark little rooms and low, beamed ceilings. They sat on a bench outside, under the hanging baskets of petunias and lobelias, and drank the local cider. Quentin brought out a map and she told him the best places to explore.

'Perhaps you'd like to come along one day?' he asked. 'Show me round?'

'I'm afraid it's difficult', Helena said. 'I can't always leave the children'.

'How many children have you got?'

'Five'.

His face changed.

Up to that time, they had been talking quite easily and happily, but suddenly, everything was spoiled. He couldn't hide what he was obviously thinking, that here was a lone woman who was desperate to offload her children on him. The conversation lagged. Helena tried, but after another ten minutes it became so embarrassing that she got up, thanked him for the drink and said she must go.

Her face was burning as she walked back to Plas Gwyn. She

hadn't gone after him, any more than she had gone after Reg, yet he had managed to make her feel utterly humiliated. Obviously, he wasn't a nice man. He was so conceited that he really believed, after half an hour's acquaintance, that she wanted to marry him, and hadn't even got the ordinary decent manners to keep his feelings to himself. Or perhaps, she thought wearily, he just hoped I'd let him into my bed while he's here. I'm sure Plas Gwyn is more comfortable than his tent.

No one had noticed her leave and come back because they were still watching television. She put on her working clothes again and started on the washing-up. So far as other people were concerned she was just poor old Len, neither maid, wife nor widow, but mother to the nth degree. It would be very foolish to become attached to a man because they invariably hurt you, and then went away.

Philippa, the youngest Maynard, turned up at the beginning of August with her sociology texts and a huge bag of washing. She'd been staying with friends for as long as they would have her, but now they had all gone to Greece where she couldn't afford to follow them and there was nothing to do but come home. Phil was twenty-one now, and had cut her mane and went round in T-shirts and blue jeans which made her look rather like a boy. She had joined a feminist group at university and thought her sisters hopelessly unliberated.

For the next fortnight she mooched about discontentedly, spending long hours in the bathroom, on the phone or in front of the TV. Helena knew better than to ask her to do anything around the house because she had said fiercely in the past that that wasn't her job. Then, after a series of phone calls, she bounced joyfully into the kitchen and said that she had a share in a house in Birmingham and was leaving in three days.

'And I'm not coming back', she finished.

'But, Phil, this is your home! And you'd have to pay rent where you're going'.

'Oh, that doesn't matter; I'll be a waitress in the Golden Egg or something. Lots of people do it; it's better than vegetating or looking after someone else's children'.

'But you will come back, Phil? For Christmas - '.

'I might, but you can expect me when you see me. Why do you think Fizz and Cecil got out as soon as they could? Only they got married, and I'm not going to bother. Our family is weird. Two of my sisters housewives, another who writes for women's mags, another who's a *nun*, for heaven's sake, and you're everyone's slave'.

'Phil - '.

'I don't know why you put up with it', Phil said, and danced out.

The next thing to happen was that Jo left with an old friend, Margia Stevens, for a tour of Cornwall. She went off in high spirits, talking about the romantic landscapes and jolly little fishing villages they were going to see. 'My next novel will be all about smugglers', she told the three admiring girls.

Next day Phil came down with her bags after lunch and asked her sister to drive her to Hereford. At Helena's urgent request, she wrote down her new address. They loaded her things into Dr Maynard's old Volkswagen, which cost money to run but was really necessary in the country, and Maggs leapt about asking if she could come too and look round the shops.

'Mummy', said Tessa, who was standing quietly in the shadow of the door, 'I don't feel very well'.

'Don't you, my precious? Well, lie down on your bed, or perhaps get into bed, and I'll have a good look at you when I get back'.

'I want to go to Hereford', Maggs said.

'Please, Maggs. See that she lies down, and give her some home-made lemonade'.

'Oh, come on', Phil said impatiently. 'I'll miss my train'.

Helena quickly said goodbye and backed the car down the short drive. The three little girls stood waving beside the red and pink hollyhocks which grew against the white walls and came well above their heads; bees were buzzing in the lavender. She would remember that scene for the rest of her life.

Philippa hadn't yet finished with her.

'I had to get out', she explained earnestly as they jolted over the country road to Hereford, leaving the Black Mountains in the distance. 'I mean, look at Ma. Some of her early books are quite good, I mean good for children's books, but now she just churns out the most ghastly rubbish and doesn't even get paid for it. I can't talk to her any more. And there's you'. Helena wondered what she was going to be accused of. 'You're an educated woman, you could have done all sorts of things with your life, but you just got married and wasted it'.

Helena tried not to sigh out loud. In the last ten years, everyone's opinions had changed so much. How could she explain that, at the time, it had seemed perfectly good and natural to get married and have a large family, and that she didn't think she had been totally wrong, even now? Once Phil would have been considered a freak but now, it seemed, she was.

'And then having all those kids!' She wasn't sure if Phil was referring to her or her mother. 'Obscene!'

'Well, Phil', Helena said, trying to lighten the atmosphere, 'if Mother hadn't had eleven children, you wouldn't be here'.

'That's irrelevant!' Phil snapped back. '*I'm* not going to have any. It's women like that who keep men in power, because all they think about is babies and nappies. Like I said, you've got a good degree, but you just live in this backwater and do the cooking and cleaning and let the kids and Ma push you around. You even let *me* push you around! Why do you do it?'

She looked as if she was going to burst into tears.

They drew up outside Hereford station. Helena said, 'I don't know really; it's just easier than arguing. Cheer up, Phil. I hope you're going to have a great time, but if you want us, we're here'.

Phil gave her a quick peck. 'Sorry, Len. You're doing the right thing, sending the kids to Reg. Let *him* look after them.

And look, there's this women's consciousness-raising group; I'll send you - No, don't get out; I must rush for my train'.

And she ran off, loaded with bags, at top speed. She'd see her again, Helena thought, of course she would, but just the same, Phil had left Plas Gwyn.

She drove the fourteen miles back. Because it was August, the traffic was heavy, and the orchards along the road, which ran in and out of the border between Wales and England, were loaded with red and gold apples and pears.

When she opened the front door, Frances was in the hall playing with the triplets' old dolls' house.

'Mummy, I've poured water into all the little cups - '.

Maggs appeared at the top of the stairs, looking tearful.

'Mummy, do you know Dr Prosser's number? I've been looking for him in the telephone book under D. Tessa's got a bad headache'.

She dropped her keys and was up the stairs within seconds.

'I pulled the curtains', Maggs said, 'because the light hurt her eyes, but now she isn't talking properly, and I don't like it, Mummy'.

Inside the green and white room, where the twins had always slept, Tessa, in her little peacock-blue shirt and shorts, lay under a sheet tossing restlessly. It was hard to see clearly, having just come in out of the bright sun, but she was making awkward movements with her head as if she had a stiff neck. She croaked, 'Mummy', and held out her arms.

Helena was with her immediately.

'What is it, darling? Have you got a pain?'

There was no answer, but the child felt very hot.

She would ring the doctor. No time to fiddle around taking temperatures; she'd coped with dozens of children's illnesses before but she instinctively felt that this was more serious. If only she had known, if only she hadn't wasted time taking Phil to meet the train. She tried to stand up but Tessa moaned and tightened her grip.

'Maggs, hold her, please'.

Maggs climbed on to the bed and cuddled her sister.

She raced to the phone and called Dr Prosser at the surgery. He was out on an emergency, his wife said, but she would tell him as soon as he came in. Helena decided not to wait for that. Her instinct was to bundle her into the car and drive at once to the hospital in Hereford, but that would mean leaving her unattended - she didn't want her to lie helpless on the back seat. She called an ambulance, and then phoned Rhiannon Jones, the mother of Evan who had been involved in the bullying incident, and asked her to look after the other two girls. Then she wrapped Tessa in a blanket and carried her downstairs. The light, moderate as it was, made her shrink and whimper. Helena pressed her face against her dress.

She couldn't get her to say a single word.

Rhiannon arrived. She took one look at Tessa and said, 'Don't worry, my dear, I'll keep them overnight; you won't want to come home till you can bring her with you'.

'I want to come too!' Maggs shrieked.

Frances stuck her lip out and started to cry. The ambulance came, after an agonising wait; they had had some difficulty finding the house. The attendants jumped out and examined Tessa closely, but said they couldn't understand what was wrong. Helena got in, still cradling the child, and an ambulancewoman sat beside her. She could hear Maggs screaming as they were driven away from Plas Gwyn.

Back over the road which she had taken less than an hour before, hearing the siren blare as they overtook horse boxes and cyclists and holiday cars with boats and camping gear strapped to the top. All this time, Tessa showed less and less response to her mother, although she did seem to like being held. She thought, nothing could go really wrong so suddenly. She had not been injured. She had always been a healthy child.

Then they were in a small room with high, grey windows, and a doctor was bending over her.

'Mrs Maynard, we think the little girl has meningitis. We'll do everything we can, but it's been going on for some hours'.

She thought, I left her. It had started and when she told me, I didn't listen.

'It's very difficult to diagnose', someone else said.

Tessa was given antibiotics and placed on an intravenous drip. She was quite unconscious now; her eyes which had been without expression for some time were closed and her face and chest were covered with small purplish spots. People came and went while Helena sat by the bed, practically unaware of them, holding the little girl's hand and occasionally sponging her with a flannel. She talked to her, but gave up when she got absolutely no response; then she talked to herself. She had taught her children that God was loving and merciful. She prayed continuously to God to spare Tessa. She offered her life for hers.

It got darker outside, but the sound of footsteps and low voices in the corridor never stopped. At quarter past eleven, Tessa died.

People were moving her out of the room. She didn't want to go but gave way to those around her as she had always done. But she caught her breath, when she heard the unexpected sound of a very young child cooing. A trolley was being wheeled towards them, and on it sat a boy of about eighteen months with a black eye. It was obvious that someone had been hitting him.

Helena stopped walking and burst into tears.

The nurse said, 'Mrs Maynard, you shouldn't be alone, isn't there anybody we can contact?'

'May I use the phone?'

A phone was given to her and she dialled Con in London. A man's voice answered, which vaguely surprised her, but a moment later, she heard her sister.

'Con, could you come, please? I need you'.

The receiver had fallen from her hands and she could see nothing but the white tiles of the floor.

Con drove through the night. She had rung Plas Gwyn several times and, getting no answer, she flung a few things into a case, filled her tank and set off. It couldn't have come at a more inconvenient time but, knowing Len, she was sure that she would not have summoned her, if it hadn't been serious.

It was light when she arrived, having turned off the motorway at Ross-on-Wye and driven cross-country to Howells. The great copper beech cast a shadow over the white gates and dew was gleaming on the lawn. *Is there anybody there? said the traveller*, Con recited, knocking for the third time and wondering why she'd never got herself a key. She had worked out that there must be something wrong with one of the children, so the next step was to try the local hospital. Then an ambulance drove up, and her sister was helped out.

'She went into shock', a woman said. 'She was so cold she had to be wrapped up in blankets'.

The man with her explained in an undertone what had happened.

'I'm fine', Helena said.

Con went inside with her. It felt unnaturally quiet. The dolls' house, which the triplets had loved to play with years ago, lay scattered all over the tiles of the hall.

'Len, I'm here now. Cry if you want to. I'll get you a hot drink'.

Helena said, 'Meningitis has to be treated straight away. I knew nothing about it. If I'd known, I wouldn't have gone off with Phil'.

'But, Len', Con said, horrified, when she understood, 'you had no way of knowing. You were only running an errand, for God's sake! You mustn't think it was your fault or you'll go mad'.

'Oh, yes', Helena said, 'it's my fault'.

Con looked round helplessly. Where was Tessa's father, who was a doctor, and who could have started the life-giving treatment? As if answering her thoughts Helena said, 'I'll phone Reg'.

'You can't; it's the middle of the night in America. Drink this. You heard what the woman said, you're in shock'.

'Con, it's only a few hours. Twenty-four hours ago everything was normal; I was thinking about the children's clothes and what to give them for supper and starting school in two weeks time. And now - '. She lapsed into complete silence, the mug of coffee growing cold beside her. Some time later, as Con sat there groping for words, she said in the same dazed voice, 'We thought it was the worst thing possible when Daddy committed suicide, didn't we? But this is worse, because Tessa was only nine. She was going to be ten on the thirtieth of August. And it still isn't the worst possible, because there are the other children and they could be next'.

The awful morning dragged on. Neighbours called, bringing flowers and sympathy cards, and officials with forms to be filled. Con should have been flying to Venice that day, spending two weeks in the sun with her new boy friend and relaxing after the book she had just finished. Now she answered the door and phone and did all the small things she could to keep routine ticking over. The cat appeared, and mewed to be fed. At first Helena just wandered round the house, clutching Tessa's Snoopy, a worn object with one missing ear, but then she said she couldn't leave the kitchen in this state, and began to wash up. It was a relief that she didn't weep, but it felt very strange.

Rhiannon Jones arrived, with an armful of fresh roses from her garden and two very distressed little girls. Maggs was screaming, hysterical, and had to be given a sedative by Dr Prosser, who was the next to call. He told Con what she didn't know, that there had recently been a small meningitis cluster in Malvern, over the county border, where a five-year-old boy had died. Nearer home, two babies had been ill, but there had been only one fatality in the Hereford district; Tessa.

No one knew quite how the rare disease was carried, or why it affected some people rather than others. They would have the rest of their lives to wonder about that.

Later, when at last they had a few minutes to themselves, Helena again spoke about Reg. She said, 'I can't get hold of Mother. She and Margia are travelling, and anyway, why should I upset her before I have to? But I ought to tell him. Con, do you know what time it is over there? I can't think straight'.

Con glanced at her watch. 'It's midday; that means they should just be waking up. I'll ring, and if it's Mary-Lou, I'll ask her to fetch him'.

In fact it was Reg who answered. Con silently handed the phone to her sister.

'Reg - '.

'Hello, Len! Ringing to check on the boys, are you? They're fine. I'll send them home in a fortnight, but we must do this again. Very nice for a man to have two strapping sons to show off'.

'Reg, Tessa died'.

Reg said, 'What?'

'She had meningitis. I don't know where or how she got it. I came back from driving Phil to the station, and it was obvious she was very ill. She was taken to Hereford hospital, and I think they did everything they could, but she died'.

There was a moment's silence, and then Reg began to shout.

'You let her die? You bloody stupid woman. You couldn't have looked after her properly - healthy children don't get meningitis - I'll never forgive you - how could you be so bloody careless - ?'

Con heard every word. She saw her sister, completely stunned, holding the receiver as the stream of abuse poured out, and stood up and firmly removed it from her hand.

'This is Con. Get off the line, you bastard, and don't ever speak to my sister again. She was here and you weren't, and I noticed that while she was alive you never bothered with Tessa. You've mucked up her life quite enough. Goodbye'.

She heard Reg snarl, 'What the *hell* business is it of yours?' before she slammed down the phone, and they both started to cry together.

Chapter 19

Out of Africa

Margot had been ill. Since the beginning of 1975 she had been losing a great deal of blood, but told no one, dosing herself with iron supplements. Then handfuls of her hair started coming out, and that was more difficult to conceal. When anyone had the temerity to say she was looking run down she just snorted, and asked if that person had seen illness in the South-west Township.

The dreadful news from home only made her more determined to carry on. She hardly knew her sister's children, having met them only once when she was in Europe seven years ago, but she keenly felt that Helena was getting far more than her share of bad luck. The text which had always puzzled her most kept going round her head, *unto everyone that hath shall be given, but from him that hath not shall be taken away even that which he hath.* Did that mean that the whites of South Africa were to go on having everything, while the poor, who only asked for a very modest standard of life, must keep seeing their children die? Not if I can help it, thought Margot, but she often felt depressed, and in her lowest moments her mind kept going back to Len. She wrote, but only once, and it was not a very helpful letter.

On 16th June 1976 Soweto hit the world's screens. Fifteen thousand schoolchildren had gathered to protest against being taught in Afrikaans, and the police opened fire. After that there was chaos and looting all over the townships and within ten days the death toll was nearing two hundred. Most of the dead were young black teenagers.

Margot's clinic became an emergency hospital as young people with horrible wounds were carried in by their friends. She had been there when the shooting started and stayed there on continuous duty for seventy-two hours. At the end of the week she collapsed.

The doctor who examined her found she was suffering from

pernicious anaemia and exhaustion. Mother Agnes immediately said she didn't have the facilities to look after her at the convent. The truth was she'd been hoping to get rid of Margot for some time; not that she disagreed with her over apartheid, of course, but the way the younger woman spoke about conservative cardinals and what she'd like to do to them made her hair stand on end. Margot was trouble; it was a mystery why she'd ever taken vows at all. Let her go back to England, where her family lived, and where she could have a complete rest.

Margot resisted but was told it was a religious order; then it occurred to her that she could use her visit home for publicity. She rang her friends in the English branch of Anti-Apartheid who arranged for her to be interviewed at the airport. She didn't, though, get round to telling her family, and that was why Con, watching the early evening news with a plate of ravioli on her knees, was electrified to hear a reference to 'Dr Margaret Maynard, a nun who treated victims of the riots'.

'My God, that's Margot! Look, Des!'

Des stopped pouring wine. 'That's your sister?'

Margot was addressing the camera from the invalid chair in which she'd been wheeled through Customs and looking very fragile. She said, 'I've treated children with bullet wounds, children as young as eleven or twelve. Some of them died on the operating table. We must have sanctions against South Africa. People must understand that it's one of the most brutal regimes on earth'.

'Well', Con said, turning off the TV as it went on to something else, 'I might have known Margot would be in the thick of whatever was happening'.

'Am I going to meet her?' asked Des.

'I've first got to find out where she is. I'll ring Len; it would be nice for the three of us to be under the same roof again'.

The obvious thing was to invite Len to stay, but Con didn't think she would agree; over the last year she had become neurotic about leaving the children. Moreover Con hadn't yet told her, or any of the family, that for the previous nine months she'd been living with Des Romano.

They'd met at the time of the Common Market referendum last year. Both were passionately pro-Europe, Con because she had largely grown up on the continent and Des because he was half-Italian. His father had come here as a chef before the war and ended up with his own little restaurant in Soho. He was extremely good-looking, olive-skinned with dark wavy hair and deep brown eyes, but what really drew him and Con together was the fact that they were both writers.

Des had an English degree, but hadn't held down a steady job in the past seven years although he had been in and out of teaching and advertising. He'd sold the restaurant when his parents died and lived for a while off the capital, and he did a little book reviewing, a little ghost-writing, all kinds of odd jobs to stay afloat. He had written a novel which was doing the rounds, like Con's, and was waiting for the day when his poetry would be discovered and make him famous. You can't give your best to art, he used to say, when you've got involved with the trappings of conventional society like a wife, a child, and a mortgage. Moving in with Con, who still had a solid income from *Seventies Style* and her romantic novels, made sense.

Des had had a wife, ages ago, and a twelve-year-old daughter, but they were in a commune in Scotland with her new boy friend and Con had never seen them. They had married when they were very young because of the social pressures in those days. He was always hard up, and Flora was always asking for money for the child's bills which he hadn't got. They weren't actually divorced but the marriage was long over; Con had made sure of that before she got in too deeply. The last nine months had been the happiest of her life.

She often thought that her mistake, in the past, was to have got mixed up with men whose line of work was different from her own. She and Des understood one another perfectly. They sympathised with each other when they got rejection slips; they rejoiced when one of Con's stories was read on the radio or when Des won a modest poetry prize. They laughed together over her Silk Slip novels and he suggested ideas for them, mostly too outrageous to use. Cooking was another thing they did together; Des made a superb ratatouille and Con had introduced him to Swiss cuisine and German wine. They'd twice been to the north of Italy where his family came from, taken the water bus round Venice and admired the Ravenna mosaics. They never quarrelled with each other, were never bored.

Through the amazing June days of 1976 (both of them were used to extremes of heat and didn't mind it) they strolled out in the long light evenings or listened to open air concerts, lying on the grass which was already beginning to turn brown. Beethoven's Ode to Joy was being played constantly and one day a streaker appeared from nowhere and ran across the park to universal applause. Life was good, Europe beckoned, the scents and sounds of summer had never seemed so intoxicating. Con didn't worry unduly about marriage. Living as a couple was quite acceptable in their circles and it wasn't as if she wanted children, but she saw no reason why she and Des should not stay together for the rest of their lives.

Margot was taken first to King's College hospital for a complete check-up. Nothing serious was wrong but she had been told to do no work for several months.

Con, who visited her straight away, thought that Africa hadn't done her any good. She was thinner and the red-gold hair which had been so striking looked dull brown and scanty, but propped up in bed, with a plastic bracelet on her wrist, she still crackled with nervous energy.

'The trouble is I might never be allowed back in South Africa', she said, 'because the Embassy saw me on the news and of course they didn't like it. I'm pretty sure that bitch, Mother Agnes, doesn't want me either. At least I won't have to keep biting my tongue'.

'But where would you go instead?'

'Oh, I could be sent anywhere. It's too early to say. America perhaps; I'd like that'.

Con was relieved. Only a few months ago the papers had been full of the case of an English woman doctor in Chile who had been tortured for treating a wounded man and not revealing his whereabouts, and she had been horrified to think that that could have happened to her sister.

'Well, Margot, I just hope it's somewhere more civilised. You seem to have worn yourself out in Soweto'.

'That's a secular attitude', Margot retorted. 'You *ought* to wear yourself out in the service of others if necessary; haven't you heard the parable of the grain of corn?'

Con changed the subject.

'Len said she'd come up very soon, but only for a flying visit because it's difficult for her to get away. And she also suggested that you should go down to Plas Gwyn to be nursed. I'll drive you, if you want'.

'Can't; I've got all sorts of people to see in London. How *is* Len?'

Con sighed. 'She doesn't tell me much, but she's obviously miserable. Tessa was a dear little girl. I don't see why one person should get all the bad luck - '. She broke off; she didn't want Margot trying to justify the ways of God to her. 'We'll fix up something; I'd love to get the three of us together'.

But as it turned out she missed seeing Helena, because a friend of Des's offered them his flat in Brighton for a long weekend, and they ended up going there. Des was good at arranging last-minute treats. When she got back Margot had been moved to a place called the Holy Child Convent, and she felt a slight inward shudder as she gave her business and was taken to the little room where her sister was resting. The nuns' dark clothes, the crucifixes, the lines of beds containing sick people, all reminded her of a period in her life she didn't wish to go back to. It seemed impossible, in the late twentieth century, that anybody could choose to live this way.

'Where were you?' Margot burst out. 'Len was here until half an hour ago with her little girl, Maggs. Incidentally I thought Mother would have come too, but she turned down the offer because she's *finishing a book*. We rang you several times. Where have you been?'

Con explained, and then found herself telling her all about

Des. She had never mentioned him to Len, partly because she'd only seen her for the odd weekend and partly because it would have seemed cruel, when the contrast in their lifestyles was so great. She knew she should have checked with her before leaving London, but perhaps she was simply selfish and wanted to avoid seeing other people suffer. To her surprise, Margot was appalled.

'You mean you're just *living* with him? Not even *planning* to get married?'

'Oh, I expect we'll get married one day. It's only a piece of paper, Margot'.

'It's not a piece of paper', Margot said forcefully, 'it's a public commitment. Can't you see, if he's only living with you, he's saying in effect to the whole world that you're not good enough to be his wife?'

Con thought of explaining about Flora, but decided that Margot wouldn't be better pleased to hear that Des had a wife already. Her sense of humour came to her rescue. It was ironic that she should be sitting here, in a convent, and expecting her sister, who was a nun, to condone her living with a man. She was just a little surprised that Margot, who held extreme radical views on so many issues, should be so conventional on this one.

'We're adults, Margot. We understand each other'.

'No man believes marriage is just a piece of paper', Margot said. 'They'll do anything to squirm out of it. You ought to see these young boys in the townships, giving the girls one baby after another. That'll be the next thing. It sounds as if this Des has got it made. He's living in your flat letting you feed him and water him, and making it impossible for you to meet anyone decent, and he won't marry you unless you insist, wait and see'.

'Please, Margot', Con said, thoroughly annoyed now. 'I hate to be catty, but you're a consecrated virgin, I think it's called, and you know nothing about this subject at all'.

'So what are you going to do without me?' Des asked.

They were having an early breakfast, on what was to be their last morning together for a fortnight. It was a continental-style meal, huge cups of milky coffee and rolls with butter and black cherry jam. The school where Des taught part-time was taking some sixth-formers to Florence on an educational trip and, because he spoke Italian, he was going.

Con poured cream in her coffee. 'Well, I'll spend the first week finishing *Love in Venice*. I think that ought to pay for our next foreign holiday'.

Des grinned. 'Then we'll go to another romantic place and get an idea for your next book. Pity you were ill last time we were in Italy, and there was another holiday that you missed, too'.

'Well, Des, that was a crisis, remember? And after that I'll probably go down to Plas Gwyn with Margot. I really ought to keep in touch with my family'.

'Good idea', said Des, whose family were all dead.

With him gone, Con set to work. Strangely enough she found she quite enjoyed having the flat to herself again, although at first she'd been a little put out to think of Des being in Florence without her. After all, he was only minding schoolchildren. She could stretch out in the double bed, and eat Chinese take-aways which he didn't like, and watch her favourite programmes without him complaining. She finished *Love in Venice*, delivered it and went to a late-night film, all by herself, to celebrate. Nevertheless, she had a problem.

She'd realised just before Des went that her period was late, later than it had ever been before. It seemed hardly possible. After all, she'd been telling readers of her magazine for years that women didn't have to get pregnant unless they wanted to, and she had always been most careful about taking the pill. But thinking back to that trip to Venice in May she remembered being very sick in the first twenty-four hours, and perhaps that had upset her system. She did not tell Des; what was the point if it turned out to be a false alarm? By the time he came back, she should be sure.

On the fifth morning after Des had gone she got up early and did the book page for *Seventies Style*; she had always been methodical and liked to finish one job before starting another. Then she looked at the time. Offices should be open now, and she had an important call to make. She stretched out her hand for the phone, but before she could touch it, it rang.

'Con Maynard'.

'Oh, Con', her sister's voice said, 'this is Felicity'.

God, she hadn't seen Felicity for ages; they lived in the stockbroker belt and didn't seem to have much time for the rest of the family. What could the girl want at this hour?

'Oh, hello, Fizz, how are you?'

'I don't know who else to ask', Felicity said tearfully, 'but you've worked on a problem page, haven't you, Con, and I certainly have a problem'.

Con sighed.

'Yes. How can I help?'

'Just a minute while I settle Timmy'.

She heard a childish voice in the background. After six years of marriage, Felicity had produced a little girl, Madeleine, and then a boy. Con calculated that they would be three and one now. She waited patiently until she returned to the phone.

'Greg's having an affair'.

Con had already worked out that this was the problem. The numbers of men who strayed while their wives were tied up with small children had always depressed her, and made her glad of her own decision to stay out of it. She hardly knew Greg and thought he was good-looking, but probably not very clever.

'Who's the woman?'

'His secretary'. So Greg was predictable as well as a rat. 'She's called Shelley, ridiculous name. I found out when I was pregnant with Timmy and that's the real reason I got post-natal depression. Looking back, the trouble started soon after Madeleine was born. He was annoyed that I couldn't go out with him every night or join him on trips abroad like I used to'.

'So it's been going on for some time. What does he want to do?'

'Oh, first he said it wasn't my business what he did away from home, so long as he was living with me, but now he's talking of living with her. Only they can't afford to buy a flat in London. The prices have gone totally insane. Con, what shall I do?'

'Have you thought of marriage counselling?'

'*I* have, but Greg wouldn't dream of coming. And anyway I don't know that I can ever forgive him. When I think how I loved that man, trusted him - '.

'Okay'. Con couldn't help feeling slightly impatient; Felicity had rung at an awkward time and perhaps she had never quite forgiven her for taking the star role in that fairytale wedding while she herself had had to stand about in the background, the ugly sister. She'd been right; their parents should never have let her get married so young.

'Are you still there, Con?'

'Yes. Now, are you all right for money? I mean, can you afford to leave your children with a good babysitter or nanny or whatever?'

'Oh, money isn't a problem', Felicity whined. 'I just feel so hurt, so rejected - '.

'I'm sure you do'. Who was Felicity to think that she shouldn't be hurt, especially when she'd had it very easy up to now? There was Con Mackenzie, dead of a brain tumour in her forties. And poor little Tessa. And Helena, who had been through the same trauma and worse. 'Can you get at Greg's bank account?'

'Oh, yes', Felicity said, suddenly matter-of-fact. 'I always insisted on a joint account, and I've got my own, too'.

'Good. Well, go out and buy some new clothes at his expense and have your hair done. Remember, the more money you spend on yourself, the less he's got to spend on her. And don't let him see you crying and complaining when he comes back from work. Let him come home and wonder where *you* are'.

'But, Con - '.

'I mean, of course, provided you can leave your children with someone reliable. Only don't ask Len, because she's already got enough on her plate. Go abroad for a holiday, wherever you like best, and do it on *his* money. You never know, you might even meet another man. Or if that's impossible, go out every night, clubbing or whatever it is you do, and there's no need to tell the whole world that you're married'.

'Is that what the problem pages say?' Felicity asked faintly.

'Probably not, but it's what I say. Do it, Fizz; at the very least it'll make you feel better. Tell Greg to go to hell. He might get such a shock that he'll beg you to have him back, then you can think about it. Or you might end up with someone else. If it does come to a divorce, get a good lawyer, don't give up your home and make him take his turn looking after the children. I doubt if Shelley grew up in a large family like we did, and it might frighten her off. But whatever you do, *don't* weep and plead with Greg, because he'll only despise you. He ought to know that he was very lucky to marry you, and if he's fool enough to play around you'll soon be snapped up by someone else. Do you understand?' Con paused, out of breath.

'Yes, but, Con, how do you know? - you've never been married yourself - '.

'Must go', said Con, and hung up.

Holding the receiver in the air, so Felicity couldn't ring her back, she looked up the number she wanted and dialled it.

'Hello, my name is Maynard. Constance Maynard. Have you the result of my test, please?'

'Just a minute, Mrs Maynard'. A pause. 'It's positive'.

'I see', Con said faintly.

'Are you pleased?' the voice said on an inviting note.

Con hung up.

Chapter 20

Con in Crisis

Of course she wasn't pleased; she was utterly appalled, and what made it worse was that she couldn't speak to the obvious person, as Des was still in Florence and not expected back for over a week. She had a phone number, but that was for emergencies and this certainly wasn't something they could discuss on an open line with the school party listening. She hadn't an address and, anyway, they really needed to talk face to face.

Con drew a deep breath, unplugged the phone in case Felicity rang again and brewed herself a cup of black coffee. The clinic she had gone to had said something about counselling, but she didn't see much point in that. She wasn't a teenager, she was a mature woman who had counselled other people in her time. No, she must think this through by herself.

The first thing that occurred to her was that, even if Des got divorce proceedings moving straight away, the baby would almost certainly be born before the decree absolute. Well, she thought she could survive that. This wasn't the nineteen fifties, but she would insist on marriage as soon as it was possible. She really didn't think they could live together as Mr Romano, Miss Maynard and their baby; society wasn't ready for that, and nor was she. But if he said no?

Des had never mentioned marriage, except to say that it hadn't suited him; had never shown any interest in his daughter. The bastard, Con suddenly thought, tears starting to her eyes; if he doesn't marry me he's not going to go on living in this flat, I'll have nothing more to do with him. Then she told herself her fears were running wild. It was Des she was thinking of, Des whom she loved and who loved her. She was getting absurdly emotional, no doubt because her hormones were all over the place. She went for a walk to calm herself down.

It wasn't really hot yet. She wandered through the park, across the parched brown grass, keeping in the shade of the trees where she could. Some of them had been cut down recently because of Dutch elm disease and there were ugly gaps. She thought, she didn't have to have this baby. She could sluice it out of her system and no one would know, not even Des because it could easily be done before he came back. It was a human right, wasn't it? Some of Con's friends in the media had been getting very passionate about that lately. She sat down on a bench and looked across at the small pond; a few children under school age were there with their mothers, dressed in tiny summer suits and shady hats and crumbling bread for the ducks. Better think very carefully, because she could be one of those mothers in another few years.

She realised that there was no point worrying about Des, because she had no idea how he would react when he knew; the main issue was the baby. And the first thing to consider was that she was now thirty-six, would be thirty-seven by the time it was born. Of course, if she and Des got married a second baby might be possible, but if they did not, she could hardly count on lining up a suitable husband before she was forty. It would be wise to think of this as her one and only chance.

Oh, damn, Con thought, looking across at the pond and the children, I'm not the maternal type, I can't be, or I would have done something about it years ago. She was forced to the conclusion that she hadn't planned her life at all well. She thought of herself as methodical and highly organised, and so she was in the day-to-day things, but she had not had any larger plan. Instead she'd put off all the big decisions for the last fifteen years, and now they were catching up with her. She should have married some nice, high-earning man who would have paid her bills while she concentrated on writing; her father had never expected her mother to work. Then she could perhaps have produced something valuable instead of all those damned Briar Rose, or Silk Slip romances. She had always been quite proud that she could support herself in some comfort. But would she be able to go on doing that, with a baby?

Con thought about it and the prospect was not reassuring. Physically a baby could be fitted into the flat, no doubt, but it was set up for adults, and she couldn't imagine herself writing, as her mother had done, with the baby screaming in the next room. She'd have to pay a woman to look after it - take it out of her sight, if possible - and that would eat into her funds. It would be best if Des could support them both for a while, until she got back on her feet, but Des hadn't done a full-time job for years and, she suspected, he wouldn't like it. Or perhaps Des could do the actual feeding and nappy-changing while she supported the three of them. People didn't now assume that a woman's career came to a full stop when she had a baby, and many couples had worked out unusual arrangements. That was certainly something a liberated woman might consider.

But so much depended on how Des felt, and she couldn't yet ask him. As she walked back, tired from the great heat, Con thought grimly that it might well end with her being really liberated and bringing up the baby on her own. Well, she could always say that she didn't believe in marriage. But the prospect of all that work, and no one to share it with, was frightening. And that made her thoughts turn to the darkest possibility of all.

Helena rang that evening and asked when she had last seen Margot.

'I'm worried about her, Con; I think South Africa's aged her. Couldn't you put her in your car and both come down to stay? I suppose she has to get permission from the church authorities, but I can't believe it would be a problem when she's been so ill. The children would love to see you and if you need to do your writing, you could do it at Plas Gwyn'.

'My writing?' Con hadn't thought about Margot all day but she had thought a lot about the effect that a baby would have on her work. 'Oh - yes'.

'Con, you sound miles away! Are you all right?'

'Fine. Okay, Len, I'll speak to her and get back to you'.

'Yes, do. It would be so lovely to have you both here'.

As she replaced the phone Con thought that her sister had her own heavy problems, and she couldn't tell her about this one. No, if she decided not to go through with it, Helena must never know. She spent a sleepless night and worried for the next two days, changing her mind almost from hour to hour. On the morning of the seventh day, a postcard arrived from Des saying that he was having a marvellous time in the Pitti and Uffizi galleries. In the afternoon, without any warning, Margot turned up.

'I was sick of lying there waiting to be told what to do. So I got my friend Bernard to drive me to South Africa House and we joined the picket for half an hour - it was boiling hot - and then he dropped me here. You've been lying very low, Con. I thought you'd have come round before, or were you working?'

'No'. Con, who had been lying on the sofa, got up rather wearily. She hadn't been able to do a thing because her stomach was aching badly, and although she had taken some pills, they'd made no difference. Probably it was nerves. 'Sorry, Margot; let's have a drink'.

As she unscrewed a jar of pineapple juice, and filled two long glasses with ice cubes, she realised that she was going to tell her. She couldn't go on carrying this burden by herself and, once out of that convent, Margot was a whole lot easier to talk to.

'I don't see the problem', Margot said. 'You told me you had a perfect relationship, didn't you? In love and all that. So ring him up and tell him. You can use the time that he's in Italy to arrange the wedding'.

'Margot, it isn't that simple. Des can't marry me because he has a wife, although they've been separated for years'. Margot said something under her breath; it sounded most unsuitable for a nun. 'Whatever you think of my morals, I had nothing to do with that. It was over long before I met him, but the fact remains, the baby would be illegitimate'.

'I see. Well, that's not the end of the world. After all', Margot said brutally, 'you've got no reputation to lose, have you? According to what you say, you've been openly living in sin with Des for quite some time'.

'You don't understand'. Con was getting increasingly annoyed. 'People are very liberal about sex outside marriage, Margot - well, more liberal in London than in, say, Howells village, but London is where I live. That isn't a problem. But when you get pregnant, that's quite another matter'.

'You *are* pregnant', Margot pointed out. 'If it's embarrassing, I suppose you can move somewhere else to have the baby. For pity's sake, young girls have always done that. But shouldn't you get on the phone to Des? I don't agree with divorce, obviously, but there are two evils in this case, and the interests of the child - '.

'Margot, I'm not sure I want this child'.

'You've got this child'.

'I could have an abortion'.

'Con!'

'Why shouldn't I?' The pain deep in Con's abdomen was worse than ever, and she was finding it harder and harder to talk normally. 'It could very well ruin my life if I have to give up work and look after it. I haven't decided yet, but I am not going to do something which is wrong for me, just because the Pope says so'.

'It's nothing to do with the Pope', Margot said, firing up. 'As a doctor I can tell you beyond a doubt, your baby is a human being'.

'I'm a human being - I -'.

She broke off as the pain stabbed again.

'Con, I'm sure you wouldn't talk like this if things were normal. Have you quarrelled with Des? Let me ring up and tell him what's going on'.

'I don't see Des with a baby', Con said faintly.

'Oh, he's one of those'.

She had never known pain like this. She had a great dislike of screaming, but she writhed and bit her lips and stuffed the corner of the cushion in her mouth. Margot's face changed. She came over to the couch and examined her.

'Let me see - where's the pain?'

'Deep down', Con said.

'I'm going to ring for an ambulance'.

She did so. Con got up and began to walk about, but it didn't help.

'Margot, do you think I'm going to lose this baby?'

'We'll soon know'.

The ambulance drew up outside in a matter of minutes, and she was helped downstairs. Margot said brusquely that it was an emergency. With sirens blaring, they were driven through the streets and unloaded at the nearest hospital. Con thought afterwards that she couldn't have understood everything that was happening, because she only remembered bits, like a bad dream. But she was aware that her legs were in stirrups, a light from the ceiling was trained on her and then someone said, 'we'll have to take her into theatre'.

'No!' she screamed. 'You can't - I haven't made up my mind - '.

Margot came up and put a hand on her shoulder.

'I'm sorry, Con, there's no choice. You have an ectopic pregnancy. That means' - for Con was still trying to argue back - 'the baby is growing in one of your tubes, and if it's left there, you'll both die'.

There were no more words. She was wheeled along a corridor and, under anaesthetic, the pregnancy she had spent so much time agonising over was taken away.

Chapter 21

The Triplets are Reunited

They had finally let her go home. Margot, who was looking ill herself, said that there'd been enough deaths in their family, and at least Con's life had been saved because she had been able to diagnose what was happening. Con had often wondered whether a doctor could have saved Tessa, if one had been around at the critical time. Within a year, she and her sister had each lost a child, but, unlike Helena, she wouldn't get any sympathy, nor could she talk openly about her grief.

She kept thinking that she ought to feel relieved. But she couldn't; she could only think of her baby, struggling against the walls of the narrow tube that had become its death cell. Margot said it hadn't been fully formed but that was how she imagined it. A dark-haired little girl, crossing her life for a few days or weeks and then disappearing into limbo. I would have loved her, she thought, crying into her pillow at night when nobody could see how the normally composed Con was behaving. I would have brought her up, alone if need be.

Alone, but not necessarily. She had still not talked to Des. Her chances were reduced, and her age against her, but it was not impossible that she could have another child.

There was a lot of mail at the flat, but no more from Des. Margot checked that she had everything she needed, and then said she must get back to the convent. Con insisted on putting her in a taxi. Then she lay down and glanced wearily through her letters - several postcards from friends who were abroad - listening to a classical concert on the radio because that was all she felt strong enough to do.

The bedside telephone rang and an aggressive female voice asked, 'Is that Des Romano's house?'

'Well - yes, he does live here. Can I help?' asked Con, although the last thing she wanted was to be disturbed just now.

'Are you Mrs Romano?'

'No, just a friend. Who is that speaking, please?'

'This is Pamela Innes, the headmistress of St Chad's, and I wish to say that he won't be welcome if he has the gall to show his face here again. If he hadn't had excellent references' (Con recalled that one of the references had come from her) 'I would never have dreamed of letting that man near my girls'.

'I thought you were a mixed school', Con said faintly.

'No, we are a private school for girls, and we pride ourselves on our educational and moral standards. Nothing like this has *ever* happened before. Marilyn Buckley's parents have been informed, and have threatened to take it further. Had she been a few months younger, there could have been criminal charges'.

'Sorry, you've lost me'. But this was beginning to sound horribly predictable, like Felicity's story. 'What exactly has Des done?'

'I don't know where you've been', Miss Innes said aggrievedly. 'I've been ringing you every hour since I knew the facts. Mr Romano was asked to leave the tour because, I regret to say, he abused his position with a sixth-former, Marilyn, who of course was in his care. It was disgraceful. Needless to say, we want nothing more to do with him, nor are we prepared to give him any reference. In fact, I shall warn my colleagues in the teaching profession that he is totally untrustworthy. Is that clear?'

'Quite clear'.

'Then I'll wish you goodbye'.

After she put the phone down, Con wondered why she felt so little. Perhaps because the baby had absorbed all her emotions, and there wasn't a great deal left over for Des. Or perhaps she had simply had enough of him; after all, he hadn't been around in what had been the most bitter week of her life.

It was two hours later when she heard Des's footsteps on the stairs and his key in the lock. She wasn't very surprised; where else could he go? During that time she'd been thinking what to do and had decided to remain calm. She'd been doing enough crying recently. Ugh! Back to work!

Des came in, smiling radiantly, wearing a blue shirt covered with little gold stars. He crossed to the sofa, kissed her and produced a box of chocolates which had obviously been picked up at the station.

'Hello, darling! I'm knocked out - the heat - and the crowds!' He crossed to the sideboard and poured out two glasses of sherry. 'I'll have a shower and then tell you about Italy'.

Con decided that she didn't want him in her bathroom.

'Des, I've found out about Marilyn Buckley'.

Des spilled his drink.

'You mean that old - '.

'Yes, Miss Innes rang up and gave me the broad picture, and I can fill in the details myself. It sounds a bit like one of my novels. Hot Mediterranean days, nightingales in the lemon groves and I suppose you were both overcome by passion'.

'For heaven's sake, Con, the girl was a nymphomaniac!'

'Oh, I don't think so, Des. I understand that she's sixteen, and you're thirty-five, which makes you more than twice her age'.

Des looked injured.

'Look, Con, I've just come off the boat-train, I'm very tired, I've had a lot of unpleasantness from St Chad's and I really don't need this. Damn it, I even brought you a present -'.

'Well, thanks, Des, but I thought we had an exclusive relationship. I've been telling the more conventional members of my family, who dislike my living with you, that we were as good as married'.

'Hang on!' Des was now looking both angry and frightened. 'We're *not* married - I never promised anything - it wasn't even talked about. Damn it, I didn't come home to be nagged! It's my life, I'll see who I want and do what I like, and if you don't like it you can get out!'

He was really shaken, Con thought dispassionately, Des who had always been such a charmer. She decided that she would never tell him about the baby; she had had enough humiliation to last for the rest of her life. She finished her sherry.

'No, Des, *you* are getting out. I hate to mention it, but this flat belongs to me'.

'I meant - '.

'You have the rest of the evening to pack your things, but I refuse to have you here overnight. You can leave your heavy stuff, if you like, until you've found somewhere to put it. But not indefinitely'.

It was almost comic to see Des's face.

'But - look, where am I supposed to sleep, for heaven's sake? It's almost dark!'

'Sleep under the stars. It's quite warm, or perhaps you could go to Marilyn's. I'm sure her parents will give you a bed'.

'My God, you've got a vicious tongue!'

He stamped out, and she could hear him in the next room, opening drawers and cursing. Con lay limply on the sofa. It wouldn't have been safe to do this to some men, but Des wasn't violent, at least. She was still bleeding; she wanted to crawl into bed; she wished he would hurry up and be gone. After half an hour, he put his head round the door, looking considerably more subdued.

'Con, I really am sorry. But could you lend me something to get me through the night, because, honestly, I'm cleaned out'.

Con reached for her handbag and took out a five pound note.

'That should get you into a bed and breakfast'. This was the man she had thought of marrying. 'But that's it, Des. Can you leave your key?'

Des dropped it on the bedside table.

'Any chance I could borrow your typewriter?'

'I'm afraid not'. Des had an old machine of his own but he had naturally used her good electric typewriter while he was here. 'Goodbye. Let me know when you want to pick up the rest of your things'.

'I've got an awful lot of poems to type', Des grumbled, heading for the door with his two cases. 'Oh, well. So long, old thing, I'll see you around'.

He was gone and there was only the box of Black Magic to remind her of him.

Con spent the next day expunging all traces of Des from her life. She packed his clothes, books and records into two tea-chests and asked the family downstairs if she might store them in their garage. Having done that, she was too tired to do more, so she arranged for a firm to give the flat a thorough cleaning and then close it for the summer. She suspected that it wouldn't feel really clean for some time, but it was the best she could do.

She was going to Plas Gwyn. Helena would always be there, and she needed a long rest. Before leaving she offered a lift to Margot, who accepted eagerly.

'Sure. I've been doing too much; I'll come'.

'You don't have to ask anyone's permission?'

'I won't bother. So many priests and nuns are leaving to get married that they have to treat those of us who are still left with a bit more respect. Do you realise this is going to be the first time for years and years that we three have been under the same roof?'

They drove down to Howells village, where Helena welcomed them with open arms and gave them the old nursery to sleep in. The hot weather continued unabated and they spent a lot of time indoors, with the French windows wide open, or under the shade of the copper beeches outside. Con did not tell her elder sister what had been happening; she would have liked to burn it out of her mind completely. But they talked a great deal about the old days.

Jo was there, of course, but had little to do with them. She exclaimed, 'My precious triplets!' when she first saw them together, but otherwise spent most of her time writing in the attic. Margot was very shocked by the change in their mother.

The boys were spending the summer helping on a farm which did pony-trekking holidays, so Con saw much more of her nieces. Maggs was very nervous and liable to fly into rages. Frances, who had just had her ninth birthday, was an enchantingly pretty little girl who filled the house with her friends.

Helena only once spoke about Tessa.

'I gave her clothes to Oxfam. I suppose I should have kept them for Frances, but I can't explain - it would have upset me to see her wearing them. Con, do you still believe in God?'

'Not really. It certainly isn't easy to explain why children should suffer. I think religion was pushed too hard in our family, and most of us have reacted against it. Except Margot, and I don't pretend to understand what goes on in her head'.

'Con?'

'Yes'.

'Do you think it was my fault?'

'Oh, for heaven's sake!' Con almost shouted. 'Of course it wasn't. You're the most devoted mother I've ever seen; there's no way I could do what you do. Don't tell me you're still worrying about what Reg said?'

'We've had no contact for a year. He won't speak to me. The boys miss him, but they can always get in touch when they're older, if they like'.

They did the cooking and cleaning together, not difficult with three of them, although Con and Margot were still so tired that they spent much of the day resting, or doing light work in the garden. The grass had stopped growing and was now completely brown. Con dug out an old photograph album filled with pictures of them as babies. She remembered how the older girls at the school had loved them, how proud Jo had been (she'd repeatedly been told) of having triplets. Certainly in the photographs they looked like three enchanting little girls. And later, when they'd left home, they had been looking forward so much to the future, but it had all gone so wrong. She remembered that girl quintuplets had been born in Canada, a few years before them, and had caused a sensation, but apparently they hadn't been very happy either. Now that they were all halfway through life, what had they achieved? Margot physically broken down, and her girlish good looks gone. Herself, just through a trauma. Apparently the removal of the tube had halved her chances of having children, and at her age, it was probably better not to think of it. Helena had her children but she was one of the walking wounded. And none of them with that most priceless of all possessions, a man.

And what about the little girls? she wondered as she watched them playing. Would they go through exactly the same thing when their time came?

Just the same, it was a good summer. Helena actually cried when they went back to London, but work was piling up for Con, Margot was eager to find something to do and it was very much cooler and more comfortable, the drought having broken just in time to spoil the August bank holiday. Their mother waved them off quite happily.

Con had been thinking. If she died, as she nearly had, there would be quite substantial assets - her flat, which was worth much more than when she had bought it, her savings and perhaps royalties, although she didn't think many people would be reading her books in fifty years' time. And if she didn't make a will it would all go to her mother or, if she predeceased her, be divided between her ten brothers and sisters in sums too small to do any good. Con Mackenzie's legacy had made quite a difference to her when she was starting out, and she thought she would like, without telling anyone, to do the same thing for Helena's children. Johnno was so bright that he was certain to do well, and Richard had the easy-going temperament which should see him through. But the little girls had got biology against them, and in twenty-five years might well be struggling, perhaps as single parents. She went to see her lawyer and drew up a will, leaving everything of which she died possessed in equal shares to her nieces, Margaret and Frances Maynard.

Chapter 22

A Wedding at the End of an Era

The first months of 1979 would become known in history books as 'the winter of discontent'. Night after night the TV news showed lorries crashing through picket lines, and piles of garbage on the pavements of big cities, but in the misnamed Golden Valley, where Helena and her children had lived for the last eight years, life was totally dominated by the snow. There were yelling winds, too, which piled it up against the sides of houses into white walls almost eight feet high. New Year's Day was, the weathermen said, the first time this century that the entire island had been covered. Struggling to the shop was a major expedition, drying damp clothes and boots was a nightmare. The children all got 'flu and she kept them at home for the greater part of the spring term; she was terrified whenever they were ill. The lowest point came in February. A young woman, whom she knew by sight, was found dead with her children, a boy of eight and girl of six, in a fume-filled car. It turned out that her husband had left her and she'd been receiving treatment for depression for some time.

Helena spent much of the next week crying. She'd seen her at the school gates, but had had little contact with her because her own children were older; now, though, she kept thinking that if she had taken the trouble to talk to her it might have made a difference. The village went into deep shock and everyone said they could never forgive her for what she had done to the children. Helena found it unbearable. The news stories from Cambodia affected her in the same way; she couldn't stand anything which had to do with children suffering. The programmes which she sometimes caught her boys watching made her furious. Why did people want to play at violence, she asked them, when there was so much actual suffering in the world?

So she struggled through the winter, spending more than she could afford on heating, feeding the children on beans with toast or shrivelled potatoes because there was little fresh food to be got. When she had the time she went for long walks across the snowy fields, feeling better if it was a clear day and she could see the white mountain peaks on the Welsh border. The exercise calmed her down, and she'd also taken valium for the last four years on the doctor's advice. Every morning she religiously swallowed one of the little green and yellow capsules and hoped it would get her through the day. Possibly there was nothing in them, but the act of taking them seemed to help. Once her mother had found the pills in her drawer and been quite curious.

'What *are* those things, dear? Some sort of tonic?' and then, suspiciously, 'Len, you're not on the pill, are you?'

'No, mother'.

It was ironic if her mother really thought she was having an affair. Who with? she wondered. With the postman, with old Mr Watkins at the general store? She hardly saw an unattached man from one year's end to the next, and anyway was convinced that none of them would want her. That way lay nothing but trauma and humiliation.

I used to be a happy person, she thought. At school, which she'd enjoyed more than either of her sisters, she had woken up each morning looking forward to a day packed with interest. She'd believed that if you loved God, worked hard, treated people as you would like to be treated yourself, everything would in the end be all right. Even after Reg left her, even after her father died, she had still got a lot of fun and enjoyment out of her life with the children. Now all that was gone, because she couldn't look at them without fearing they would suddenly be taken away. My little Tessa, she thought as she waded through the deepest snow, I would have done anything, anything. I'll never understand why God took you, instead of me.

In April, out of the blue, she received a letter from an old school friend, Clemency Barras. It had been sent care of Con and invited her to her wedding, which was to be held in London later that month. It was a second marriage, of course; Clem was some years older than herself, and she was thirty-nine.

'It's such ages since I've seen you', the letter said. 'Do come, and I've asked Con too - I only wish we could have Margot! A few other Chalet girls will be there, and we can have a jolly talk about old times. Let me know if you'd like a bed, that will be no problem, but *come*!'

Helena was tempted. It would be good to see old friends, and stay the night with Con, perhaps. But Con, when she rang her, said rather curtly that she would be out of town that weekend. Not for the first time Helena thought there might be things in her sister's life which she knew nothing about. The other problem was that she was nervous of leaving the children, even for a day. But when she talked it over with the family they all urged her to go.

'You're ridiculous, Mum', Johnno said. 'Go up early, and you can come back in the evening, and I'll stay around all day and keep an eye on the younger ones. I promise faithfully that I'll call Dr Prosser if there's the slightest trouble'.

Johnno was sixteen and had shot up in the last few months, after worrying most of his life about being shorter than other boys. Now he was half a head taller than his mother and had an unexpectedly deep voice, but was still very thin. He'd got a string of As in his GCSE exams, last year. Richard, smilingly eating cornflakes at the present moment, plodded a long way behind him. His great passion was horses and he spent every spare moment at the Black Mountain farm.

Maggs flounced in, heading for the refrigerator without condescending to speak to anyone. She was the problem child, having been hit even harder than the rest by the loss of her twin, or perhaps it was her age, which was thirteen and a half. Little Frances, looking like an angel in her blue dressing-gown, piped up, 'Yes, Mummy, it's quite safe to go'.

'Of course you must go, dear', Jo said briskly. She was preparing the huge cups of milky home-brewed coffee, such as they'd drunk in the Tyrol, with great efficiency. 'You can't miss the chance of meeting so many Chalet girls. *I'll* be here to see that the children are all right'.

Helena didn't know what to make of her mother.

Sometimes, as now, she was perfectly reasonable, other times she was off in a world of her own. She'd loved Tessa, she had undoubtedly been devoted to her husband, yet she had somehow managed to cut each of them out of her mind, quite ruthlessly, when they were no longer around. It was a great strength; she wished she could have done it.

Besides, she was aware that her own behaviour was not rational. So she wrote back to Clem, saying she would like to go.

There was an election campaign under way. Helena sometimes thought how extraordinary it was that one of the major parties should be led by a woman, who indeed looked more and more like becoming Prime Minister. That would have been inconceivable even a few years earlier.

'I don't like that woman', Jo said. 'She ought to be at home with her children. What do *you* think, Len? Isn't she frightful?'

Helena took some time, seeing that it was probably the right thing, to listen to Mrs Thatcher giving a broadcast. The strength of her reaction surprised her. She was quite non-political, she had never voted, and certainly she had seen plenty of women doing responsible jobs. She decided, though, that this time she would definitely vote against the prospective first woman Prime Minister.

On the last Saturday in April she got up very early and drove to Hereford to catch the London express. Her one decent outfit, a light blue two-piece, had been cleaned and was in a carrier bag. The children were all well, otherwise she wouldn't have gone. She'd also brought a good silver jug, in the possession of the Maynard family for fifty years, as a wedding present.

Clem lived in a small but charming house near Wimbledon Common. When Helena knocked, later in the morning, she was shown into a front room full of people she remembered vaguely or not at all. There were three or four girls from her school, but they were all older than herself, and had changed, and another woman was introduced to her as the lawyer who had handled Clem's divorce. The bride, in shirt and slacks, welcomed her with hugs and kisses.

'Len - I'd have known you *anywhere* - it must be twenty years - it's so kind of you to have come all this way. Sit down and have some coffee and Danish pastries and we'll toddle along to the registry office when we feel like it'.

'I've never been to a registry office wedding ', Helena said.

'Well, last time I had the full works', said Clem, 'cathedral bells, two hundred guests, six bridesmaids throwing rose petals, and you know how that turned out. And Perry' - she looked fondly at the unimpressive little man - 'has also been married before, so a church wedding was not on. This time we're going to be more modest and more hopeful. Just a small party with friends'.

Helena wondered whether she'd have known Clem if she'd passed her in the street. Her hair, which had been red-brown at school, was now red-gold, and she looked considerably smarter and more sophisticated than the plain-spoken girl she remembered. The house looked as if there was money around - modern paintings and prints, Habitat furniture, a long garden and a great deal of light and air.

'How are your family?'

'My parents are dead, but Tony's coming up from Bristol for the day, and I've got a nephew and niece. How many children have you got?'

'Five - four'.

'Clem', the bridegroom said, 'I hate to rush you, but we do want to be on time, don't we?'

'Right. Come upstairs, Len, and we'll change'.

They went to the main bedroom, where Helena got into her blue suit and Clem into an apricot silk outfit, talking all the time.

'Well, Len, I've been through the mincing machine, just like you have, since school. Vince, my ex-husband - you never met him, did you? - was pure poison. I sweated blood to help him set up the gallery, sold several of my father's paintings to raise money, and then, when I'd put up with his nasty habits for more years than I care to think of, along came this woman. I actually gave her a job as my assistant. I was sorry for her, because she spun me a hard-luck story. And when she went off, she took

Vince'.

Though it was her wedding day, Clem was obviously still feeling extremely bitter.

'But I decided at once that I wasn't going to let the bastard destroy me. Jean, who you met downstairs, got me a good settlement, and luckily we never had any children so I was free to make a fresh start. I bought a whole new wardrobe, joined the best marriage bureau I could afford, and then I met darling Perry totally by accident. Someone asked us both to dinner and that was it. How do I look? Tell me honestly'.

'Fine. You look lovely, Clem'.

'Then let's stagger downstairs'.

They did so. Helena thought she might be starting a headache; Clem's reference to children had struck her painfully, but she refused to dwell on that just now. While they were getting dressed, more wedding guests had crowded into the sitting-room. She was startled to find herself being kissed by a good-looking, fair-haired man in a Harris tweed jacket. Tony Barras. Everybody seemed to greet each other this way nowadays.

'Len, how nice to see you after all these years! You haven't changed at all. And this is my wife, Christine'.

A very pretty woman a few years younger than herself smiled a greeting. There were also two tow-headed children, a boy and girl. A moment later she met Clem's godfather, Peter Young R.A., and his wife Gillian, whom she had known in her schooldays as Miss Linton. Quite a surprise; her dark hair was silver now, but she was still pleasant-looking. She immediately began asking about her family.

'Right, folks!' the bridegroom shouted, 'let's go'.

They took a fleet of cars to the nearest registry office, where the deed was done, then drove back to Clem's, where Tony kept posing them for photographs. Helena smiled through it until her jaw ached. While they were out, a buffet lunch had magically appeared, and they each took a plate and went out into the garden. She found herself sitting next to Christine Barras, who said apologetically that she was just a housewife.

'I've run a playgroup since the children started school', she explained, 'but that's about all. Clem says I should send them away to board and get a high-powered job to pay for it, but I could never do that'.

'No, I wouldn't either', Helena said. 'But I think people had a different attitude in the last generation - my brothers all went to public school, and I suppose we did too, though our parents were just round the corner'.

'How did you like your school?'

'Oh, I loved it'.

She remembered it so vividly; the snowball fights, the summer meadows with their wild flower tapestry, the troops of friends. Miss Annersley telling them to be strong self-reliant women.

'Yes, I've heard it was rather special', Christine said, 'but we wouldn't send our children away from home even if we could afford it, which we can't. Tony was very unhappy at boarding school'.

'I always say', Tony said, appearing with a bottle of champagne, 'that if you've survived a British public school, a Third World jail is no problem'.

'It happened in the Congo', Christine explained. 'He goes to all sorts of remote parts of the world to get photographs'.

Tony dropped down on the grass and poured out some fizzing liquid for both of them.

'Do have some, Len; for once it's the real thing. Well, how are you, and how are your sisters? I saw Margot on the box talking about South Africa'.

'Margot was banned from going back, but she's in Buenos Aires now. She's talking about specialising in TB'.

'Yes, I should think that's needed. I've seen a lot of it in the shanty towns. Not that it couldn't creep back here', Tony added, suddenly looking quite worked up, 'if that woman gets in'.

'Tony, you *do* exaggerate - '.

There was a commotion, and they all got up to wave to the bride and groom. Clem embraced her.

'Goodbye, Len - it was nice of you to come - we're probably

moving to France very soon, but I'll keep you informed. Perry works in computers, did I say? They're the great thing of the future - oh, all right, I'm *coming*!'

And they drove off, with the Barras children running along the pavement and flinging old shoes at the car until it disappeared.

Helena returned to the party. It all seemed to be couples, successful middle-aged people on a day out. She found herself thinking of people who had been stabbed, walking around and behaving quite normally when all the time they were bleeding to death. Her head swam and she wondered if it was the unaccustomed champagne. She saw Tony looking at her, obviously concerned, and then Gillian Young came up.

'My dear girl, are you sure you're all right? You look sadly run down'.

'Honestly, Miss Linton - sorry, I mustn't call you that now - I'm fine. I just ought to leave soon, because I have to catch a train to Hereford'.

'Then we'll drop you at Paddington. It's no trouble'.

And in less than ten minutes they were away. Helena stared at the dirty streets, with their election posters, and then dredged up something polite to say when they dropped her at the great station. It was nearly empty, a typical Saturday afternoon in London. A man looked at her and then looked away. For a moment she saw herself through his eyes, a woman nearing middle age, nicely dressed, perhaps looking younger than her years, but too thin, too haunted by the past.

Her train wasn't due for another half hour. She wandered along the platform, going as far as possible.

Trains were drawing in and out all the time. A pigeon fluttered under the great glass roof, struggling for a way out. The film *Anna Karenina*. Greta Garbo with smoke drifting across her tragic face. The twins cuddled up on her lap, bewildered, and Tessa asking her, 'Mummy, why did that lady jump under the train?' Tessa. She began to sob hysterically; there was no one near her just now and she could let herself go.

But in a moment she sat down on the nearest bench and

wiped her eyes, because she had been taught never to make a scene in public. A train nearby made snorting noises and began slowly to move away.

If you jumped under a train you couldn't possibly survive, and you would know almost nothing about it. It would be so quick, so simple, and she didn't think she could endure any more pain. Her father had been a very serious Catholic and known that suicide was the ultimate sin, but that hadn't stopped him, when the pain became bad enough. Probably, like her, he had reached the point where he simply didn't want to go on.

Where was Con? It was ridiculous that she should be in London, and not see her. Perhaps she was keeping away on purpose, perhaps she was like Typhoid Mary, bringing bad luck wherever she went. Helena felt she must have been suppressing an awful lot of anger in the last thirteen years. Anger against Reg, who had invaded her life when she was only fifteen, against her parents, who had encouraged him, against whoever or whatever had killed Tessa. But she was no good at being angry with other people; she could only turn it on herself.

The train wouldn't come in for quarter of an hour and she was too tired to get up and look for another one. She stared along the line, waiting for it, and tried to think of a good reason why she should not kill herself. After all, once she had jumped off the platform, it would be too late to change her mind. She worked it all out - how she would leave her handbag on the seat, so that she could be identified with no trouble.

She thought first of the driver. It seemed a mean thing to do to him, but it would not ruin his life, surely. Then she thought of what her death would mean to Johnno, Richard, Maggs and Frances. They would be terribly upset, of course, but they had survived other traumas in the last few years. Children were very resilient.

Only who was going to look after them, if she died? She went through all the alternatives, growing more and more depressed as the arguments stacked up against her. Her mother - impossible. Reg's parents were long dead. Reg himself, she was sure, would not accept all four children. The most she could hope for was that he would grudgingly take the two boys, and after all, did she want her boys brought up by Mary-Lou? Con perhaps would have the girls. She wouldn't turn her back completely, but she was not really interested in children, and would rather give them presents than her time. Or Margot; would she be expected to give up her important work and come back to England to raise the children, when she had never wanted any of her own either? She thought about her married brothers and sisters - excluding Felicity, who was now divorced - and did not see how she could ask any of them to do it. Steve's wife, in particular, was quite capable of being unkind to them. If she died, her children would be, at worst, put into care, at best, divided between several people who didn't want them, and they would also be damaged for life.

The train began to come in.

No, she thought wearily, getting up from the bench, I can't do it; I must wait until Frances is grown up. After that nobody would need her, and she could look at her options again. She got into the train, and the doors slammed behind her. Thankfully there was no one to see the open misery in her face. The train began to pull out of the vast dirty city, which she would not see again that decade.

THE END OF THE NINETEEN SEVENTIES

THE NINETEEN EIGHTIES

Chapter 23

Into the Eighties

By the end of 1982, Jack and Jo would have had sixteen grandchildren. Apart from Tessa, they were all alive and healthy, as were the eleven original Maynards. But not all of them were living as their parents would have wished, and of the six who had married, four had been divorced.

There had been Maynards at Plas Gwyn, on and off, for the last forty years, and people in Howells village were quite used to old Mrs Maynard and young Mrs Maynard - as they called them - and to the children who came and went. Old Mrs Maynard, completely grey now but still tall and vigorous, was a familiar figure, always stopping to chat with anyone she met on the roads, and it was said that she had been a distinguished novelist, although she hadn't published a book for ten years. Early in 1980 she surprised her family by announcing that she was getting a job.

'I'm tired of hearing, Len, that we haven't got money for this and haven't got money for that. I shall do my bit towards expenses. The school is advertising for a dinner lady and that will suit me very nicely; I've always got on with children'.

'But, Mother - '.

'I know what you're going to say, dear. You're afraid it may interfere with my writing, but I shall do that in the morning and then have a complete break from mental work. Artists ought to have regular contact with the real world, you know. It's just a pity that Anna went back to the Tyrol. I don't know why but we never had to worry about money in those days'.

And, against all expectation, it had been a success. The children loved her, the wages, though very low, were a help and she went happily off to the infant school each day and came back full of news.

'Things have certainly changed since my own schooldays.

Some of the little boys' language is quite dreadful; it wouldn't have been tolerated by my sister or Miss Annersley. And, do you know, several of the mothers are not married. They're quite open about it. Very strange'.

Her daughter also worked part-time, as a supply teacher in Hereford, and she would give language lessons to anyone who wanted them, although she refused to leave home if any of her children were ill. People who knew Helena said she had never got over the death of her daughter in 1975, but she didn't talk about it, and she was generally considered a nice woman who had had bad luck. Her children had turned out reasonably well, too, or better than you'd expect from a one-parent family. Johnno could have got into university on his languages alone but had chosen to do history and was at Christ Church, Oxford. He'd spent a summer working unpaid on the local newspaper because he wanted to go into journalism. He was a bit abrupt, but polite in a formal way and extremely hard-working. Richard had left school at sixteen with no qualifications and had a job in the local stables. His mother had begged him to stay on but he'd stopped trying to compete with Johnno years ago and had always loved ponies. He had his own circle of friends at the Young Farmers' club.

Maggs was trouble; the older residents said that she was the image of her grandmother forty years earlier but she had a wild streak they'd never seen in Jo. Whether it was rioting on the school bus, or drinking under age in the Green Dragon, Maggs was always in the thick of it, and she had a habit of talking German to her family in front of other people and shrieking with laughter when they looked baffled. Nothing serious so far, but that girl was clearly going to give her mother a lot of grief one day. And Frances, now fifteen, was just a quiet little schoolgirl.

Con was occasionally seen in the village, visiting her sister, but there could hardly have been a greater contrast in their lifestyles. She had a highly-paid job on her magazine, *The Eighties*, she travelled and was seen in public a great deal, and she still published a romantic novel every year under a pseudonym. The only mystery to her family and friends was why such an eligible woman was not married. They were not to know that Con had briefly joined a dating agency, soon after the Des disaster, but the men she met were so dreary that it was all too obvious why they hadn't got married under their own steam. Of the two who wanted to see her again, one talked only about his digestion while the other turned out to be obsessed with Elizabeth Taylor and wanted Con to dress and make up to look like her. Con decided it was ridiculous for a woman of her age and status to waste her time like this, and let her membership lapse.

Sometimes - not all the time or every day, for she was very busy - she mused about her luck. If you married the first man you met, like Helena, it would probably go wrong, but if you waited until you were more worldly-wise all the decent men would probably be already married. But she had her good job, her comfortable flat, foreign holidays, interesting friends and absorbing hobbies. In no circumstances would she have wished to change places with Len.

Neither of them had seen Margot since 1976, the summer of Con's pregnancy, after she had been barred as an undesirable from South Africa. The Order had packed her off to Buenos Aires, where she lived in one of the shanty towns or *villas miserias* scattered around the capital and worked pretty hard in the field of preventive medicine. Her letters said that the health care was good, but the dictatorship much worse than people realised. They knew that she was involved with the Mothers of the Disappeared, a group of women who were the only people who dared to demonstrate, holding vigils for their student children of whom they didn't know if they were alive or dead. When the Falklands crisis broke out, in April 1982, they wondered whether Margot would be on the government's side for once, but in fact she was implacably opposed to war. She wrote that the British community in the Argentine all thought Thatcher was mad and couldn't believe that even she was prepared to kill people for two barren islands which, if you looked at a map, were obviously not a part of Britain. Helena and Con listened appalled to the talk of dropping a nuclear bomb on Buenos Aires where their sister was. Con even wrote to an old boy friend, the Labour MP Alan Marshall, who replied that he agreed with her but an election was coming up and he couldn't afford to sound unpatriotic. Helena looked at her sons, then aged eighteen and nineteen, and had nightmares about boys dying in the freezing sea.

About six weeks after the end of the war, Margot returned to England. It wasn't clear whether she had been sent or just come, but she told Con that the junta was going to fall, and that she had done all the good she could.

'It's too comfortable. I want to do some serious work on TB'.

'TB?' Con had hardly thought about it since her childhood. 'But that's all over, isn't it?'

'Everybody thinks that'.

They had been brought up in the shadow of TB, the great white scourge, as it was then called, which their father and uncle had dedicated themselves to fighting and which had claimed the lives of several people they knew. It had practically died out in the 1950s in Europe and that was why the sanatorium on the Gornetz Platz had had to close. But, Margot explained, it had never died out in the Third World and was still a big killer in Asia. It could also come back in advanced countries which had pockets of poverty because it thrived on malnutrition, bad housing and dirt. She was keen to get the BCG vaccine to children before the disease could get a hold on them.

'Well, Margot, I hope you're not going abroad again immediately'.

'Don't count on it', Margot said.

Helena arranged a reunion in Plas Gwyn so that Margot could meet up with her brothers and sisters, and ten out of the eleven Maynards came. But it was all spoiled when she and Steve had a row about the Falklands war; she accused him of enjoying bloodshed and he accused her of being disloyal. And after she had stormed out Steve's wife, Sue, said that poor Margot was quite neurotic and it was probably something to do with sexual frustration. It cast a shadow over the whole weekend. Steve had grown very conventional; he was doing well in his job as an engineer while Sue worked for a firm of financial consultants. They had two boys at boarding school. The triplets, who still thought alike about most things, privately agreed that Steve and Mike were both obsessed with making money, but Steve would have been a much nicer person without Sue.

Charles was the only Maynard who didn't come to the reunion. He'd said something about summer 'flu; Helena worried that he might be really ill and she might not know. But it was just as likely that he had invented it because he couldn't face meeting people. They very rarely saw him, though he paid his share of the family bills without complaint and sent a cheque for the children at Christmas. He was not married, and had never, so far as they knew, had a woman friend; Sue, that same weekend, had asked in hushed tones, 'Do you think that Charles is *normal*?' And Helena, for once, got quite angry and said she didn't agree with speculating about people's private lives. In fact she did not believe that Charles had anything to conceal but that he had simply turned away from relationships at an early age because he found them too difficult. He was now a reader at Durham University and was respected by a very small circle of scholars in Europe and America.

No two brothers could have been more different than Charles and Mike. He and his wife Rosemary, whom they all liked, had produced two girls, and then a boy, after their hasty marriage in 1971. As an estate agent he'd done very well out of the boom in house prices and bought his own boat, on which he spent all his spare time. This had brought him into contact with a smart set; so much so that when the serial *Howard's Way* went out a few years later, with its saga of boating and adultery in the Home Counties, everyone said it must have been based on the lives of Mike and his friends.

For that marriage had not lasted. A good-looking man, still only in his early thirties, Mike began to feel tied down and started an affair with the bored young wife of one of his Yacht Club friends. There was a brawl, which got into the local papers, and a particularly nasty divorce. Con had only just attended his second wedding, which felt weird, she said, with the bride almost bursting out of her Yves St Laurent dress. And now they were here, with their new little boy, whom Mike doted on, and it was as if the first wife and children had never been.

Felix looked and behaved very much the same but, being that crucial few years younger, had never felt the need to marry the women he got involved with. Quite a few attractive actresses had been seen with Felix but he believed in travelling light, and none had lasted more than two or three years. He was affable and easy-going but people who knew said don't be fooled, Felix means to get to the top. He'd often given his brothers and sisters tickets for his shows and they were impressed by his professionalism.

Felicity, his twin, was doing as badly as Felix was doing well. She was bitter about the divorce, and complained that Greg gave her hardly any alimony and took no interest in his children. At thirty-three, Felicity was a very discontented young woman. She looked good and dressed expensively, but the girlish bloom had gone and she blamed her parents loudly and often for letting her get married so young. As if anyone could have stopped her, Con said. Felix still had some affection for her and took her to theatre parties in London, but most of the rest of the family were fed up. Helena had got used to her turning up on the doorstep of Plas Gwyn, asking if she could look after Timmy and Madeleine while she went abroad with the latest man. She was glad to do it, because she loved the children and kept hoping that one of the men would be right for her sister. But they never stayed around.

And again, her younger sister's life was completely different. Cecil had married Hywel Davies in the year of her father's death and they now lived in Cardiff, where they were heavily involved in teaching and performing music. They had two little girls, both dark and exquisitely turned-out like their mother. Hywel was jolly and pleasant, and they were the only couple who had never dumped their children on Helena. Cecil had actually managed to find a nice man who was devoted to her.

There remained the younger twins, Geoff and Phil, and it was remarkable how their lives had diverged, just like Felix and

Felicity. Geoff, the elder by an hour, had none of his sister's forcefulness. He'd drifted through his teens without any idea of what he wanted to do, and now, in his late twenties, was the same vague good-natured, apathetic person. Everyone had thought that nothing could be safer than a job in the car industry, but it wasn't, and now Geoff was unemployed and waiting passively for something to turn up. It was a comedown for a man who had been to public school, but did not seem to worry him. Back in 1978 he'd married his girl friend Jennifer, who was pregnant, but the marriage had broken up when their little boy Kevin was a few months old. Not his fault, Geoff assured everyone; Jenny had just got fed up with him. Helena worried about the child, growing up cut off from his father's family, but no one else did and least of all Geoff. He still lived in Birmingham and spent his days in the pub and watching daytime TV, as more and more young men seemed to be doing, although he turned up occasionally at Plas Gwyn with his dirty washing when he wanted a break and a meal.

Philippa also turned up at the reunion, from her good job in Brussels, though she said that the family was an outdated institution and she certainly wasn't coming home for Christmas or anything like that. She, too, managed to quarrel with Margot, who had told her that Western feminists were some of the most privileged people on earth. Phil snapped back that she wasn't letting any priest run *her* life. When Mike jovially asked when she was going to get married, she said she had a meaningful relationship with a Belgian diplomat but had no intention of becoming his property.

'Len got married. So did Felicity. And look how it turned out'.

'Oh, I say', said Mike, who thought that all women wanted nothing else.

These were the Maynards at the beginning of the 1980s, the meanest and most vulgar decade in British history.

Chapter 24

Margot goes to Greenham

December, 1982. It was bitterly cold, and still dark when the van dropped Margot and Pauline near the perimeter fence of the U.S. Air Force base at Greenham Common. There were woods on the boundary, and the tall bare trees loomed black against a greyish sky; they could also see little clusters of candles where women had camped overnight. A group of them were singing quietly. Margot recognised the Welsh carols she had occasionally heard in Howells village as a child.

The driver was a bearded man in a duffel coat who looked like a leftover from the Sixties. He said, grinning, 'I'm sure nuns didn't behave like this in my young days'.

'You ain't seen nothing yet', Margot said.

Pauline had a flask of coffee and they drank it black from paper beakers, walking about to keep their circulation going in the keen cold. The last stars faded; the fence became visible, a twelve-foot wall of chicken-wire supported by stout concrete pillars and stretching as far away as the eye could see. The common must have been a nice place once, with gorse bushes and dog-violets, but it had been enclosed for so many years that only the older residents of Newbury could remember what it had looked like. From where they were they could see only a few insignificant-looking buildings, but somewhere, hidden from the public eye, were the Cruise missiles, the smart bombs which could go round any corner, hit any target.

Margot had not worn a nun's robes for years. She was dressed plainly and sensibly in a navy skirt and thick jumper, with strong shoes to keep the mud out and gloves to protect her hands. She'd met up with Pauline, a former Pax Christi friend, soon after her return to England. Pauline was also a doctor, working with disturbed children.

They'd been talking for hours, while they were travelling down from London, and hadn't got to the end of it yet. Most people listening to them would have been baffled. Margot asked,

'So did you ever think of leaving?'

'Often', Pauline admitted, 'but I never quite got there. I think God probably wants me to stay on as a thorn in the Church's flesh'. They both smiled. 'What do you think of this Pope?'

'Bloody awful', Margot said. 'He's doing all he can to squash liberation theology. There won't be any progress till they elect a man from the Third World'.

'A man? Couldn't it be a woman?'

'Don't dream *too* hard, Pauline'.

Now that it was getting light coaches from all over England were drawing up, and more and more women were approaching them through the trees; white-haired granny figures, young girls, respectable-looking women who were obviously mothers of families and a few in wild fancy dress. Some of them were carrying banners which they proceeded to prop against the fence:

       THOU SHALT NOT KILL

and

       WOMEN AND CHILDREN
       THE MAJORITY OF THE HUMAN RACE
       SAY NO TO WAR.

And the opposition was also showing itself. They could see a few men in uniform inside the fence, and a ring of policemen at strategic points to stop the women breaking through. Pauline remarked, 'Why aren't they dealing with the child molesters?' and wandered over to talk to one. Margot was about to follow when a girl's voice called, 'Hey, *Margot*, is that you?'

She turned round and, after a moment's bewilderment, recognised her niece, Maggs. She had met her at Plas Gwyn that summer and noticed the striking resemblance to her grandmother, but now the girl looked more extraordinary still. Her abundant dark hair had been given a Mohican cut, and dyed pink, and there was a pin in her nose.

'Do you like it?' Maggs asked, grinning. 'Mum nearly fainted when I came home like this'.

'Well, it's certainly different', Margot said. Why were women always doing things to their hair and faces? 'Is your mother here?'

'No. I wanted her to come, but Frances had a cold, so she panicked. Hey, it's great to see you. My friends all think I'm really weird, having an aunt who's a nun'.

'Your friends -'. Margot was struck by an unpleasant thought. 'Don't you go to a Catholic school?'

'Nope. First there wasn't one near us, and then Mum stopped going to church, when Tessa died'.

'I see'.

Pauline came back. 'That policeman was really nice; he hates the missiles but can't say so. Hello'.

'This is my niece Maggs', Margot said.

'Lovely to meet you', said Pauline, and they started talking, but a moment later a crowd of younger women came up, and swept Maggs away.

Margot sighed. She had probably, personally, saved hundreds of children's lives by vaccinating them at the right time, but the memory of the ones she hadn't saved always troubled her. And it was a particularly depressing thought that her sister's child, who lived in a developed country, had died. You're never going to get a perfect society, Margot thought, edging closer to the wire fence, there's always that hard core of selfishness and perversity in human nature, but we certainly make it an awful lot worse than it need be. Those missiles, besides being designed to kill people, each represented tons of food, powdered milk, anti-polio drops, all the things she wanted for the Third World. Sitting snugly in their bunkers with armed men protecting them. Why people call them heroes, she thought, I'll never know.

They had reached the fence. It was decorated with hundreds of small objects; tinsel, branches of holly and mistletoe, family photographs, a baby's woolly mitten. She and Pauline looked at each other and then moved to another part of the fence, which was bare.

'Got your wire-cutters?' Pauline asked.

Margot produced them. They both started clipping and had soon made a small hole, which grew wider as other women came up and saw what they were doing. Then an armoured car drove towards them from inside the base and there was a scrum.

'You're all bloody lesbians', one man shouted.

'I am not!' an earnest-looking young woman with fair hair shouted back. 'I'm doing this for my children'.

They were being pushed up against the fence. The concrete pillar was swaying; any moment, Margot thought, it was going to come down. Pauline had been grabbed and taken off, but someone else seized her wire-cutters and went on widening the hole. It was just about big enough for a small woman like Margot. She dived through, began to run towards the sheds and was brought down a moment later when an SAS man jumped on her. Other women streamed through the wire.

Plas Gwyn was getting ready for Christmas. Johnno was home from Oxford, Richard was having a morning off and the girls had just been let out of school. Helena, as she always did, had decorated the house with holly from the huge tree by the back porch and with branches of fir. She was filling mugs of coffee while the children - heavens, not children any more, they were all teenagers - sat around the kitchen table with their heads in their comics or books.

'Mum', Frances said, looking up from her girls' magazine, 'do you think, if I cut my hair short, I might look like Princess Diana?'

Johnno, who was reading the *Life of Bismarck*, rolled his eyes to heaven.

'I wouldn't bother, darling; your hair looks lovely'.

'At least it isn't *pink*', Richard said, guffawing, 'like Maggs'.

Maggs flared up. 'Don't make personal remarks!' She gestured at the front page of the *Guardian*, which carried a large picture of Margaret Thatcher. 'Why did you call me after that awful woman, Mum? It's really embarrassing'.

'Maggs, your great-aunt wasn't an awful woman. She

started a school in the Tyrol on practically nothing, and built it into a remarkable place'.

'You and your old school', grumbled Maggs.

Helena thought it wise to ignore her daughter when she was being stroppy. Maggs was seventeen, one of the brightest in her sixth form, she had lots of friends, and she'd been to Greenham and come back unscathed. She was going to take a year off before university, working at a hotel in Lausanne to improve her French. It frightened her a little, but she knew how important it was for the children to keep up their languages. They had all spoken German in the Oberland - even Frances, who had been not quite four when they left - and she'd never let them get out of the habit. So it was just as well that Maggs should take this chance.

But when she looked at Maggs, she saw her twin. Tessa would have been seventeen, would have been tall and dark and strikingly attractive, reminding so many people of her grandmother Jo. But Tessa had been a very quiet and timid child; it was impossible to imagine her dyeing her hair pink or snapping at her brothers or going off like a firework in all directions. She would probably just have trailed admiringly after Maggs. And if Maggs had been ill, she would have screamed until everyone knew.

'Hey, Mum!' Maggs was looking up from the newspaper, black eyes blazing. 'Here's another bit about Greenham. Just listen - "A forty-three-year-old nun, Sister Margaret Maynard, appeared before Newbury magistrates with six other women. They refused to pay a twenty-pound fine and were jailed for one week"'.

'Oh, my God', said Helena.

'I shouldn't worry, Mum', Johnno said, after the paper had been passed around. 'Margot's quite tough'.

'You don't understand', Helena said, fighting back tears. 'Margot isn't tough; she was terribly delicate as a child and had to be sent to Canada because our parents thought she'd die. And then she overworked and had that breakdown; I don't think she could survive in prison. I'll ring Con'.

Johnno stood up. He was very protective of his mother, beneath his rather gruff exterior, and he knew that apart from him and the other children she cared more about her triplet sisters than anyone else. 'Okay, Mum, you do that. And then I'll do some ringing round myself and find out where she is'.

Con was concerned, but tended to agree that Margot would probably survive anything they were likely to do to her. Meanwhile, Johnno phoned the *Guardian*, and a few other numbers, and established that she was indeed in jail. 'Gave the magistrates a real telling-off', someone informed him. He wasn't surprised.

So it was that the triplets met in Newbury, late that afternoon. The town was covered with cheap Christmas decorations and carols were being piped to shoppers. Con was smartly dressed in mauve and black, Helena in her normal working clothes. They waited while their sister was brought up from the cells.

Margot looked small and vulnerable, with immense bruises under both eyes.

'Why did you come?'

'We couldn't leave you - ', Helena began.

'You look rotten', Con said. 'Come on; Len wants to take you home for Christmas. Tell me what your fine is and I'll pay it'.

'If you do that, I'll never speak to you again'.

'But, Margot, you can't just stay here and suffer - '.

'Why shouldn't I suffer?' Margot demanded. 'Other people do, the whole of their lives. I know this isn't South Africa but you only keep your rights if you're prepared to fight for them and we'll never get rid of these missiles, until a lot of respectable women are prepared to go to jail'.

They were unable to change her mind and at the end of quarter of an hour a warder said, 'Come on, Maynard', and she was taken away.

'I don't know what to do', Helena said. Funnily enough, although she had had a much harder life than Con, she was the more distraught. 'It's terrible to think of Margot being in prison, just for her beliefs, and she's so obstinate, we can't - '.

'Excuse me'.

A tall man with thinning fair hair had come up, smiling diffidently. He wore a grey shirt and dog-collar.

'You must be Margot's sisters; the resemblance is unmistakable. I'm Bernard Martin. Do let me get you some coffee and then we can discuss what to do'.

Thank God, Helena thought with deep relief, Margot's got some respectable friends, at least. She was already worn out with the preparations for Christmas and the long drive to Newbury. She followed him without arguing.

'Are you a priest, Bernard?' Con asked, when they were all sitting round a table with cups of instant coffee.

'Not a very good one, I'm afraid, but yes, I met Margot several years ago in Pax Christi and we've kept intermittently in touch ever since. How did she look when you saw her?'

'Awful'. Helena roused herself to make him understand the situation. 'You see, she's never been strong - I'm very worried - and now she refuses to let us pay her fine'.

'The fine has been paid. She may not know it yet, but they're going to let her out in the next half hour and then I'll drive her to London. I agree, she's taken quite as much as can be expected'.

'And how do the church authorities feel?' Con asked curiously. Catholic priests didn't often come her way these days and she thought this was an interesting man.

'Oh -' Bernard smiled. 'Well, Margot has a tense relationship with them, as you can imagine, but she insists that she's doing only what her conscience tells her. Which is absolutely sound theology. Her friend Pauline has been reproved by the Bishop but is refusing to apologise, and people like me are doing our bit behind the scenes. She won't like it when she knows about the fine, but I'll deal with that'.

They went back.

Margot was brought up from the cells in her everyday clothes. Her eyes went to Bernard but, for once, she seemed speechless.

'How are you?' he asked.

Margot said, 'The woman in my cell was a prostitute. She had needle marks all over her arms and she'd tried to slash her wrists. She's sixteen'.

None of them knew what to say. Margot took a step forward and went on, tears streaming down her cheeks, 'It's just so bloody awful - the missiles - and people are dying, here in front of our eyes and we don't care, and all those young men joining the army and not even thinking, not knowing that there's such a thing as conscience or morals - I can't stand -'.

'It's all right, my dear girl', Bernard said.

Helena and Con stared, and then looked away, at the sight of their sister sobbing her heart out in the arms of this perfectly strange man.

Chapter 25

Re-enter Mary-Lou

Con's plane circled Heathrow and she looked down at England for the first time in two long months. Two months in New York which had started so promisingly, but had ended in the most awful humiliation of her life.

That summer, 1983, she'd managed with a little manoeuvring to get herself attached to a big English conference as the tutor in romantic fiction. There were, she was told, several American housewives who would pay good money to learn to write like she did, and indeed, that part had gone very well. Her plan was to spend the evenings socialising with the other conference-goers and then take a holiday, looking up old friends and going in a relaxed way round the main sights.

But at the conference she got acquainted with one of the other tutors, a professor (they all called themselves professors) of Victorian studies at a minor university. He told her that he was separated from his wife, about to get divorced, and Con had been prepared to take him very seriously. So after the students went home they headed for his apartment and spent two blissful weeks there. They went to museums and concerts, he introduced her to a circle of interesting, well-informed people and she began to think there was no reason why she shouldn't relocate permanently in New York. And then, one Sunday morning, it all blew up in her face. Jethro was not separated from his wife, although they clearly had major problems; she had merely gone on holiday and come back early (tipped off, Con suspected, by a friend), and made an unspeakable scene.

Dreadful. There she'd been, peacefully squeezing orange juice in her dressing-gown and wondering whether to take the bagels from the oven, when this woman had erupted into the flat and begun to scream at her. She'd called her a home-wrecker, an English bitch, a goddam tramp. It was particularly wounding when she had always been so careful to keep away from other people's husbands. And Jethro had just stood there and then bleated, 'Honey, she doesn't mean a thing'. There was really nothing to be done but leave them yelling at one another, get dressed, get packed and phone a cab.

She felt sick, physically battered (although the woman hadn't actually hit her) throughout the journey home. And her mood didn't improve when she picked up a magazine and her eye fell on an article, 'People of the Rainforest', with photographs by Tony Barras. Lovely photographs, he was just as good in colour as in black and white, and although he wasn't a household name he was an F.R.C.P. and it was obvious that his work was respected. It would be something to be the wife of a man like that; every so often, when she was feeling low, Con would think her life might have been different, if she and Tony had managed to get together when they were young. There was another woman sitting nearby, with a little girl. Con calculated that she must be six or seven, the same age her child would have been. Her father didn't seem to be around but perhaps that didn't matter; several single women were bringing up families now. Odd how that little girl followed her round, turned up in unexpected ways.

Wearily, she went through customs, took the Piccadilly line, and was soon on the last long lap of her journey home. She was at Green Park and about to get on another train when a lady getting off fell on her with a delighted cry.

'Con! It *is* Con Maynard, isn't it? You don't look a day older!'

With a sinking heart, Con watched her train pull away. The woman looked a typical middle-aged housewife, rather plump, not very fashionably dressed and Con couldn't place her at all.

'I'm Ros - Rosamund Lilley - how wonderful to bump into you like this! It must be twenty-something years since we all left school. How are the other triplets? Is Len in London?'

'No, she lives very quietly with her family, near the Welsh border'. It was coming back, although Ros looked quite different. 'What are *you* doing?'

'I'm married, my husband works at the British Museum, and we've got three lovely children. Oh, and I still do a lot of gardening when I can find the time. Look, Con, we're having a very special party on Friday and you must come. There'll be a few old Chalet girls'.

'Sure'. Con wasn't at all keen to miss the next train, which was due in a minute; the one thing she wanted was to get back to her flat, pour herself a drink, fall into a hot bath and then go to sleep in her own bed. 'Here's my card. Lovely to see you again, Ros; I'm jet-lagged and have to go. If you ask me, I'll come'.

As she boarded the tube, she thought how curious it was that Ros, who had been a lovely girl, and was now quite matronly, should have changed so much while she hadn't. Rosamund Lilley had been one of the very few working-class girls ever to come to the Chalet School; some of the others had given her a bad time over that. She had been Len's friend rather than hers, and Con quickly forgot her. But only two days later an invitation arrived.

It was from Ros and Giles Carthew and was for a silver wedding party, which meant, Con calculated, that Rosamund must have got married almost as soon as she left school. Well, why not go? She bought herself a new cyclamen suit (for she was still feeling quite vulnerable), had her hair styled and turned up at the appointed time.

A pleasant house, if rather lived-in; Con accepted a glass of Beaujolais and was soon at the centre of a laughing group. Ros's husband, though some years older and going bald, seemed a nice man, and there were two boys of university age and a little girl. And then, just as she was beginning to relax and feel better than she had for days, Mary-Lou walked past the door.

She was unmistakable. Some people don't change even in twenty-five years, which was about how long it was since Con had seen her, and besides, she was talking to somebody, and those bell-like tones were unmistakable too. The same tall figure, fair hair cut fashionably short, a blue dress which matched her eyes and made her look not much more than thirty. That was deceptive, Con knew; Mary-Lou must be all of forty-six. Horrible woman; she would never forgive her for ruining her sister's life.

But what, for heaven's sake, was Mary-Lou doing here? She was supposed to be in Boston; Con had even wondered if she might bump into her during her recent trip to the States, though knowing how unlikely that was. Her mind raced. The British Museum - archaeology - that must be the connection. As soon as she could get a word with Rosamund, who was surrounded by friends, she asked her in a light voice if she was dreaming, or had she just seen Mary-Lou.

'Oh, *yes*. She's over here for six months. We always thought Mary-Lou was going to do something remarkable, didn't we? She's very eminent now'.

This didn't surprise Con, because she knew that a lot of people who were eminent in their own field had never been heard of by outsiders. But what did surprise her about her presence this evening was that Rosamund had always been very fond of Len.

'Is her husband here?'

'No. She's got a husband, but I'm not sure of his name because she's liberated and calls herself Mary-Lou Trelawney. Giles can tell you exactly what she does, but I can't. Oh, sorry – excuse me -'.

That was it, Con reflected, as her hostess was pulled away; Ros had no idea what had happened back in the 1960s. She probably thought that Len was still living happily with Reg and their eight point four children, because she herself hadn't got round to telling her about the divorce. Well, the question now was, what was she to do? A moment's reflection convinced her that she couldn't make a scene.

About ten minutes later, when they were all streaming into the kitchen for a buffet supper, Mary-Lou caught up with her.

'Con, how lovely to see you'. Evidently she'd found out that Con was here and had time to prepare herself. 'What are you doing these days?'

Damn, how she wished she was a household name and had written novels that got displayed in W.H. Smith's. Or at least had a husband on her arm. Smiling like a sphinx she responded, 'I'm fine, thanks; I write the book page on *The Eighties*. And how about you?'

'I'm here to pick up an honorary degree from London University'. Damn, Con thought again. 'Actually, I'm thinking seriously of moving back to England'.

'Oh?'

'Yes; there's a job at the Museum of Mankind that looks interesting'. They moved up the line and began to help themselves to an excellent home-baked quiche, prawns and salad. 'Incidentally, Con, I don't know if you know that Reg and I have split up'.

Con almost spilled her Beaujolais.

'Sorry; did I startle you? Yes, I'm afraid we just outgrew each other. Got enough? - well, shall we grab a seat outside?'

A number of people had taken their plates out of doors, where the last of the light still lingered. It was an extremely pleasant town garden, with creeper turning red against a massive wall, giant cacti in pots and a drift of mauve flowers Con couldn't identify. Ros had always been a good gardener, she remembered. They sat down at a chunky wooden table.

'Reg turned out to be not at all what I thought him. It was agreed that we should each concentrate on our own careers and leave one another free, but in fact he expected me to drop my work when it suited him and be a good little housewife. For instance, if we were between maids for any reason, I was supposed to pick up his dirty clothes where he'd dropped them and cook him steak-and-kidney pie like his dear old mother. Perhaps it's his northern working-class background, but I wasn't prepared to put up with it'.

She paused. Con, desperate not to say too much, could only manage, 'I never liked Reg'.

'No, I'm afraid he's got a lot of growing-up to do. Len's well out of it. How *is* Len, by the way?'

'She's absolutely fine', Con said, 'and so are all the children'.

'I'm so glad. Len is an excellent mother, isn't she? Well' - Mary-Lou tossed down the last of her drink - 'I must circulate. See you around, Con'.

Unbelievable, Con thought, ducking her head over her plate

in the hope that no one would speak to her. Reg was probably just as bad as he had been described, and she would have agreed that her sister was well rid of him, if it hadn't been for all those children. And the great love affair for which he had unhesitatingly smashed up his family had ended just like all the rest. Oh, God, Helena should never have married Reg; their parents should never have smiled on it; she ought to have cut loose at Oxford and found herself somebody decent, since she was into marriage and children. Then she shook herself. What was she doing, sitting here like a limp rag and letting that woman think she was upset?

She talked to Mary-Lou a few more times in the course of the evening, and made a point of staying on till a respectable hour. Then, when it was after eleven and people were beginning to drift away, she thanked Rosamund for a lovely party and said how glad she was to have met her again. Then she headed for home.

She parked the car and then stopped dead. That was a woman in her little doorway, just sitting there on the cold ground with her head in her hands. God, Con thought, the homeless haven't got this far, surely? The woman got up. It was Margot.

'What are you doing here at this hour?' Con asked, amazed.

Margot's eyes blazed at her under the lamplight.

'I've walked out'.

Chapter 26

Sisters Keeping Secrets

'I sat there for two hours', Margot said. 'The people downstairs said you were back from America, but wouldn't let me in. I don't know what I'd have done if you hadn't come. Slept on the streets, probably'.

'Haven't you any money?'

'No'.

Con had taken her upstairs, lit the fire - because Margot's teeth were chattering - and switched on the percolator. She checked that the spare bed was made up and then poured two generous measures of brandy.

'Get this down you. I think I need one too'.

Margot swallowed it automatically and then gagged. 'I'm not used to this'. She fell back in the armchair, looking scruffy and out of place in Con's comfortable flat. 'It all happened very quickly in the end, but please don't tell me to go back, because I'm not going to'.

'Why would I do that?' Con asked. 'It was never my idea that you should be a nun'.

Only a few minutes earlier she'd been thinking that this was getting too much for her; three major shocks in one week and two on the very same night. But as she moved about, preparing coffee and adding hot milk as they'd done in the Oberland, she was feeling happier by the moment. It was as if, after twenty years, she had got her sister back; there had been a barrier between them all the time she'd been a nun, just as there had been between herself and Len when she'd had a husband, all those years ago. She resolved to be very careful and say nothing which could conceivably make Margot change her mind again. After all, who knew what she might think was her duty?

'Drink this. You look awful'. Outside, it had begun to rain; it was frightening to think that her sister might really have had to sleep rough. 'But, Margot, why did you just turn up? I could have been anywhere. If you'd told me or Len what you were going to do, one of us would have come and got you'.

'I didn't know what I was going to do till I'd actually done it'. Margot was still shivering, her hands around the warm mug like a talisman. 'Of course, I've thought for years about leaving. So have lots of other nuns and priests, though they don't say so in public. But I told myself that people like me and my friends were the real Church, not the bishops who bless nuclear weapons, and that those people would be only too delighted if I got out. Still, I suppose everybody has their breaking-point'.

'What happened?'

'It came to a head when I got arrested at Greenham. You can imagine how the respectable people reacted; I was a nuisance, an embarrassment to the Church. My friend Pauline's been subjected to medieval tortures. I won't go into that. Well, I kept my head down and went on with the TB project. I told you I wanted to do some serious work on it?'

'Yes. Go on'.

'But all summer they were mulling over what to do with me. I asked to be sent home from Buenos Aires because it was too easy; I wasn't being stretched. And since coming back to England I've got involved in - oh, various things. Well, they wanted me out of the way, somewhere I wouldn't make trouble, and finally they came up with a great idea. I was to go to a mission hospital in Zaire, hundreds of miles from anywhere, and it's a dictatorship so I'd have got into real trouble if I'd stuck my neck out'

Con sat cold with horror.

'That was the original idea; I didn't like it but I would have gone, because it's the job I volunteered to do, after all. But then someone remembered my breakdown, and thought I might be ill again if I went back to Africa. As if I cared. Then they looked at my file and saw that one of the family was a nun in Canada'.

Con thought of her aunt Robin, whom she had not seen for over thirty years.

'So then they came up with another idea; I was to be sent to a convent in Newfoundland, a nice middle-class area, and get a job at the local Catholic hospital. That would mean that all the work I've done on tropical disease would be wasted, and I would probably never see any of you again. She called me in and gave me my marching orders - '.

'Who did?'

'Mother Priscilla. That woman should have been a wardress in a concentration camp. Nothing since about 1500 ever happened, so far as she's concerned. I tried to reason with the old bat. I said that any doctor could work in a developed country, and the Third World hadn't enough of them, and I would agree to go anywhere that my special skills could be used. She told me there was nothing to discuss. I was to pack my bags, say goodbye to my family and next week I'd be put on a plane. And did I remember that I was sworn to obedience, like a soldier in an army?'

It was true, Con thought; that was what Margot had promised.

'And I thought, damn it, I am *not* a soldier in an army; I tried to talk to soldiers at Greenham Common. My whole argument with them is that they're giving up their right to independent judgement and killing people just because they're ordered to do it. It was the worst thing that she could have said. And I thought, I'm an adult, I live in a free country, this woman can't actually force me to do anything. So I walked out - wandered round a bit - then I looked at some maps of London, walked for miles, and came to you'.

She fell back looking exhausted in the chair.

'You didn't even pack a change of clothes?'

'I don't own anything'.

'I'll take you shopping tomorrow', Con said, 'and get you an outfit'.

'What? Oh, thanks very much, Con, but I don't mind what I wear. I'll have to start looking for a job immediately'.

'Well, Margot, thank God you're a doctor so that won't be a problem. I hate to think what you'd have done if you'd been a contemplative nun'.

'That would never have suited me. Do you know', said Margot, firing up, 'all my life I've been indoctrinated into thinking that the greatest virtue is obedience? You remember? We were told that we had to obey our parents, obey the prefects or the Head or whoever else was in authority. Well, I'm through. From now on I'm not going to obey anything but my own conscience. Damn it, I have got a sense of right and wrong, I was never one of those people who freaked out in the Sixties'.

Con got up.

'Come on; I can hardly stay awake. I'll find you a toothbrush and night clothes'. She remembered that she hadn't yet told her about Mary-Lou but instead she said, 'Margot, I don't want to pry, but - this isn't anything to do with wanting to get married, is it?'

Margot went crimson.

'Honestly, Con, you're just like those dirty-minded people at the top of the Church. Each time a priest or a nun leaves, they think there's a woman or man involved. No, I am not planning to get married, but if I do I won't ask their permission. I've left it very late, but after all, it isn't a sin'.

And it would be ironic, Con thought, as she finally drifted into a deep sleep, if Margot should be getting interested in men, just when she herself had practically decided that they weren't worth it.

'And that's the whole story', said Con. 'I decided I couldn't give you two major bits of news over the telephone, which is why I'm here this weekend. Margot wouldn't come. She sends her love, but she's gone to see some people in Liverpool. Really, she's being very mysterious'.

They were in the garden at Plas Gwyn. It was a perfect September afternoon, and their mother was in the orchard sorting apples into a cardboard box; she hadn't told her anything yet. Frances, who had had her sixteenth birthday that summer, sat some way away from them sketching on an A3 pad. She'd turned into a lovely girl, with very pale reddish fair hair.

Helena said nothing for a moment; her head was throbbing. In the last few minutes she had learned that her ex-husband had split from Mary-Lou, his wife for fifteen years, and that their sister, who had been a nun for even longer than that, had walked out. Con seemed more interested in the second fact but she kept thinking, most painfully, about Reg.

'You haven't said anything, Len. You're not shocked?'

'No. I would have been once but all sorts of things seem to be happening which would have been inconceivable when we were young. Do you know, there's a couple in the village who just had their second baby, and they're not even talking about marriage?' She sighed. 'How are we going to tell Mother, Con? *She* might well be shocked; she was very proud of Margot being a nun'.

'I should let Margot deal with that herself. She's got absolutely nothing, you know, nothing after twenty years' hard labour. I took her out and bought her some basic clothes, and then dragged her along to my hairdresser. She looked a lot better with her hair washed and styled. But, as I said, Len, something strange is going on'.

'How?'

'Well, Margot keeps talking about the Third World, but I can't see that she's actually planning to go there. In fact, only this morning she mentioned a possible job in Scotland, among down-and-outs. I also can't help wondering if that rather nice man we met, Bernard, is more than just a friend'.

'But he's a Catholic priest, Con!'

'I'm not sure how much that means, these days'.

Helena sighed; these days! How much simpler it had been when they were all at school, and you assumed that soon after you left school you got married, and that was it for the rest of your life. Her headache was getting worse and she said, 'I'll go in and make coffee'. The house was quite quiet now, that had once been full of children. Johnno was in Germany; Maggs working in Lausanne for her in-between year; Richard was out with his ponies all day. Only Frances was around for much of the time and, nowadays, you never knew what she was thinking.

Left in the garden, Con got up and walked across to see Frances's sketch. Now it seemed she wasn't going to have any children of her own, she had become quite interested in her nieces; she'd taken Maggs to Paris in the autumn of last year and a trip to Madrid with Frances was being discussed. She'd benefit from seeing the great art galleries; she was quite talented. She had drawn a wasp and a peacock butterfly, next to some Michaelmas daisies, and was now carefully colouring them with mauve and orange pastels.

'That's good, Frances'.

Frances smiled briefly but didn't reply. What went on in teenagers' heads?

Helena came back, took a mug of coffee to their mother, who waved cheerfully, and sat down again beside Con.

'How did Mary-Lou seem?'

'Very much the same. One of life's winners. But I've wondered, Len - at first I believed what she told me but now I think she just wanted me to hear her version. I'm sure Reg was a pig around the house, as she says, but I wonder if he wasn't really the one to walk out'.

'Why should you think that?'

'Well, he's done it before, hasn't he? And there are lots of women younger than Mary-Lou'.

Silence. They both gazed across the garden at Frances, out of earshot and crayoning busily. Just as Con had never told her about the baby, Helena had never told Con, or anyone else, that she had thought seriously of taking her life. Looking at her youngest daughter, she felt thankful that she had resisted the temptation. It would have been very hard for a vulnerable girl to survive without either parent, for she could certainly not have expected any favours from Reg.

'Do you miss him, Len?'

Helena shook her head to clear her thoughts. 'Not now. Although I would have done anything I could to keep things together'.

'Len, where did we go wrong? We're middle-aged women now, and we've neither of us found a man. Perhaps they're not worth having - I often think so - but this wasn't what we hoped for, was it? And Margot thinks she made a lot of mistakes, too'.

'But Con, I'm sure you could still get married if you wanted to. I always thought you preferred living alone. You look lovely, and you've got so many friends'.

'I suppose so', Con said. 'It's true, I could have married Roger Richardson'.

'Roger? Heavens, I never knew you were even going out!'

'It was a long time ago. And he's probably a very good husband to some other woman. But what about you, Len? After Reg cleared off, why didn't you go to parties, or join a dating agency or something?'

'Oh, I was too busy. And anyway I don't think it would have been a good idea'.

'I know the children were a problem - ', Con began.

'It wasn't just that'.

'What, then?'

A longer silence. They could still see their mother, busily sorting the good from the bad apples. At last Helena said, 'Reg told me I was frigid'.

Con snorted. 'So would I have been, with Reg'.

'Well, Con, it must be true, or I would have done something about it. I just didn't feel I could go out like a teenage girl on the hunt for a man. And if I'd ever got close to one, he would probably have ended up very disappointed'.

'That's nonsense - '.

'Seriously, I think some women are only good at being mothers. I don't mind about much else, so long as the children are healthy'.

'They're lovely kids', Con said. 'You must have done something right'.

'I did worry about them not having a father. The girls don't remember him, but Johnno does, and I think he'd like to make contact again. But Con, it's not my business of course, but I really wish I knew what went wrong between him and Mary-Lou'.

'Mum, what do you mean?'

Frances was standing behind them, blue eyes wide and shocked.

'I heard that! Are you saying Dad and Mary-Lou have

quarrelled?'

'Well, yes, I suppose so', Con said after an awkward pause. 'I bumped into Mary-Lou at a party, as I've just been telling your mother, Frances. She's looking for a job in this country, and she says the marriage is over'.

'I knew he would', Frances said. 'I knew he'd see through her in the end'. She turned to her mother with a radiant face; she looked like a Botticelli angel. 'Mum, you do see what this means? He might come back to us!'

The two women looked at each other.

'I don't think so, Frances'.

'But you don't *know*. He's never even seen me, and I'm sure he'd like to, now he's away from that woman's influence. Mum, wouldn't it be incredible? Daddy might come back!'

Chapter 27

Maggs

The bus stopped opposite the old post office, after a long rambling journey from Hereford, and the tall dark girl who had been sitting quietly at the back with her two heavy bundles got out. Luckily she didn't see anyone she recognised. After nine months abroad Maggs looked different; her hair had gone back to its natural colour and was falling luxuriantly over her pale blue raincoat, and she'd taken the pin out of her nose too. A strikingly pretty girl; she'd got many admiring glances during her long journey home by train, boat and bus from Lausanne.

And now she was here. The same dead-and-alive place as always - church, pub, bank, one shop and nothing else - but there were dandelions flowering all over the roadside and the hawthorns, scattered on the slopes above Howells village, were white with may. She picked up her bags, which felt more awkward and lumpy than ever, and began to walk, dragging her feet, towards Plas Gwyn.

She'd left in August 1983, and had not been expected home till this autumn, when she was to take up her place to study English at Birmingham University. 1984, Maggs thought; it had always sounded so terrifying before it happened and there'd been a lot of jokes in the run-up to the New Year. She'd seen a calendar with a picture of George Orwell, winking knowingly at the date. But now it was actually here, everyone had got used to it. Well, 1984 would certainly be a year to remember for her personally.

Maggs had always done whatever she wanted to do easily and stylishly. She had a lovely singing voice and was in great demand for school concerts, she was more or less bilingual, she'd passed her driving test first time, she'd got three good A levels, she'd got masses of friends. Only she hadn't got her sister.

Thinking of Tessa made her eyes fill with tears as she came in sight of the familiar white gate and copper beech tree. They had planned to explore the world when they were nine-year-olds;

she used to get the atlas and look up Switzerland, where they had been born, and the Tyrol, where their grandparents had once taken them for a marvellous holiday, and they'd drawn little lines over it in red felt pen and cut out pictures of all the places they wanted to see. They would have had such fun going round Europe together, and she probably wouldn't be in the mess she was in now because they would have talked it over first and Tessa had always been the sensible one, the one who stopped and thought.

But that was nearly ten years ago, and what had happened had happened. The car was out, which meant her mother was probably in town. Frances, her silly younger sister who was no sort of substitute for Tessa, wouldn't be back from school yet. She got out her key, which she'd carried all over Europe, and let herself into the house. Nobody was there but her grandmother, sitting at the dining-room table with her glasses on and reading *The Dogs of War*, by Frederick Forsyth.

'Oh, hello, Maggs', she said without surprise. 'I thought you were in Switzerland'.

She didn't get up or offer to make her a drink or anything. Her mother would have done that, Maggs thought resentfully. She went into the larder and poured herself a glass of elderflower cordial.

'Where's Mum?'

'She's got a little job, dear, in Hereford at one of those peculiar modern schools where girls and boys go together. She's really in great demand because of her Spanish, and she has people who come to the house to be taught too. Of course she doesn't want to work full-time yet - Frances has her A levels next year - but when all you children are off her hands, she might get a very good position'.

Maggs sat down at the table, keeping her coat on.

'So what's that book for, Gran? I wouldn't have thought it was your style'.

'It isn't'. Jo took off her reading glasses and rubbed her eyes, sighing. 'The fact is, Maggs, I've been having a bit of a blip with my publishers; they keep saying my work is old-fashioned'. Maggs felt suddenly terribly sorry for her, even forgetting her own preoccupations for an instant; she knew her grandmother had been quite a celebrated children's author in her day. 'So I thought I'd read some of the writers who are popular now, to see what's wanted. But it's hard work; the characters are all very unpleasant people'.

'I expect so. Why don't you try some women novelists? Margaret Drabble or Iris Murdoch?'

'Oh, I have, dear, but I couldn't get on with them either. All these married or unmarried people having affairs, which has never been part of my world. Your grandfather was devoted to me and I was to him, so it always seemed very simple. Of course your mother hasn't been so fortunate'.

There was the sound of the front door opening, and Frances, in her school uniform, bounced in.

'*Maggs*! I thought you weren't coming home for ages'. She rushed across the room to embrace her sister, who winced. 'Mum's here too'. She turned round to call, 'Mum, Maggs is back!'

Helena, looking startled, came through the kitchen door with a bundle of books under one arm and a shopping bag on the other. Maggs' heart sank, but she couldn't go on hiding for ever. She stood up so that they could all see her swollen stomach under her loose coat.

'I can't believe this', Helena said. They were in Maggs' little green and white room, the one she'd shared with Tessa, where she was squatting on the floor with her black hair streaming over her slacks and her head on her knees. 'We talked it over before you went abroad, and you said that you knew all about it and weren't interested'.

'Oh, don't be so smug, Mum! We were in love'.

'But you could have waited till you were married - '.

'Well, you did', Maggs snapped back, 'at least I suppose you did, and look where it got you!'

Helena took a deep breath and decided that at all costs they mustn't say unforgivable things. It was the usual pattern; she had been jogging along quite nicely, glad of the chance to do a few bits of work, earn some money and get out of the house, and now something cataclysmic had happened. Her heart ached when she thought of her daughter pregnant in a foreign country, and all the time writing postcards and making breathless phone calls to say that everything was fine. This, of course, was why she hadn't come home for Christmas. She'd thought she was having a marvellous time and surrounded by friends.

'When's the baby due?'

'Around Frances's birthday. July'.

'And isn't there a chance that this man, whoever he is -?'

'*No!*' Maggs shrieked, and burst into tears.

Frances came up with two mugs of tea and said, 'Cheer up, Maggs, it might be quite fun having a baby. My friend Sharon's got one'.

'Thanks, Frances. Can you distract your grandmother, if she wants to come up here?'

'Oh, she's reading her book', Frances said.

When she had gone Helena got down on the floor and put an arm round the sobbing girl. Maggs shuddered and didn't respond.

'Come on. Drink your tea and we can plan - '.

Maggs said in a muffled voice, 'I know what you're thinking. Tessa wouldn't have behaved like this, but she's gone and I'm here, and it's my fault she's dead'. She sobbed and sobbed.

'Maggs -'. Had the child really been blaming herself all these years? 'How could it possibly have been your fault?'

'I was in the house. You left me in charge, and at first I didn't think there was anything wrong with her, but then I got frightened and couldn't think what was the right thing to do. I should have rung 999 straight away. All I remember is hunting through the phone book - '. She flung herself into her mother's arms and literally howled.

Helena grasped her tightly until she had cried herself out. She felt something move; obviously the baby had been disturbed by all that shouting. A little foot briefly kicked her hand and then went back into the depths. As soon as the girl was in a state to listen she said, 'It was nothing to do with you, because you were a child, and if anybody was to blame it was me. I think now that probably no one could have saved Tessa, unless a doctor had actually been on the spot at the time. But for years and years, just like you, I believed it was my fault'.

'And you don't think so now?'

'I do when I'm depressed, but Margot says - she's seen a lot of children die - that most of them could have been saved, but occasionally something goes wrong, which they can't understand. And the family always feel terribly guilty, but it's not reasonable'.

'I hope this baby is all right', Maggs said between tears.

'I can't see any reason why it shouldn't be. Now dry your eyes, and we'll work out what to do'.

Later, she heard most of the story. The baby's father was an American, working temporarily in Lausanne, and had got to know her when he came to drink at the hotel where she was doing her turn behind the bar. He was twenty-eight, which made him, Helena thought with cold fury, a lot more sophisticated than Maggs. The girl had fallen desperately in love with him - all the people she'd dated up to now had been schoolboys, whom she hadn't taken seriously - and perhaps, for a while, he had felt the same about her. But 'he sort of assumed I was on the pill', said Maggs, 'and I didn't want to look naive; I mean everyone else of my age has already done it'. Why she hadn't actually put herself on the pill was not explained. That was typical Maggs.

When they found out about the baby he had said that was great, and he'd 'stand by her', but marriage was 'uncool'. Maggs, who wanted very much to be married, had hung on hoping he'd change his mind. They went through a long cold winter like this and then he was recalled to Germany, and said he'd gone off her because her hormones were all over the place and she was always crying. Terrified of telling anyone, Maggs had gone on working at the hotel until her condition became obvious and they sacked her. After that there was nothing to do but come home.

Helena listened to all this without saying more than a few reassuring words. Indeed, words failed her. At first, of course, she'd hoped that the man could be persuaded to marry her daughter, but having heard the details, she now thought that he could not stay too far away from Maggs and her child. Indeed, Maggs thought so too. 'I'm glad I never gave him this address', she said, perhaps a little too vehemently. 'I loathe him. I'm going to wash him right out of my hair'.

'Good. Now', Helena said, as cheerfully as she could, 'we must think about how to look after this baby'.

'Well, a baby might be interesting, at least. But, Mum' - Maggs dissolved into tears again - 'what are we going to do about my place at Birmingham? I've thought and thought'.

'I'll see what I can organise', Helena said.

When Johnno came back from Oxford, confident that he had done well in his finals and that he would get the job at the BBC he was trying for, he was furious.

'You shouldn't have done it', he said, glaring down at Maggs who was lying on the sofa, looking enormous in a green smock. 'You know it's only going to make more trouble for Mother'.

'I suppose *you've* never done it with anyone?' Maggs retorted.

Johnno went dark red.

'Johnno', Helena said at the same moment, 'will you please stop talking about me as if I wasn't here?'

'Rotten hypocrite', Maggs added. 'Men are all the same; they keep on and on at you to do it and then if you do they call you a slag'.

'Mum, will you do something about her? she's talking very indecently'.

Helena firmly took her son's elbow and steered him out of the room.

'Leave her alone, Johnno, please', she said when they were out of earshot. 'Maggs is having the baby very soon now and I don't want her upset'.

'But what are you going to - ?'

'We'll manage just as other families have managed before'.

It was difficult for Johnno, she thought. He had worked so hard, done so well, been almost painfully polite and well-behaved since that one disgraceful incident nearly ten years ago. Maggs could have been a high-flyer too, if she hadn't got pregnant, but there would be time to think about that later on. She said, 'Now, Johnno, I'd like to hear your news'.

Johnno's frown relaxed slightly.

'I *think* they'll take me at the BBC's foreign desk. It obviously helps that I speak German, and I'd like to be a foreign correspondent, one day, but of course I'll have to work my way up. And, Mum, you know that essay competition?'

He had worked on it over Christmas, a six-thousand-word study of the causes of war in Europe. He took that very seriously. Understand the past, he kept quoting, and you can stop the same mistakes being made again. She wondered if the seed had been planted when Margot was arrested at Greenham, and how pleased she would be with the way her nephew, for all his minor faults, was turning out.

'Yes?'

'Well, I won'.

'Johnno!'

'I was just going to tell you when Maggs distracted me. The prize is two weeks in Washington this summer. And Mum, I wondered - '.

'You'd like to see your father?' Helena asked.

'Well, yes. Although I don't know if he'd like to see me. But it seems a good opportunity, and we haven't been in touch since 1975. He never wrote, you know'. Johnno suddenly looked as forlorn as a small boy. 'Only I'm not going to tell him anything about the baby. I shall tell him we're all doing very well'.

'Come on, Maggs, *push*! You're almost there'.

'I want to go home', Maggs sobbed.

'You can go home when you've got your baby and not before'. The midwife's voice was brisk; she sounded as if she'd dealt with a lot of silly girls in her time. 'Mrs Maynard, come and have a look if you like. The head is showing'.

'There's something I haven't told you', Maggs said suddenly.

'What's that?'

But there was no time for any more because the next contraction had started; Maggs clung convulsively to her mother's hand so she was unable to see what was happening at the other end of the bed. The baby plopped out into the midwife's hands and immediately began howling. It had taken eight hours.

A boy. Quite big, a clump of dark hair and obviously healthy to judge from the way he was yelling. Then Helena saw both midwives look surprised and realised what it was that Maggs had not told her. The baby had enormous dark eyes, never seen in European newborns, and his skin was the colour of coffee with milk.

Chapter 28

The Fourth Generation

'Not all black Americans are poor', Maggs said. 'Conrad comes from quite a well-off family in Baltimore, and he has a good job; he prefers it in Europe because he says people are less prejudiced. There was an awful lot of mixing between masters and slaves. So Robin is about one-quarter black'.

'Robin?'

'Yes, I decided on it last night'.

The name brought back memories of her aunt, Jo's adopted sister, who had left them to become a teaching nun all those years ago. They were very faint now, but it still seemed strange to hear a boy called Robin. Secretly she'd been hoping for a girl, because that would be easier for Maggs and because it would have felt like a link with Tessa. But she'd forgotten all about that when she saw the actual baby. It was the most extraordinary emotion; it was like falling in love at first sight.

Robin had been dressed in a miniature white gown and a plastic nappy. His hands and feet stuck out like a doll's and his dark velvet eyes looked around with a surprised expression, as if he didn't know quite what to make of his new surroundings. He hadn't cried for long because he seemed too dazed by what he'd been through.

'Mum, isn't he gorgeous?'

'Lovely'.

'You do like him? You're not upset that he's here?'

She held the baby, who gripped her finger strongly, and couldn't find any words for what she was feeling. After nine years of more or less total unhappiness, which she had concealed only for the sake of the other children, it was too painful, it was like blood streaming back into a frozen limb.

They took him home. His eyes immediately focussed on the black beams running across the white ceiling and they decided that he was highly intelligent. Four weeks after his birth, he was smiling; shortly after that, he was making cooing noises and showing definite signs of recognising his family. Even Johnno and Richard (who had also been annoyed with Maggs, because she'd embarrassed him in front of his friends) were bowled over fairly quickly by his charm.

Helena was keen that the boys should pick up and play with him, since there was no other man in his life. She worried about that. She'd also had a taste of the prejudice he was likely to come up against when she took him to the clinic and got a few strange looks. Black faces were not exactly common in Hereford and she was sure she'd heard one woman whisper, 'disgusting'. She realised, too, that they assumed it was her baby. Heavens, did she still look young enough for that, although she had always looked young for her age?

But she refused to let it frighten her. Robin was a full member of the family, although her mother, Jo, seemed to be not quite sure who he was and kept saying that the real Robin was her little sister in Canada. They loved him, they were proud of him, and other people would just have to take him as he was. Even in her lifetime things had changed, because she could remember a time when women thinking of marrying 'out' were advised not to do so because it would be unfair to the children. There was much less of that sort of talk now. No, she believed that his mixed race would not have been a major problem, had his father been around and involved.

She also worried, of course, about Maggs. Birmingham University had agreed that she could have the year off and take up her place in the autumn of 1985, while her mother looked after the baby, and it was close enough for her to visit at weekends. That was an enormous relief. She didn't want her daughter's life to be spoiled by one mistake, and she was actually quite looking forward to having sole charge of Robin.

He slept with his mother in the green and white bedroom, and by the age of eight weeks was going happily through the night. After his early morning feed, Maggs put him down for another few hours and had breakfast with the family, dealing with his nappies and damp night-suits when she was dressed.

Then she usually disappeared into the garden with a book. Helena would listen for him as she went about her jobs and, when she heard little sounds from his room, would quietly open the door. Robin would invariably be gazing up at his mobile (three little yellow ducks and one ugly duckling), with his dark brown eyes, and his face when he saw her would break into a dazzling toothless smile. She'd change him, give him a wash, and carry him downstairs to be played with until it was time for Maggs to feed him. Or Frances, who adored him, would take him walkabout round the village. It wouldn't be so easy when the school year began, but just now he could easily be passed from one person to the next so there was no question of him being fractious. He blossomed under all the attention and affection and moved forward very fast.

Con turned up at August bank holiday, with presents for the baby and for Maggs's nineteenth birthday. Margot hadn't seen him yet. She was working in Edinburgh, and although she'd sent a rabbit and her best wishes, she had not found time to make the long trip south.

'It *is* odd, though', Con said, when she'd admired Robin. 'She told me she was walking out of the Church because they wouldn't let her go back to the Third World, and now that she's free to go where she likes, she hasn't gone. Mind, I don't *want* her to go off again, and from all I can hear she's doing a fine job. But she hasn't appeared in London for six months'.

To Maggs, while Helena was making supper, she decided to do some straight talking.

'You do realise, don't you, Maggs, that when you begin university, your mother will have to look after your baby?'

Maggs glowered.

'My mother's *always* looked after children. She likes it'.

'I know, but just the same, she was beginning to build up a quite nice part-time career, and this is going to put a stop to it'. Nothing but concern for her sister could have made Con break a lifetime's habit and lay down the law. 'And don't forget that the cheques from your father will stop coming as soon as Frances is eighteen. The baby is very nice - '.

'He's much more than very nice', Maggs said indignantly.

'Okay, but I don't think you want another baby every year, do you? Anybody can make one mistake, but please don't do it again. I know you think your Mum is just your Mum, but she's also my sister, and I'd hate her to spend the next twenty years bringing up your illegitimate family'. Maggs leapt to her feet, speechless. 'I can tell you where to go for birth control, if you like - '.

Maggs drew herself up to her full height, black eyes flashing.

'I think that's really sordid. I know all about that, thank you very much, and I'm not interested, because I'm fed up with men. I don't mind if I never see one again'.

Johnno came back from the States two days later. He was jet-lagged and seemed depressed.

'I did see him', he said after his mother had given him tea.

'And it went well?'

'Oh, yes. He said he'd always intended to have me for another visit but hadn't got round to it. And he was pleased about my job with the BBC. I took a few photographs; do you want to see them?'

Helena took them, rather apprehensively; one of Johnno with his father and one of Reg by himself, standing on the beach. His hair was grey, and his shoulders had a stoop that she didn't remember, but otherwise he hadn't changed a lot. Just a well-preserved, rather commonplace middle-aged man whom she had once thought was the centre of the world. It was very strange to see it; she'd always had a feeling of unfinished business since Reg had left home without telling her he was going for good.

'I'm glad it was a success', she said.

'I wouldn't have done it if you'd objected', said Johnno. He hesitated a moment. 'Mum - '.

'Yes?'

'There's one other thing'.

She thought she could guess.

'He's getting married again. The woman's quite young -

about twenty-five - glamorous if you like that type. She's called' - Johnno pronounced it with distaste - 'Cindy Anne Callender. Stupid name. I talked to her of course, politely, what else could I do? The wedding is at Palm Beach and it's actually next week'.

'Well', Helena said, 'Frances will be disappointed. She really hoped, when Mary-Lou went off, that your father and I might get together again'.

'And you don't mind, Mum?'

'I don't think so, Johnno. It was a very long time ago'.

'That's all right then', Johnno said. 'I suppose I wanted to see him, to get things sorted out in my mind, but I'm not in a hurry to do it again. I didn't mention Robin, by the way'.

Autumn came. Johnno started his new job and got a small flat in London, Richard moved out to live over the stables where he worked, so the household at Plas Gwyn now consisted of four women and a child. They all went on being absolutely delighted with Robin. He got bigger and stronger by the week, he was obviously bright and showing him new things was a continual pleasure. Helena would take him out into the garden, well wrapped up, and prop him in his bouncy chair while she sorted the apples or got on with her other jobs. He would look at the wide sky and falling leaves, waving his short arms and crowing.

It was not that Tessa's little shadow would ever go away. But Robin was so much fun, so responsive, such an entirely lovely child that the past nine years now seemed like a nightmare she'd woken up from. She was happier than she had been since the early years with Reg. Of course it wasn't an ideal situation, of course she would have preferred Maggs to be married to some nice man and living round the corner, but she didn't argue with her own happiness because she knew how quickly it could be taken from her. People who saw her proudly wheeling Robin to the shop noticed her radiant looks and stopped talking about Maggs's bad behaviour, and Robin soon made a few friends on his own account.

After an exhausting day she would sometimes fall into bed with one of Con's novels, of which she'd brought a stack on her last visit. She now openly acknowledged to her family that she wrote Silk Slip romances for money, and Helena thought they were quite amusing and helped her to unwind. Then, one evening in late October, there came a phone call about Margot.

Chapter 29

The Nun's Story

Margot looked at the swans on the polluted water. It was an almost deserted stretch of the Union Canal, with the towpath on one side and on the other derelict buildings, boot factories and print works from the days when every man had a job that supported his family; their windows smashed, the bricks blackened and creepers climbing up the massive walls. A lot of the city's waste went into that canal, syringes and condoms and the occasional body; germs and disease multiplied in the water. But the swan floated on the surface, apparently untouched.

That was what she'd tried to say to Bernard when they'd come here the night it all began. The water was black and yellow where the rays of an occasional gas lamp streamed over it, and they'd walked up and down the path for hours talking about her decision to leave. No one else around, except a few other unhappy couples. She'd argued that the swan was like the human spirit, somehow rising out of the perversity, violence, meanness which was always trying to submerge it.

Oh, my God, she thought, where did we go wrong?

Only that was a year ago, and this was a bitter autumn morning in Edinburgh. She walked along the canal bank until it grew lighter, then back to her tiny room in Lower Gilmore Place. Nothing there except a bed and an electric plate, on which she could heat meals, and she had the use of a dirty bathroom. Back to the streets, where early morning traffic was very heavy. There were buses loaded with office workers, children heading for school. No one looked at her; she was just a small, insignificant woman, plainly and cheaply dressed. Yet I've seen things, Margot thought, which would make their hair stand on end. People said she was so lucky to live in Edinburgh, where she'd done her medical degree over twenty years ago, but the city had a downside like everywhere else. There had been a significant little cluster, recently, of AIDS cases, all from one estate where a group of young people injected drugs and then passed the virus on to the people they slept with. Margot suspected that disease was going to become quite big. She walked through some more streets and then came to the office she had marked down a few days ago. It was just opening.

'Can you give me a test?'

The grey-haired Scottish woman who had let her in welcomed her warmly and said her name was Joan. Margot also gave her first name. She didn't trust herself to do this test; she'd tried, but although it had come out negative that had been some time ago and she was not sure it was accurate. She sat down and looked wearily at the pictures on the wall, diagrams of the baby in its early stages of development. How many women had sat here, she wondered, hoping they were not pregnant?

Years ago when she was a medical student in this city she'd had to listen to a lot of jokes about nuns who had thrown their babies down wells in the Middle Ages or who used their robes to cover a swelling stomach. People didn't any longer respect celibacy; if you chose it, they thought you must be peculiar in some way or have some hang-up which made you afraid of men. Actually that wasn't true. She knew all about men, having had five brothers, and she had been quite aware that one of the Richardson boys, Rod, had been besotted with her when she was sixteen. But he was too young, and Margot refused to take him seriously. He was in New Zealand now, must have forgotten her long ago. Then, at Edinburgh University, she'd thought long and hard about scrapping her careful life-plan to marry Angus Ross. She liked him; he was tall, fair and very good-looking, and it was pleasant to go to lectures and the cinema with someone so devoted. She was nineteen, living away from her family for the first time, and none of them had ever known about that friendship. Her parents were quite pleased with her decision to become a nun but if she had told her sisters she was thinking of getting married they would certainly have encouraged her. But, in the end, they had not had enough in common. He respected her religion, was prepared to have any children brought up in it, but there was no way that she could have married Angus and still been a medical missionary.

So as far as men were concerned, she'd been there, done that. It was like chocolate, she had once told Con, pleasant but you could live perfectly well without it. She had serious work to do and no time to spare. And then when her conscience, or whatever it was (perhaps just a dislike of being pushed around) had driven her out of the Church, she hadn't at first thought of Bernard as anything but an old friend.

They were both free agents. They could walk into a registry office and get married tomorrow because the law had no interest in the vows they had taken. Bernard was impressed by her courage in having walked out. He hadn't yet gone so far himself, but he had applied for laicisation so that he could continue as a theologian and lecturer but be allowed to marry. It could take years, because this Pope wasn't keen on priests who changed their minds. Fortunately he was employed by Liverpool University and not the Church. They had walked along the canal, after dark, looking at the swans on the black water and talking endlessly. He told her that he hated being celibate and longed for a normal life with children.

And it had been so sudden, so shattering that neither of them knew what to do with their new-found emotions. Bernard said, 'We're ridiculous, Margot, we ought to have been doing this in our twenties', and she couldn't disagree. Certainly she would never have become a nun if she had felt like this about Angus, or any other man.

And that had been the pattern of their lives for the last twelve months. He was in Liverpool, she was in Edinburgh. Snatched weekends, long exhausting train journeys, letters during the working week (lovely, jokey, erudite letters) telling her what a difference she had made to him. It seemed too hard sometimes, working at full stretch and then living an intense hidden love story in her time off. That was why she had hardly phoned or written to her sisters for ages. She hadn't had the strength; she frequently had violent headaches or felt dizzy after a meeting with Bernard, and besides, what was she supposed to say? It was beyond her to make light conversation with the two people who knew her best when there was only one thing on her mind. If they had got married at once, as she'd always wanted, it could have been out in the open. Now she could only say that she and Bernard were waiting for permission from Rome, and that, as he knew very well, was humiliating.

Only she was quite sure that he would marry her, if there was a child on the way.

She lay back in the chair, as the woman took her sample and made her preparations to do the test, and thought, it hasn't all been awful. Loosen up, Margot, Bernard had said, we're going to have fun. Fun had not been a big part of Margot's life since she was a teenager but she'd gone with him to the Cairngorms, last winter, and rediscovered a youthful love of skiing. He had taken her to galleries and concerts in Liverpool, given her meals in good restaurants, even tried to teach her about wine, although that was a lost cause. It had all been very modest by some people's standards, but they'd had some extremely happy times. They were an odd couple but they got on; there was no other man she could imagine being that involved with.

So what went wrong, she thought again, so why am I here?

'You didn't take any precautions?' the woman was asking her.

'No'.

'And how old are you, Margot?'

'Forty-four'. Something made her add, 'I know that isn't too old for a baby, though it's unlikely '.

'The problems which you're experiencing are quite common at that age. Let's see, we'll have the result in a minute'. Margot stared at the diagrams. Was there really one of those creatures swimming in her body? It seemed inconceivable; she didn't feel any different from usual, except that she always felt ill. 'Do you have a job, I mean outside the home?'

What would this nice woman say if she told her that she had been a nun for twenty years? And she didn't want to admit to being a doctor, in the circumstances. She said hastily, 'I'm an aid worker. Have you the result?'

'Coming up'.
A short pause.
'It's negative'.

So that's it, she thought, as she went out and the bitter wind blew grit into her eyes. Heavy traffic rumbled by. Negative, and it could not be a false result, as she'd told herself last time, because she had had no chance of getting pregnant for six weeks. And she would be forty-five very soon and might as well accept that it had been a feverish dream. Len's daughter had a baby, nothing could be easier for these young girls, but if she had been going to have one, she should have done it twenty years ago.

Could she have looked after one? she wondered as she trudged down the steep hill towards the Old Town, catching occasional glimpses of blue sea water and the distant shores of Fife. Well, of course. But it was Bernard who really wanted children, and Bernard, for all his deep scholarship, perhaps didn't know an awful lot about a woman's reproductive span. Or perhaps he had not even thought of it when they first fell in love; they had neither of them been in a state to make logical plans for the future. It hadn't seemed possible then that anything could go wrong, but something had.

How she knew it had gone wrong, Margot couldn't say. They hadn't quarrelled - well, once, perhaps, but that seemed worse than it was because it was less easy to have a real reconciliation when you were living apart. Edinburgh to Liverpool, two hundred and twenty-five miles. And lately he'd always seemed to have conferences at weekends or be unable to see her for some other reason. Talking to him was not easy - neither had a private phone - and recently Margot herself had put off writing because she wanted to know the result of this test. She had hoped to find a letter when she got home, but there was nothing. Well, she thought, as she climbed the stairs to her grim little room and packed her bag, it could not go on like this. The weekend was coming up. She would catch the night train, and find out where she stood.

It was early morning when the two cathedrals of Liverpool reared up on the horizon and Margot got off the train, jaded after a bad night trying to sleep in her seat. She'd done a lot of thinking. It was term time, so Bernard couldn't be far away, and with any luck she'd arrive before he was out of bed. He might not be pleased to see her, but this situation had dragged on long enough. He could either marry her or break with her; if the latter, she would not argue but would go away quietly. She would even agree to wait for however many years it took for the Church to release him, only provided she could be sure that he really wanted it.

Bernard lived in a modern block of flats belonging to the university. Having pressed the intercom and got no response, she tried several other buttons until a young man appeared and said he'd look for him. He came back and reported that the flat seemed empty.

'He hasn't been around much lately'.

Well, Margot thought, walking back to the station through the Saturday morning crowds, what now? It was inconceivable to go home without knowing. The only person she could think of who might help was Bernard's sister, who lived in Manchester where they had once visited her; unfortunately she did not have her phone number but she did remember the address. She caught the Manchester train.

Why am I doing this? she asked herself several times during the short journey. The message is obvious, isn't it? I'm never going to let another man do this to me, but I must see him at least once.

In Manchester, which she didn't know at all, she got a taxi and was driven past a number of streets with almost identical terraced redbrick houses until she came to the one she was looking for. By now it was about half past one. She breathed deeply; if there was nobody there, she would really have come to a dead end.

The door was opened by a tired-looking middle-aged woman. A little girl of about two ran up behind her, gave Margot a disappointed look and then went off again.

'Hello, Anne'.

'Margot!' Bernard's sister seemed even more surprised than she would have expected. 'Were you looking for - ?'

'Yes. I've just come from Liverpool, but he doesn't seem to be anywhere'.

'Come in, dear; I'll make you a cup of tea'.

Margot followed her into the kitchen. Somehow she was in no hurry now to get answers; she was fairly sure that they would not be those she wanted. Anne was explaining that her husband and sons were at football and that the little girl didn't seem too happy. They went into the front room, which was very neat and tidy, with a crucifix over the fire and a picture of Pope John Paul II. It was quite a modest house; Bernard had been the brilliant one of his family. Anne pressed her to have tea and a slice of cake and she accepted, because by now she was feeling rather faint.

'Well, Anne, I'm sorry to burst in on you like this, but it was all I could think of. I would just like to have a few words with Bernard and don't worry, I am not going to make a scene'.

'Oh, dear!' Anne was looking at her with concern. 'He hasn't written to you, then?'

'No'. There might be a letter on its way to Edinburgh.

'I don't know how to say this, Margot - ', Anne began.

'Just say it'.

'Well, my dear, he's married'.

'Married?' It had crossed her mind, in the last few weeks, that there might be another woman, but this was too sudden and took her breath away. 'But - when - ?'

'It was in Liverpool, this morning. In a registry office, because they couldn't get married in church, of course, and then he and Delia came on here by car, left the little girl with me, and went out to lunch with some friends'. Margot began to get up. 'Don't worry, dear, they said something about a matinee and they won't be back for hours. Sit down and finish your tea'.

Her heart was racing, so violently that she thought she might really be going to have an attack.

'How long has he known this woman?'

Anne explained that she was a mature student whom Bernard had met through his teaching duties. She was twenty-nine and had a little girl, born in a relationship - not a marriage - which had broken up before she enrolled at the university. 'And the child seems very fond of him', she concluded. 'But, Margot, I had very little idea what was going on, because Bernard knew full well that I wasn't happy about it. I believe that once a priest, always a priest, but he's made his own decisions for years'.

It made sense, Margot thought, as she let it sink in. A much younger woman, known to be fertile. The little girl ran in and out of the room, prattling and dragging her plastic telephone. Even if Bernard still had any feelings for her, Margot could do nothing to threaten her security.

'Well, I must go', she said, standing up.

Anne rose too.

'Are you sure you're all right?'

'Oh, yes, I shall survive'.

'Well, Margot, I'm very sorry to have been the one to give you this news. But I'm sure they'd have you back in the Order, if you asked them'.

'I'm sure they would, but I'm not going to ask'.

'Good luck, then, my dear'.

Into the streets again. She wandered about a bit, till she found a bus going in the right direction and got to Manchester Piccadilly. There seemed to be football fans everywhere. She looked at the timetables; there was a choice between the fast train to London or the slow train to Hereford. Or back by various ways to her little room in Edinburgh, but she didn't think she could face that yet. Neither could she face Con after the things she had said to her when she had her own crisis. She decided to make for Plas Gwyn.

That was why Helena received a phone call, that evening, to say that a lady had been taken ill coming off the train and was asking for her.

Margot lay on a bench at Hereford station. She could hardly stagger to the car, but seemed to recover a little as soon as she saw her sister. Once they were out on the dark country roads, with only a few scattered lights from lone farmhouses visible, she jumped and said, 'Oh, God, I've got to be back at work on Monday morning. I must find out about trains - '.

'You're not going anywhere', Helena said firmly.

Back at Plas Gwyn Jo, who was watching TV, gave her a preoccupied greeting while the two girls stared with all their eyes. Helena steered her into Johnno's old room and said, 'Go on, get into bed, and I'll bring you a tray. But first you must see my grandson'.

Robin, fresh from the bath, was brought in with his hair sticking up and scattering smiles in all directions. Margot looked at him, noting with a professional eye that he was obviously healthy, but she felt too beaten, now, to do anything but sleep.

She woke up halfway through a fine Sunday morning to hear voices from beneath the window; it was Maggs playing with her baby. The rowan and apple trees with their yellowing leaves were visible without her moving her head. She began to cry and was still crying when Helena came in with a continental-style breakfast of coffee and rolls.

'Oh, God, Len, I've made such a mess of things'.

'That's nonsense'. Helena sat down on the end of the bed. 'Margot, I'm no good at saying these things, but think of all the lives you've saved'.

'I've mucked up my own life'. The tears flowed freely, now that she was awake and remembering. 'I'm not saying you should have stopped me, because I probably wouldn't have listened, but I made a great mistake by becoming a nun'.

'Is there a man behind it?' There usually was, in her experience. 'Only you don't have to talk to me, if you don't want to'.

'No, I'll tell you'. Her head felt as if it was going to split. 'But can I have an aspirin, please? I'm not fit to talk yet'.

Helena rang the clinic and left a message that Margot wouldn't be back for a while, then set about making the family lunch. Early in the afternoon she checked on Margot for the fourth time and found her awake.

'Mother asked me why I wasn't in South Africa'.

'She doesn't understand much these days. Can't I get you anything, Margot? You must be starving'.

'No, I'd be sick', Margot said.

Gradually she told her the whole story, breaking off from time to time to sob, while Robin chortled happily from the garden below. Helena didn't know whether she was more shocked by Bernard's treatment of her sister or the fact that Margot, who had never been maternal, had tried to have a baby for the sole purpose of hanging on to her man.

'It's better as it is', she said brusquely when she had finished crying.

'How can you say - ?'

'Bernard's quite a good man really, whatever it looks like'. Helena bit her lip, although she too had found him attractive. 'And that girl will probably have quite a nice life. He's a typical academic, you see. Humanitarian views, a social conscience and all that, but his books come first. I wouldn't have fitted in'.

'But, Margot, if you had been pregnant - '.

'I'd have managed. Con sometimes wishes she'd had a child, did you know? But now that I'm definitely not pregnant, I can get back on course again. I've been planning it, over the last few weeks since I began to suspect that Bernard was slipping away'.

Helena listened.

'I'm hoping to join Medecins sans Frontieres. I always wanted to work in the Third World; the mistake was thinking it could only be done through the Church. It just shows you how besotted I was with that man that I was prepared to give it up. This way I could be sent anywhere in the world, wherever the need is greatest, for a long or short time, and still have a base in this country. And no one would try to order me about', Margot ended with a ghastly smile.

'Margot, that's a wonderful idea! You could live here at Plas Gwyn whenever you're not abroad'.

'I'd like that. I suppose, as you get older, your family does get more important'.

Chapter 30

Frances

Frances would be eighteen in July 1985. Throughout June, she and her friends would be taking A levels and they were all walking around looking pale and tense. Not that she had any real reason to worry, her mother believed. She was doing art, German and Spanish - she could speak both languages - and needed only a very moderate result to be accepted at a good art college. Frances wasn't as striking-looking as her sister, Maggs, but she was a pretty girl, with very pale reddish-gold hair (nobody would have believed that she was Reg's daughter) and a fair skin that flushed easily. Over the last year or two she had become very silent, but that was normal for teenagers, and occasionally she proved that she was aware of what was going on round her by giving her mother an unexpected hug or making a fuss of Robin. She was a hard worker, too. She was always leaving little drawings around the house or scribbled in the margins of newspapers, tiny people with enormous heads and turned-down mouths, animals and butterflies and creatures from outer space. When she got around to colouring them she worked very slowly, with rich reds and blues, and they ended up looking like a medieval manuscript. Her teacher said she had much more talent than she thought.

It was a Friday near the end of May in a cold, unpleasant spring. Day after day they'd hoped to see the sun but it hadn't happened. Helena had just finished putting Robin to bed; he was crawling everywhere now and didn't like to be left out of anything. She left him rattling the bars of his cot, in his little blue sleeping-suit, and came downstairs. Her mother, who loved police serials, was watching TV in the back room. Maggs was reading *Middlemarch*; she planned to start at Birmingham that autumn and had been working seriously. And Frances was still in the bathroom; she was due at a party in Hereford. Her exams would start in four days and they all thought she could do with a break.

'Are you sure you're all right for a lift?' she asked through the door.

Frances's voice came back sounding muffled. 'Yes, Scott Dawson's taking me there and back'.

Helena knew the boy by sight; he was one of those people whom everyone knows. A good-looking boy, in the same year as Frances, with a mop of dark hair and a ready smile. And she had seen him driving his mother's Porsche all over the village. It still shocked her slightly that some of these young people turned up at school in cars which their teachers could never have afforded.

A few minutes later Frances came downstairs, wearing a cream-coloured blouse and long blue skirt, and with her hair loose. She had never looked so lovely. Then the bell rang; her escort had arrived but at that moment a howl and a thud from upstairs told her that Robin was in trouble, so she rushed up to check on him and didn't actually see her daughter go.

It was nearly two hours later. Maggs had insisted on lighting a fire and it was crackling comfortably as she stretched out on the floor reading. Helena had brought her library book into the sitting-room, but couldn't concentrate. She looked up at the big photograph above the white marble mantelpiece, of herself and her sisters as teenagers. Frances didn't look so different now from how they had looked then. She hoped that the boy would not drive too fast, that he was not planning to seduce Frances. But she was a sensible girl; she had surely learned from her sister's mistake.

'Hey, this is good', Maggs said. 'Listen - "If we had a keen vision and feeling of all ordinary human life, it would be like hearing the grass grow and the squirrel's heart beat, and we should die of that roar which lies on the other side of silence" '.

'Who wrote that?'

'George Eliot'.

The telephone rang.

Helena groaned inwardly; she knew it was probably for one of the children but she also knew that no one else would be bothered to answer it. She got up and lifted the receiver.

'Mrs Maynard?' a voice asked. 'Mrs Helena Maynard?'
'Yes'.
'Have you a daughter called Frances?'
'Yes'. Now she was beginning to feel alarmed.
'This is Hereford hospital. Could you come - ?'
Oh, my God, that boy must have crashed the car.
'No', Helena sobbed. 'No, no, no!'

Maggs had bounded up and taken the phone away from her. She heard both voices - 'No, there has been no car crash'. Maggs demanding, 'Is my sister dead?' 'No, but she's been taken ill and we think her mother should come at once'.

Maggs replaced the phone. 'They won't tell me any more. Come on, Mum. I'll drive; you're not in a fit state'.

'But what about Robin -?' She knew that anything that could go wrong, would.

'Gran's here, isn't she? Come on!'

She raced out to get the car. Helena had just enough self-control to throw ash on the fire and ask her mother to keep an eye on Robin. Then they were driving madly towards the distant lights of Hereford, fortunately meeting no other traffic on the dark and narrow country roads.

Maggs kept saying that it couldn't be meningitis, it only affected children. But Helena had read enough to know that a girl of seventeen was not necessarily immune. Either there was some rare genetic condition, striking down her family one after the other, or they were the victims of unbelievable bad luck. She cried a good deal, from shock, while they were in the car, but was calm by the time they arrived at the hospital, a building she had grown to hate. Possibly having her mother beside her could make all the difference. She hurried into reception.

A group of four teenagers, two boys and two girls, all of whom they knew, were standing round looking upset. She went up to them, Maggs behind her.

'What's happened?'
'She just fell over - '.
'I think it was the pills', a boy said.
'What pills?'

'Scott's at the police station, answering questions - '.

A girl sobbed, 'I told her it was all right; I've *taken* them lots of times, I told her that they gave you a great feeling'.

Maggs had burst into the centre of the group and seized her by her shoulders.

'You did that? You encouraged *my sister* to take things? You slag. If she dies, I'll cut you into little pieces. I'll have your picture in the papers so everyone knows about you'. She shook her violently and a porter came up and dragged them apart.

'Come on, we can't have a brawl'.

Helena was breathless; she leaned against a wall to support herself. 'Can someone please tell me where she is, and what's going on?'

'She's in intensive - '.

The other girl said, 'Scott had a lot of pills, he knows where you can get them. He's short of money, they fired him from his Saturday job. Well, like, he was selling them to everyone else for five pounds, but he just gave one to Frances because he wanted to impress her. And we danced some more for, like, half an hour, and then she started feeling ill'.

'Scott still had some in his pockets. He's going to get in real trouble - '.

'He sure is!' Maggs screamed. 'I'm going to kill him myself'.

A doctor had come quietly up and touched Helena's arm.

'Will you come with me, please, Mrs Maynard?'

Frances was on life support, just as Tessa had been almost ten years ago. Her fair hair streamed out on either side of a face that was colourless, almost expressionless, as if the personality had already gone. Helena sat beside her holding her hand.

She'd told Maggs to go home and look after Robin, so she didn't have to worry about both of them. She sat there and let people do things to Frances's inert body while the sounds of the hospital, which was never quiet, receded into the far background of her mind. The doctor told her that they hadn't given up hope, there was still a chance, but obviously the longer she remained in a coma the greater the danger.

She talked to her, because she'd heard that some people who appeared to be deeply unconscious could still understand what was said to them. She told her that they all loved her and were waiting to take her home. She talked about Robin, about small happenings round the house, and when she ran out of things to say she kept repeating 'you're all right, Frances, I won't let you come to any harm'. She asked her to press her hand if she understood, but there was no response.

Some time in the middle of the night she remembered how she had written to Reg, just before Frances was born, and offered to give up this baby if it would save the marriage. She had done that very reluctantly and now she wondered if she was being punished for it. Or had she, perhaps, been too locked in her grief for Tessa, or given too much attention to Robin, and failed to realise what was going on in her daughter's mind? All her life she'd assumed that only extreme degenerates took drugs. But a boy whom she had known for most of his life had given them to her lovely, vulnerable Frances, and Frances had accepted them, there was no getting round that. Had she seen her swallowing tranquillisers and thought they were some sort of cure for pain? Was it somehow her fault?

Day broke, and there was still no change. Maggs came in, crying bitterly, and said the police had been to the house and Scott's mother was in a terrible state, having had no idea what her son was up to. The doctors were looking serious. She thought they must know that she'd already lost one child.

Meanwhile, an enterprising young reporter whose sister had been at the party had got hold of Frances's photograph from mutual friends, and it went out on the front page of the local free Sunday newspaper with the story that a young girl who had taken a banned substance was fighting for her life.

Frances began to come out of her coma on the Saturday evening, having been unconscious for nearly twenty-four hours. By the time the newspapers were plopping on to doormats, and bells were ringing from the cathedral across town, she was off the life support machine and crying feebly in her mother's arms. The doctor had said that she should make a full recovery and there was no brain damage.

'But why did you do it?' Helena asked as soon as she could speak. 'The school warned you and I warned you'.

'I was depressed. They said the pills made you feel good'.

'But, my darling, what have you got to be depressed about?'

Frances wouldn't say. She seemed very unhappy; the tears splashed out of her blue eyes and fell all over the sheets, but she was aware that she'd had a narrow escape and promised willingly not to do it again. She slept a great deal, only waking up occasionally and looking round to make sure that she wasn't alone. Around midday Helena was told that there were some people to see her, and crept out into the corridor to find Maggs and Richard.

'Look!' Maggs said tragically, waving the newspaper. 'Some rat got hold of her picture and it's spread all over the front page. I haven't told Johnno or anyone, but now they'll have to know'.

Helena glanced at it. She couldn't summon up much feeling, after all that had happened, but it clearly was not good news.

'I can't think why she did it', Maggs went on. 'She certainly never seemed at all interested. I mean, everybody's smoked cannabis a few times - '.

'I haven't', said Richard. 'I'm not a complete fool'.

'Maggs! Do you mean *you* - ?'

'Oh, Mum, it was years ago, and it didn't do anything for me anyway. I did it once when I was sixteen and I'm not going to do it again, but the point is, you can't muck around with pills. I mean, ninety-nine people might take them and be all right but the hundredth might have some physiological thingy and it could kill them. Or do things to their brain. I'd be terrified'.

'Yes', Helena said. She suddenly realised that she was almost dropping. 'Well, I shouldn't think anyone in our family will ever touch them again. Come in and see her'.

They went back inside the ward and looked down at Frances, who was fast asleep, and still looked wretched, but now had a little more colour in her face. There was a big bunch of lilac at the end of her bed from friends in Howells village, and her school friends had brought sweet peas and roses.

'Anyway, Mum', Richard said, 'I've come to take you home'. He looked reassuringly square and sturdy; he was the biggest of all her children. 'Maggs says you've had no sleep for forty-eight hours'.

'I can't - '.

'I've brought my book', Maggs said, 'and I'll sit with her till whenever you come back. I'll do days and you do nights. I mean I ought to, like, get some sort of relationship with my sister'.

In the end she gave in. Richard drove her back to Plas Gwyn and then went on, as he had to get back to the farm. It was a relief that he at least gave her no cause for worry; Richard was happy in his low-paid job and had a large circle of friends. The house was very quiet. Her mother had gone for one of her long walks and Robin, she had been assured, was safe with neighbours. She took off the caramel jumper and crumpled navy skirt which she'd worn since Friday morning and got into her dressing-gown. She was to relieve Maggs at nine o'clock. She'd planned to have a bath and make some refreshing tea but, in the end, she just fell on top of her bed and went to sleep.

She woke up, two hours later, to the sound of the bedside telephone. The room was filled with unaccustomed sunlight. She stretched her hand out, too dazed even to wonder if it was more bad news. Johnno's voice said, 'Mum, where have you all been?'

She couldn't think what to say.

'I tried several times', said Johnno, 'but it was either engaged or no answer. Mum, I've got some news. I don't know what you'll think'.

At least, Helena thought, it didn't sound like a major disaster. She said cautiously, 'Yes?'

'It's Dad'.

Understanding was coming back; it could be nothing to do with her children, or her sisters. Margot was in the Horn of

Africa and Con, she had no doubt, was safe. 'Reg?'

'He had a heart attack, Mum. He died'.

She thought, but Reg is a young man, and then remembered, no, he'd only been young when she'd last seen him.

'Cindy phoned me. It happened last night, about midnight our time. There was no warning at all but she said things about not enough exercise - Oh, God, I'm just waffling on. It's a big shock. She said she'd put off the funeral if I wanted to come over'.

'Yes, go if you like, Johnno. I wouldn't be offended'.

'I don't see the point', Johnno said bleakly. 'I suppose I'd go if it was in this country, but it's not worth flying the Atlantic twice. They're sending me to Germany next week, by the way; it's good news. So I'll just send a wreath from myself and the other three. Do you think that's the right thing to do?'

'Yes'.

'Sorry but I must go now, Mum, I'm in the middle of a big job. You're all right?'

She assured him she was. Then, as she put the receiver down, she realised that she had been too stunned to tell him anything about Frances.

She walked about the house, all thoughts of sleep forgotten. The man she had married, the only man in her life (how old-fashioned that seemed, these days!) Gone, just like that, and she had never been able to talk to him, to work out in a calmer atmosphere where they'd gone wrong. She had always felt cheated of something because they hadn't done that. She tried to recall how he'd left her at the door of their chalet nearly nineteen years ago, with the children clinging to her skirts, Johnno shrieking 'Daddy come back soon!'. He'd told her that he would see her at Christmas or in Boston early the following year. Possibly he'd been lying, had never intended to have any more to do with them, but she couldn't know and would never be sure now. He had genuinely had some affection for the boys.

And it struck her, after a while, that Reg must have died around the time that Frances was emerging from her coma. It surely couldn't be the case that someone up there had decided that Frances should live and Reg should die. But her own feelings frightened her; she was so glad that it had not been the other way round. She was indescribably thankful that she had still got Frances.

She thought, the tears starting to flow - though it was shock, much more than grief - that Reg had never seen his youngest child and never known anything about Robin. And there was his poor wife. But she was young and had no children. As the phone began to ring again she walked towards it with tears streaming down her face. It was Con.

'Len, is that you? Johnno rang me because you were out. Look, I've got some news - '.

'I know', Helena said. 'So have I'. With her sister she didn't need to keep anything back. 'I know about Reg, but Frances is safe. Thank God, Frances is all right'.

Chapter 31

Summer of '87

When little Robin Maynard had his third birthday, at the beginning of July 1987, he was still living at Plas Gwyn with the female members of his family. Johnno was long gone, you could sometimes hear him on the radio using the name John Maynard, and Richard was happily settled at his Black Mountain farm. Helena had had a lot of grief, people said, from those two girls, and with her mother getting more and more disoriented. But Robin was a favourite, even among people who had originally thought that he shouldn't exist, and they gladly let their children attend his party, which was held in the garden with masses of balloons and ice creams.

If Helena had been asked, only two years ago, she'd have been hopeful that by this time both her daughters would be away at university. But it had not happened. Maggs came to her, only a week after they brought Frances home, and said that she'd decided not to take up her place at Birmingham, after all.

'Mum, I can't do it. I couldn't bear to leave Robin. And Frances isn't better yet; I can't just let you cope with everything'.

Helena had tried very hard to change her mind. She wanted Maggs to make a fresh start; she had secretly hoped that she might meet a nice man when she was away from home with Robin not too obviously in the picture, and if they preferred to leave the little boy to be brought up by her she would not object. But Maggs was definite.

'I've been thinking about it for some time. I can do an Open University degree at home, I'm going to work till I drop, and with that and my languages I'll be qualified for a good job by the time he's at school. And then there's your teaching, Mum. You can carry on doing it if I'm around'.

So that was how it had finally worked out. On the days when she was teaching, Maggs looked after Robin; the rest of the time she took him while Maggs studied. She was getting As and

Bs for her essays so it seemed to be going well. But Frances was more of a problem. Frances had never really got over that terrible weekend.

After she came home they had to break it to her that her story was in the local papers, and they also had to tell her that her father was dead. No one had expected her to be much affected by that, but she seemed quite heartbroken.

'But, darling, you didn't know him', Helena tried to console her.

'That's the trouble', Frances sobbed. 'I always wanted to know him and now I never will'.

'He was nothing very special, Frances', Con, who was there, said tactlessly.

Frances looked at her with red-rimmed eyes. It cut both women to the heart to see her looking so miserable. 'How would you like it if I said *your* father was nothing special? I've got half his genes, so if he was no good nor am I'.

Later, when she'd tucked her up in bed, Frances confided to her mother, 'I wrote to him, you know'.

'When?'

'After he broke with Mary-Lou. I asked him if I could come and see him in America, because the boys did, years ago. And I put in my best photo. But' - Frances burst into tears all over again - 'he never answered'.

There wasn't much she could say. She wondered if Reg had never forgiven his daughter for being born, or if he'd thought she was trying to get something out of him, or if he simply couldn't be bothered to reply. The pain from that marriage hadn't stopped when it was legally ended. She only wished she had known that Frances had been brooding about her father, all these years.

She went on being very depressed. There was nothing they could do but surround her with affection, and a few things - like drawing, or giving Robin his bath - seemed to cheer her up. But she was badly shaken, prone to crying fits and convinced that no one outside the family liked her. It had been impossible for her to take her A levels, so all plans had to be put on hold. She did take them in the following year, and passed quite creditably. In autumn 1986 Helena drove her to the art college in Canterbury where she'd won a place, a bit apprehensive, of course, but hopeful that her daughter would be happier among new people who didn't know about the scandal. A week later the phone rang. Frances was having panic attacks.

They brought her home and got her to a specialist. He said that she wasn't yet ready to leave her mother and would have to continue living at home, with as much family support as possible. There was no mental illness and she wasn't malingering, either; she was just one of those abnormally sensitive people who find quite ordinary stresses and strains hard to bear. She could just about manage to get herself on the bus each day to Hereford College of Art, and to do the work she was given, but otherwise she didn't want to go anywhere. All that winter she huddled into her coat and pulled the hood over her face; she was convinced that everybody was looking at her and remembering the time she had made herself ill.

Maggs was very good with her sister. She herself was having quite an active social life - even boy friends, although none of them lasted more than a few weeks. If they didn't like Robin, she said, that was it. Some nights she took the car and went to see people in Hereford, always inviting Frances to come too, but she never would. Other times her friends came to the house and sat around for ages drinking cider. Frances would sit in the corner, hardly speaking.

In the spring Helena got a letter from her cousin Josette Russell, who had lived in Australia for the last thirty years. She said that her son, James, would be touring England that summer with a friend, and could they pitch their tent for a few nights in the garden of Plas Gwyn? Helena said of course, they'd be welcome to stay in the house itself, then forgot about it.

Much of her life seemed to be spent entertaining a stream of children and young people. Maggs drew people to her wherever she was, and Robin's little friends were always trooping into the house. That spring, too, Johnno began to come down bringing his girl friend, Katie Shaw.

They'd met through Con, of all people. When the house of which Con's flat formed part was sold to Katie's mother and stepfather, she had given a barbecue to welcome them and Johnno had looked in. He hadn't meant to go, he said, he'd just happened to be at a loose end and didn't want to be rude to his aunt, but as soon as he and Katie met that was it. She was a thin, frail-looking girl, very quiet and polite, with a bush of dark hair. The next time Helena talked about their concern for Frances, Johnno confided that Katie had been anorexic as a teenager.

'It was when her parents got divorced. She was quite ill for two years, but you can see she's fine now'.

Helena wasn't convinced of that. She fed Katie well when she was there, on meat and two veg and apfelstrudel with cream, all the things she normally discouraged, and after two or three visits she and the girl became very good friends. Even Johnno seemed to have relaxed a little bit, and the relationship looked serious.

When two young men turned up at her door, very sunburned and carrying backpacks, it was immediately obvious which was which. James was tall and dark, very like his mother, whom Helena remembered well. He was also distinctly good-looking, whereas his friend, whom he introduced as Spike Andrews, was a rather plain young man. He had a dark complexion, a broken nose, and only came up to James's chin, though he did smile at her quite pleasantly and said he hoped they wouldn't be in her way.

'It's lovely to see you', Helena said sincerely. Frances was hiding somewhere. 'This is my daughter, Maggs, and my grandson Robin'.

Robin, who had never even considered that anyone might not like him, rushed up and Spike lifted him into the air. Maggs glowered in the background. There was always a slight awkwardness when anyone saw them together for the first time.

'Before you ask, Robin's father was an Afro-American, and we weren't married. In fact I haven't seen him since before Robin was born. Just so you know'.

Helena sighed inwardly; she did wish that Maggs wouldn't

be so bristly. But she kept up a flow of cheerful talk as they went into the sunlit dining-room where she had laid out a cold meal. James produced a bottle of rather good Australian chardonnay and soon they had relaxed. It turned out that they had both just finished degrees in law and were spending the summer on the move before starting work at a legal aid centre. James had been in Europe fifteen years earlier, with his family; Spike had never before left Australia.

Towards the end of the meal Jo wandered in from her writing-room and was introduced. She was delighted to see James.

'I remember your mother well. She was a splendid head girl'. Then, turning to Spike, 'Do tell me, are you Maggs's husband?'

There was a splutter from Frances but Spike replied quite calmly, 'I'm afraid not, Mrs Maynard. I only met her this evening'.

'No'. Jo sighed as she looked at Robin, who was making bananas with his yellow playdough on the floor. 'They tell me that little boy is my great-grandson, but I don't believe it. He's very nice, but he isn't a member of the family. It's the colouring, you see'.

She wandered off again.

'Sorry about that', said Frances.

'I don't mind', Spike said. 'I'm a little bit of a mixture myself. My mother's mother was an aborigine'.

Maggs stared.

'They took Mum away from her family in the 1950s, when she was five, and they were trying to persuade the mixed-race kids to think they were white. It seems incredible but they thought they were doing them a favour. She gets depressed about it even now; she didn't find her way back home for twenty years'.

'And my Mum was always into aboriginal rights', said James, 'so I had it drummed into me'. They talked for the next hour about the minority groups in Australia, and were still talking when the girls followed them out on to the lawn to put up their tent.

The idea had been that they should stay in Howells for only one or two nights and then move on. But after the first twenty-four hours there did not seem any reason why they shouldn't just remain where they were, and explore. Both of them steadily refused to move into the house and cooked most of their own meals. As it was the school holidays Helena didn't need the car, so the four young people packed into it and went for long trips, to Oxford, to the Three Choirs Festival (they all loved music), even to London. Sometimes they took Robin with them and went fruit-picking, or taught him to swim at the Hereford baths. She was delighted that they were having such a good time. Even Frances seemed to have emerged a little from her shell.

One day they took a picnic to Llanthony Abbey, and Helena found herself sitting on a fallen stone, with Robin turning somersaults nearby, while the other four wandered off. It was hundreds of years, now, since the abbey had been sacked and the high arches left open to the sky. The afternoon was warm and quite peaceful, and after a while Robin cuddled up to her and started talking. He said, 'I like James and I like Spike'. And at the same moment she saw Spike and her daughter a long way off, near the ruins of the altar, kissing passionately.

After that, it was more difficult. Maggs and Spike didn't try to hide the fact that they were totally absorbed in each other, and James grew restive. He began to say he wanted to see a bit more of England, so they would drop him in Hereford to catch a train and then go off by themselves. Frances, who had rather liked James, began to mope once more. And Helena worried, of course.

She couldn't see how it could lead to anything good as, whatever else happened, the two boys had to be back in Melbourne by the beginning of October. She supposed they could write to each other but it was a long way and Maggs was going to be very depressed, when he left. And of course there was the danger that her daughter might get pregnant a second time. It was just as well that the young men were still sleeping in their tent and the girls in the house.

But she took more trouble to talk to Spike, not to discover his intentions in the old-fashioned way but simply to get to know him better. What she found out, she liked. At twenty-five he was two years older than James, though they'd graduated at the same time; he came from a working-class family and had put himself through university by working as a bus conductor and long-distance driver. He was very serious about using the law to help aborigines and other exploited groups get their rights. She also noticed that he always gave a hand with the washing-up, and was very patient with Robin. However, she didn't feel she could say that she really knew him. It was the gap between generations.

This was how things stood when Maggs came up one evening, about midnight after she and Spike had put the car away, and announced that they were getting married.

'You know he's got to be back on October the first?' She was sitting on Helena's bed, still in her outdoor coat, her dark eyes blazing with excitement. 'I'm sorry about the rush but there's no other way; he's talking to his parents on the phone now. He wants to adopt Robin'.

'Robin's starting playgroup next week', Helena said foolishly.

'Mum, you don't understand. Robin's coming with us'.

She must have been in shock. Her daughter talking blithely about taking herself and, worse still, Robin, to the other side of the world with a man she hardly knew.

'Maggs - darling, I know I ought to be pleased, I like Spike very much, but do you really think it's a good idea to get married when you've known him for less than two months? I only want you to be all right - '.

'But, Mum', Maggs said patiently, 'we can't wait, because, as I said, Spike has to get back to Australia. I *know* what I'm doing. I've met literally hundreds of men at school and when I was working in Lausanne, and none of them is the same sort of fantastic person as Spike. Sometimes you find out these things very quickly. I mean, look at all those people who live together for years and years, and then split up. So they probably never really wanted to be married'.

'Maggs -'.

'He likes you, you know. He thinks you're great, and he loves Robin. I wouldn't even have considered it otherwise'.

'I don't want to lose you', Helena almost sobbed.

'Yes, I know, and it's not what I *want*, Mum, but have you thought, we can't keep Robin protected in this house for ever? Once he starts going to school, he'll stick out like a sore thumb'.

It was true. The tiny children Robin played with were colour-blind, but once he got a little older, he could expect to be brutally teased. If this marriage had to happen, at least Robin would be living in a cosmopolitan city and with a man who looked as if he could be his father. She was just desperately afraid that it had flared up too fast and would not work.

'Oh, yes, he's a *very* nice young man', said Josette, at the other end of the telephone. 'I've known him for three years, and I should say Maggs couldn't do better. But, Len, you never told me that she had a baby'.

'I suppose I'm old-fashioned and didn't want to spread it far and wide. Josette, you will keep an eye on them, won't you?'

'Of course. And you must come out and stay with us'.

Even if she could find the fare to Australia, Helena thought, she didn't see how she could abandon her responsibilities here. But matters were rushing ahead very fast. Maggs and Spike went up to London several times, to visit Australia House and to get a passport for Robin, and although they'd said they didn't want an elaborate wedding, there was still an awful lot to arrange. Con was invited down to Hereford for the day. Margot couldn't be reached.

Robin had been told to call Spike 'Daddy', and went round the house practising the new word. Helena kept him away from playgroup because she wanted to spend as much time with him as possible. When they all gathered at the registry office, in the last week of September, he sat on her knee saying, 'That's my Mummy' and 'That's my Daddy' to anyone who wanted to know.

Maggs looked almost frighteningly beautiful, in a pink dress, with marguerites in her dark hair. After the ceremony, which only took about five minutes, they went back to Plas Gwyn for cake and sandwiches and Australian sparkling wine. Con took her niece to one side while everybody else was talking.

'Maggs, I'm sure everything will be fine. But if you ever need to get back, and there's a problem, let me know, and I'll send you and Robin the fare'.

'It's okay', Maggs said blissfully. 'Thanks, but I'm only coming back for visits'.

And after they'd gone off to spend a two-day honeymoon in Stratford-on-Avon - 'we've got tickets for *three* plays', Maggs boasted, and James asked what kind of a honeymoon was that - the two sisters cleared up, and tried not to talk, or even think, of the marriages which had gone wrong. Helena kept Robin very close to her; she couldn't imagine what her life was going to be, without him. Her family was shrinking fast.

Chapter 32

Con Steps Sideways

On a chilly Saturday morning in November, six weeks after Maggs's wedding, Con was sitting in front of her word processor, doing the last page of her latest novel. She had got plugged into the new technology as soon as possible; she'd found it cut her working time by almost half. Some people of her age hadn't got the hang of it yet, and the older generation still used typewriters, but she herself hadn't touched one of the antiquated things for several years.

But today she was finding it hard to concentrate, because she was seriously considering whether or not to go for a winter break in Egypt. Some friends wanted her to join them on a luxurious cruise up the Nile, they had even said they would bring a man for her, although Con suspected that this particular man, a bachelor in his fifties, wasn't into women. She was tempted. The price was horrendous, of course, but she'd enjoy seeing the pyramids and the famous temples and she could always set her next Silk Slip novel in Egypt. She was going to spend the weekend thinking about it but, on the whole, and subject to a check on her bank balance, she thought she would go.

But first, there was this novel to wind up. Con turned back to the screen but her mind kept wandering to what she would do next; go to the delicatessen, perhaps, and get a wedge of apricot cheese, roam around a few bookshops and then spend the afternoon reading that new biography of Florence Nightingale which she'd just taken home to review. And tomorrow, she might go to the British Museum and refresh her memory of the glories of ancient Egypt. Yes, that would definitely be worth doing.

Sighing, she embarked on the last paragraph of *Annabel's Lover*:

Annabel's golden hair streamed over the turquoise sheets of the king-sized bed. His arms entwined her and she could hear the strong beating of his heart. They both knew that their love was eternal and unshakeable and -

The letterbox clattered. Con half rose, but she knew she could spend hours over her post, depending on what was in it, and she hadn't got where she was by being badly organised. She'd finish it off and then check.

.... eternal and unshakeable and would last for the rest of their lives.

There! Con pressed the SAVE button and ran downstairs joyfully to pick up her letters. There was only one, bearing her publisher's logo. She carried it back and put on the coffee-machine before opening it.

Dear Miss Maynard, (she read)
I very much regret to say that after we have published your current novel, **Annabel's Lover***, we shall not be able to offer you future contracts. I am telling you this now to avoid wasting your time. Unfortunately, due to economic pressures, Silk Slip has had to rationalise its list and we have decided to keep only best-sellers and younger writers who can offer fresh perspectives on modern life. In your case we feel that your work is a little old-fashioned and does not reflect the reality of women's lives today.*
May we wish you luck in whatever you decide to do next and thank you for your many years of service to Silk Slip.
Yours sincerely,
Serena Maxwell (Editor).

Her first reaction was to tear the letter in half and throw it in the waste paper basket. Then she got it out and read it again, her fury deepening with each hackneyed phrase. 'Many years of service to Silk Slip' - what rubbish! She'd only done it for the money. 'Fresh perspectives on modern life' - 'the reality of women's lives today' - absurd! Who'd ever thought that Silk Slip novels bore the faintest resemblance to the way most women lived their lives?

What she means, Con thought with cold fury, is that I'm middle-aged, that I grew up before the permissive society, and that I can't churn out endless pages of soft porn like Yseult Pertwee. Some people might think that *Annabel's Lover* was soft porn but she knew better; as she grew older she felt more and more uncomfortable writing about people thrashing round in bed. (How long was it since she'd been to bed with anyone herself? Damn, four years). Yseult was the same age but she was at the top of her profession; she was forever appearing on chat shows, with her blonde hair floating round her diamond earrings, jabbering about what she called 'women's needs'. Yseult would not be getting an insulting letter. And she can't even write decent English, Con thought fiercely, and I can. True, her own books weren't great literature but they were good of their kind, well-crafted and they'd given pleasure to a lot of people. She'd written - how many could it be? - *twenty-seven* novels since she first met Liz Arnett in 1966. She recalled briefly that Betty Wynne-Davies had died at the beginning of the year. Well, she didn't mean to complain to Liz, that was certain. What she did mean to do, she wasn't sure.

First she poured herself a mug of strong black coffee. Then she took out the disc marked *Annabel's Lover* and parcelled it for the publishers; she'd get every penny she was owed on that book and she would not be going over it to give it a final polish as she normally did. She paced up and down the room, trying to work out her next move; it was a very, very long time since she'd been so upset. She could forget Egypt, she thought after a while; there would certainly be no money for extras. She would tell her friends that she herself had broken the connection with Silk Slip because she wanted more time to write seriously. But, Con thought bleakly, they would then immediately ask what was she going to write instead?

Always she'd believed that she was doing these people a

favour, by supplying the kind of silly novels they wanted, and now it turned out that they thought she wasn't good enough. How had she got into it, she who had dreamed of being a great writer through all the years she was at school? Her eye fell on the birthday cards standing on her mantelpiece - not many, because she didn't tell that many people her age. Forty-eight last week, and what had she achieved? No husband, no child, no book of the slightest consequence. Only those twenty-seven novels which would be forgotten long before she was dead, and a mass of frothy articles. Even her nephew Johnno was a more serious journalist than she was; he at least hoped (though he was probably wrong) that his work might do some good. Looking back, she couldn't see that she had done a single worthwhile thing.

One of the cards was from Miss Annersley, who was immensely old now and living in a home but faithfully wrote to the triplets every fifth of November. Con stopped pacing. She and her friends used to laugh at the spinsters of that generation, women like Miss Annersley and Miss Wilson who had never been to bed with a man. But now she wondered, in what way was she superior to them? They had believed wholeheartedly in their work and encouraged the girls in their charge to make the best possible use of a freedom they had never enjoyed themselves. What she had done with her freedom didn't bear thinking of.

She wandered miserably about the park, went to a film and didn't take in a word, kept asking herself if she had done anything with her life, other than earn a living. Well, there were a few short stories, mouldering in the files of various little magazines. Annersley had been quite complimentary about the one she'd heard on the radio. She was prepared to stand by her stories, but she hadn't taken the necessary time to write more of them, and, anyway, short stories didn't sell. Or I could try biography, Con thought suddenly. That life of Florence Nightingale which she'd just received, that was certain to be popular. But, she thought despondently a minute later, I haven't done it before, and probably all the important figures have already been done.

She had a horrible night. She lay awake, listening to the young people in the garden having a raucous party, dreamed and dozed and dreamed again. She imagined she was one of three little babies in a basket, tossing on the sea. Her mother had told her several times how they'd had to be evacuated from Guernsey weeks before the Channel Islands were invaded in 1940. How lucky that they hadn't drowned, or would it have mattered so much after all? Mary Helena, Mary Constance, Mary Margaret. The sort of names devout parents gave their daughters a generation ago. Last night the queen had four Marys, this night she'll have but three. Where did that line come from? Mary Wollstonecraft, Mary Godwin, Mary Shelley - .

Con sat up. In a flash, she had got the idea she was looking for. She switched on her lamp, wincing as the light hit her eyes, snatched the pad she kept beside her bed in case inspiration struck in the night and scribbled:

THE TWO MARYS.

The next day, Sunday, Con consulted all the reference books in her flat and made a great many notes. She wandered about London in the cold sunlight, looking at the red poppies on the war memorials and slowly getting things clear in her mind. On Monday she rang Kermit Jones' literary agency and asked for an appointment. He sounded pleased and suggested they meet for lunch.

She'd seen Kermit on and off in the twenty years since they met at that disastrous party, and although nothing had ever been said, she knew that he had a soft spot for her. But she had never thought she needed a literary agent. Over lunch, at a jolly little Greek restaurant, she sketched out her idea.

'Mary Wollstonecraft and Mary Shelley. People have written about them before, but not a double biography. Or else they've concentrated on the men in their lives. They're probably the most famous mother and daughter in history'.

'I'll take your word for that', Kermit said.

'One life ends as another begins'. Like my own, Con thought in passing. 'Mary Wollstonecraft died when her daughter was born. She was the first English feminist, she lived through the French Revolution, she had a baby outside marriage and tried to kill herself and led an extraordinary life. And the second Mary ran away with the poet Shelley, experienced a lot more tragedies, and wrote *Frankenstein* when she was pregnant and only eighteen. How many people who enjoy the Frankenstein films know the first thing about her?'

'I did vaguely know that *Frankenstein* was written by a woman', said Kermit. 'Go on, Con. I'm listening'.

'It's got everything, you see - sex, death, childbirth, love triangles, condition of women, revolution. It's going to be a scholarly biography, every detail will be accurate, and I speak French and Italian so I can go to the places where they lived and check the history. But I also know how to write for a big audience, so if it's marketed in the right way it could be a best-seller. The feminists will like it and also people who are into horror stories'.

'Could be'.

'But, Kermit, it's got to be marketed, or not enough people will hear of it. It's got to be plugged in the colour supplements before publication, seen in W.H. Smith's, entered for the big prizes and so on. And some quotes on the back jacket from the right people could help too. What do you think?'

'Hm!' Kermit looked into his glass of sour red wine and tried to read the future. 'I think it's an interesting idea, Con - I like a good biography - suppose you write me an outline and a specimen chapter, and I'll read up a bit about the two ladies in question. Then, if it still seems a good idea, I'll see what I can do'.

Before they parted, Con asked the question she had been saving for the end.

'Do you ever see Tony these days?'

'Who?' Kermit asked abstractedly. 'Oh, Tony. No, I haven't seen him since they moved to Bristol'.

And that was that, Con thought, as she made her way home, planning how she would go to the British Library and sort out the necessary books. Kermit liked her; he wouldn't have agreed to an idea which was no good but he might be prepared to put in that little bit more effort because she was the person concerned. But Kermit had a wife, like most men of his age, and she had never found him all that attractive anyway. The men she did find attractive invariably seemed to end up with someone else.

Chapter 33

Johnno

Helena was washing the kitchen floor when she heard a familiar name, on the PM programme to which she often listened while she was making supper, and then a voice that sounded familiar too. Miss Betty Landon, minister at the DHSS. It seemed amazing, but she thought it must be the same Betty Landon who had been in her year at school. Margot had nearly killed her once by throwing a paperweight when in one of her rages. And it was just as well that Margot couldn't hear her now, because Betty was saying that many young people sleeping on the streets had perfectly good homes to go to and were only there because, in effect, they liked it. No doubt if she had been more political she'd have noted Betty's progress years ago.

Well, she thought as she sluiced the dirty water down the sink, it certainly shows how far we've all travelled in different directions. Betty being interviewed on the radio, herself cleaning the floor. When they were schoolgirls it would have seemed inconceivable that women would be popping up all over the place, reading the national news, being members of governments, doing almost all the jobs which had once been exclusive to men. But it made no difference to her own situation, none at all.

It was now over six months since Robin had gone to Australia. Maggs's letters said that he was going to nursery school and his new grandparents loved him, and every week he sent her a little drawing. She herself intended taking a law degree and getting qualified to help Spike. Well, the three elder children were settled. Richard had a girl friend, a little dark creature called Olwen who had been around for years although nothing had been said about marriage. Johnno and Katie were driving down for the weekend. It would be good to have them all together for Sunday lunch; the house seemed very quiet when it was just herself, her mother, and Frances.

She looked out of the window and saw it was a fine May evening, white hawthorn on the trees and cow-parsley scattered over the meadows, just as it had been when Maggs had come home to announce her pregnancy four years ago. Listening to Betty had made her wonder what had happened to all the girls who had once been her friends. Clem happily remarried, Rosamund married, a few others divorced, some in responsible jobs, many more in obscurity; there was no way of keeping in touch. And Margot, who was in England for about six weeks of the year and would usually head home to recover. She had put that traumatic experience behind her and dedicated herself to the worldwide struggle against TB. Margot would burn herself out and die young, if necessary, doing that work. And she - what was she doing? Well, just keeping house for the remains of the family; she had made the wrong choice years ago and must live with it. One day Frances would leave home, and then she and her mother would grow old together at Plas Gwyn.

Now, where is everybody? Helena wondered, as she checked that supper would keep, set the table and left the floor to dry. Frances was watching TV, sucking her sleeve and surrounded by soft animals. It was one of her better days; other times she'd just come back from Hereford, shut herself in her room and cry. Her mother had last been seen going upstairs to her study, but now that she thought about it, that had been some time ago.

The doorbell rang.

Her mother was standing in the drive accompanied by a tall young policeman. She looked furious; her cheeks were scarlet and her eyes snapping.

'Sorry to disturb you, madam', the policeman said, 'but I thought it best to bring your mother home. And you'll also have to pick up your car'.

Jo marched past him into the house.

'But - Oh, dear, what's going on?'

'Well, it's a long story, Mrs - ?' the officer began as she showed him in.

'Maynard. I use the same name as my mother. But what happened?'

'Well, Mrs Maynard, this lady was seen driving your car

along the lane near Vowchurch at approximately seventy miles per hour, and on the wrong side of the road. A police car gave chase, but she declined to pull up, and was only stopped by a flock of sheep coming in the other direction'. Those country roads were often completely blocked when sheep were moved from one field to another. 'And I'm afraid one of the ewes was killed'.

It could have been a child, Helena thought.

'I see. I'm very sorry'.

'It's nonsense to say that I was on the wrong side', Jo said haughtily. 'It was the right side, that is right as in the hand you write with. I *always* know whether I'm in Britain or on the continent and of course I can tell left from right like anyone else. Len, please tell this officer to go away. I can't understand what this is about, and he wouldn't let me bring the car home although I offered to drive him'.

'But, Mother, what were you doing in the car at all?'

'I wanted a little spin, dear. I could see the mountains, and they reminded me of the Tyrol, though of course they're not so high or so picturesque. So I took the keys from your bag and set off. I didn't disturb you because you were obviously busy, and I would have been back long ago if people had left me alone'.

'I see'. She would have to keep her keys hidden in future. 'Well, Mother, why don't you sit down with Frances and watch whatever's on TV?' Although perhaps too much TV had caused this problem; perhaps she thought she was taking part in a thrilling car chase. 'Look, here's Johnno; perhaps you could talk to him'.

Another car had just stopped in the drive and Johnno got out. She could see that he was looking depressed and Katie wasn't with him. Her mother went out, greeting him warmly - she'd always been devoted to him, as the first grandchild - and Helena explained the situation. It took a long time. Just before the policeman left he said, 'You know, Mrs Maynard, she might really be happier living in a home'.

She tracked down Johnno in his room. He was lying on the bed in his outdoor coat and staring at the ceiling.

'Johnno, are you all right?' She thought he looked dreadful. 'Where's Katie?'

'She got out at Hereford. We had a row'. A tense pause and then Johnno said in an exhausted voice, 'Katie's pregnant'.

Helena sat down on a corner of the bed.

'That isn't a disaster', she said cautiously. 'You and Katie always seem very happy together, and I'll be glad to - '.

'It feels like a disaster'.

'Why? If she wants to go on working, the baby could be looked after - '.

'Oh, it's not that. She doesn't like her job'. Katie had a degree, but had only been able to find work in a tourist agency. 'She isn't very happy at home either. No, she wants to marry me, be a full-time mother, make a proper home and so on'.

'You could afford to support them, couldn't you?' Helena asked. She knew that wasn't the real issue, but Johnno was doing extremely well in his profession and his flat, though rather bleak, was big enough for two.

'I'm prepared to do that. I'll acknowledge the child and let it have my name and I don't want to give up on her, but - The trouble is, Katie's got this thing about marriage'.

'Where *is* Katie?'

'I suppose on her way home. I told you, we were having an argument and she demanded to be put down so she could catch the train back to London'.

Helena tried very hard not to show how appalled she was. A pregnant girl, travelling on her own in a state of extreme distress; a baby rejected by its father. Johnno looked at her pleadingly and said, 'What could I do? She seemed fed up with me, and I - well, I just wanted to be left alone. I wouldn't have come back at all, but I was almost here, and I knew you'd worry'.

'When did you find out about this?' Helena asked.

'Last night'.

'And you've been arguing ever since?'

'Yes'.

'Well, Johnno, you look worn out; you're in no state to make important decisions. Let me get you something to eat, and you must rest here overnight. But perhaps you should just check that Katie got home safely'.

'She won't be there yet', Johnno said. He half rose, but then dropped down on the bed again. 'I don't think I can face Gran'.

'Then I'll bring you a tray'.

She went downstairs and got him a plate of brown bread and vegetable stew, with a glass of cider. Johnno ate hungrily. The bedroom had hardly changed since he was a schoolboy; there were his framed certificates on the wall, along with his astronomical charts and political maps of Europe, evidence of hours of concentrated work. Everything in Johnno's life had gone according to plan, up till now. When he had finished he put down the tray and sighed.

'I know what you're thinking, Mum; I just don't see why I have to get married yet. I've told her, I won't walk away from the child'.

'But, Johnno, you *are* walking away from the child and her, if you won't marry her'.

'Mother, do you know that you're almost unbelievably out of date? This is the 1980s, not the 1950s. Half the people I know who have children have had them outside marriage. A lot of women are feminists and don't believe in it'.

Helena thought that perhaps she would never understand modern life.

'But Katie does mind?'

Johnno sighed. 'Yes'. There were black shadows under his eyes; no doubt he'd been up arguing all night and done a full day's work before driving to Plas Gwyn. He looked terribly young to have this on his mind. After a moment he added, 'We could always make it official later on, if we feel like it'.

'But the baby would still be illegitimate!'

'I told you, that's not important. Robin is illegitimate, and you never seemed to hold it against him'.

'Of course I didn't', Helena said with spirit. 'I love Robin. But I never pretended that he had the best possible start in life. And I think if you don't offer to marry her now, when it matters,

Katie will resent it'.

'But, Mum, you wouldn't want us to get married if we hated each other?'

Helena sighed. 'No. I know that you and your friends think I'm very old-fashioned, but even I am not quite as old-fashioned as that. Although I would still want you to take an interest in the child. But that's not how you feel, is it?'

There was a long silence. Eventually Johnno said, 'No, I think I love her. I do love her. But I'm just so damn terrified of doing the wrong thing. If I lived with them the child might get attached to me and then be upset if it didn't work out. You remember when Dad went away?'

Helena remembered vividly; the cold morning, a red sun coming up behind the pine trees, and the little boy Johnno, with his shrill voice and earnest manner, who had burst into tears when Reg drove off, run to the gate and refused to be comforted.

'I knew he was going for good. Don't ask me how, but I stood at that door with you and the little ones and I knew he was itching to leave, and that he wouldn't come back. I've never forgotten it. If he made a mess of it, why shouldn't I?'

He sighed and stood up.

'Well, I suppose I'd better ring Katie'.

Helena said gently, 'Just to check she's all right'. Inwardly she was wondering if Reg's walking out on his family long ago was going to have a ripple effect down the generations. Her boys terrified of commitment, Maggs rushing into the arms of an unreliable man, and Frances's awful depression. Where would it all end?

Johnno came back a minute later looking worried.

'No answer. I know her parents are away'.

He took out his filofax and started phoning friends. After about five minutes he had got nowhere.

'Try Con', his mother suggested. 'She may have seen her come home'.

Con had given Katie hot tea and sympathy, after finding her weeping and incoherent on the doorstep. She'd offered her a sherry - her generation never believed it did any harm to drink while pregnant - but Katie shook her head violently and started crying all over again.

'I'm not going to give you any advice', she said. 'Only I think you should do nothing in a hurry, because whether you have this baby or get rid of it, you might regret whichever you do for the rest of your life'.

'I'm not getting rid of the baby', Katie sobbed. 'I'm getting rid of Johnno. I can't tell you, Con, how selfish and how arrogant that man is. Just because he's brilliant he thinks that my feelings don't matter. He says that I can live here with the baby, and it can have his name, but I'm not good enough to have it. And he'll come and visit us occasionally. I'm supposed to be that man's sex object and not interfere with his career. I just hope the baby isn't a boy because it might remind me of him. I'm going to tear up - '.

The telephone rang.

'Yes - she's here', Con said after a moment. 'I'll hand you over'.

She gave the phone to Katie who immediately cried, 'You fucking bastard, I've fucking well had enough!' Helena at the other end heard Johnno shout, 'Where the fucking hell have you been? I've been worried to death'. Each of the older women winced. At exactly the same moment, they slipped away and left the young people to get on with it.

Chapter 34

'They shall mount up with wings like eagles'

They were getting near the end of the service.

'All flesh is grass, and all its loveliness is like the flower of the field.

'He brings the princes to nothing; He makes the judges of the earth useless.

'Scarcely shall they be planted, scarcely shall they be sown, scarcely shall their stock take root in the earth, when He will also blow on them, and they will wither, and the whirlwind will take them away like stubble.

'Even the youths shall faint and be weary, and the young men shall utterly fall.

'But those who wait on the Lord shall renew their strength; they shall mount up with wings like eagles, they shall run and not be weary, they shall walk and not faint'.

The three women stood beside the open grave, with a bitter wind from the Black Mountains whipping their dark coats and uncovered hair. It was the dead time between Christmas and New Year, and the weather was vicious, but they'd still managed a good turn-out for the funeral of old Mrs Maynard. A stroke had killed her, quite painlessly and unexpectedly, on the twenty-third of December. The *Guardian* and *Telegraph* had each printed a short notice about the death of a once well-known children's writer, and many neighbours had left the TV to pay their respects, as she had been very popular in Howells village. Ten of the eleven children were there, and nearly all the grandchildren, the boys in dark school suits and the girls in black and white outfits. Johnno, the eldest, stood a little apart from the rest, looking grim. Some of them knew that he was John Maynard whom they had heard on the BBC World Service, and that he was here only for a few hours as his wife, Katie, was about to have a baby. A band of rain swept down from the hills, blotting out the muddy fields and tiny Norman church, and those who had umbrellas put them up. The three women were the closest to the grave.

Helena was thinking, 'I'm glad I kept her at home and did everything I could. She would have hated to go into an institution. And I'm glad she was able to block out the truth about Daddy and the other awful things that happened, and stay cheerful right to the end. She was an extraordinary person; I don't think any of our generation match up to her'.

Con was thinking, 'I shouldn't have left it all to Len, but what could I do? I couldn't have left my flat and my life in London to vegetate at Plas Gwyn. There are going to be some big changes. I noticed Steve and Mike with their heads together before we left for church'.

Margot was thinking, 'I wonder if Mother's spirit is watching us. I wonder if she and Dad have finally got together. Ashes to ashes, dust to dust, but certain things endure'.

Flowers were thrown into the grave.

Johnno left immediately after the ceremony. The rest went back to Plas Gwyn, where the neighbours joined them for sherry. A lot of flowers had arrived while they were at the church, some of them from people they hadn't heard of for ages; Liz Arnett, Clem and Tony Barras, Madame Simone de Bersac, Roger Richardson, Peter and Gillian Young. Helena had prepared hot soup and a buffet lunch and several trays of mince pies. People said things like 'it went very well', and 'there was quite a crowd' and 'pity Phil couldn't come'. Phil had fallen downstairs at a Christmas party in Brussels and broken her leg. After they'd eaten, the young people went off to watch a James Bond film and the Maynards with their husbands and wives took their coffee into the sitting-room, which had been decorated for Christmas before the tragedy. A fire was burning and the white marble surround was covered with jugs of holly and swathes of ivy.

Con could see Sue's sharp little eyes moving round the room, assessing the value of what was in it. Nothing priceless, but there were some good bits of oak furniture, the cups they were drinking from were 1950s Wedgwood, and the outstanding photograph of three young girls must be worth something too. They got settled and Stephen, as the eldest son, opened the proceedings.

'Well, folks, I'm glad so many of you could be here, though it's a sad occasion. I'll put you in the picture. As you may remember, Dad made a will in 1971 which left this house to Mother for her lifetime, and after her death it's to be sold and the proceeds divided between us. I'm no expert, but it must be worth quite a bit, wouldn't you say, Mike?'

Mike, the estate agent, nodded.

'Much more than it would have been two or three years ago. I'll walk round before I leave and do a valuation. And as prices are still going up most satisfactorily, it's worth hanging on to try and get a bit more'.

'Well, personally', Felicity said, 'I could do with the money right now. I'm always hard up, you know, and the children are very expensive'.

Con reflected that no one would know Felicity was hard up from the way she dressed.

Charles was looking pained by all this talk of money. Steve was about to move on to the next point in his notes when his wife, Sue, said blandly, 'When do you think you could move out, Len?'

It was a shock. She knew, of course, that the house was much too big for her and Frances - had been too big even before her mother died - but she had not expected to be asked to leave straight away. For a moment she was speechless.

'Oh, really', Felix said, 'Len's obviously got to stay here and look after the house till it's sold, which may not be so easy. Most people don't want to live in the back of beyond. And of course she needs a bit of time to make plans'.

'Yes', Sue inquired, 'what *are* your plans, Len?'

Helena had pulled herself together.

'I'll probably try to get a full-time teaching job. But, if you all agree, I'd like to go on living here until June, when Frances takes her final exams. I'd prefer her not to be disturbed before that'.

'She had a nervous breakdown, didn't she?' asked Sue.

Helena had hoped that wasn't generally known.

'Frances is much better now, but her education has been disrupted several times and she really needs a quiet life. We'll move out straight after her exams, if anybody wants the house'.

'No problem', Mike said, 'these things always take ages. I stopped in Hereford and looked in some agents' windows - '.

Margot, totally bored, put down her cup and went out.

Sue's eyes followed her. 'I suppose, if Margot had gone on being a nun, we could have divided it into ten parts instead of eleven. They don't own anything, do they?'

'No', said Con, 'but in case you've forgotten, Margot ceased to be a nun several years ago. And she's entitled to her share'.

Using the excuse of making more coffee, Helena went into the kitchen. She found Margot there, gazing out at the tossing apple branches. Some dry snow, the sort that doesn't stick, had begun to fall.

'God, aren't they all mercenary?' she said.

'Not all'. Helena began to stack the dishes. 'Charles doesn't care; he's one of those people who can live on very little. Margot, what are you going to do next?'

'Flying to India in two weeks. I can't stand these family conferences'.

Well, Helena thought as she moved about the kitchen, doing her usual jobs with slightly shaking hands, Margot at least knows where she's going. I wish I did. Of course, she'd got no savings; all the money she had ever had had been swallowed up by the children's immediate needs. Reg had left them nothing; his estate, which was considerable, had been willed to his third wife. Through the window she could see the poplar in the field below Carn Beg, where Mary-Lou had walked into her life and ruined it. She thought, I don't mind going, really, I'd be glad to have no reminders of the past.

Back in the sitting-room, Con had started a new topic.

'Listen, you lot, I think we ought to talk about Len. Unlike the rest of us, she has no home of her own and no money, and I don't want her to do badly out of this. I think that once the house is sold, she must be left with enough to buy a little flat. Even if it means that we all have to go slightly short'.

'I don't agree', Sue said at once. 'Len's been very lucky, living in this big house rent-free all these years. Of course it's unfortunate that she lost her husband' - she sounded as if he could easily have been kept, given reasonable care - 'but we don't *owe* her anything'.

'Oh, yes, we do. All that time she's been looking after Mother, remember? It would have cost the estate thousands of pounds to keep her in a home, or perhaps you'd have liked to have her living with you, Sue?'

Hywel, Cecil's husband, said after a glance at his wife, 'That's right. Helena's kept open house for this family for the last seventeen years, and we couldn't agree to her being left without a roof over her head'.

'There's no question of *that*', Sue snapped.

'Hang on', Mike said, 'we can settle this quite easily. Con, I'm sure the house will go for over a hundred thousand, with values what they are now, and Len's share would pay a deposit on a modest flat. And of course no one wants to hurry her. I'll have a chat with her and see what she thinks of doing'.

By the time Helena had come back, with tea and Christmas cake, the tide had already turned in her favour. All her brothers and sisters had an affection for her and, while they wanted to get as much money as possible from the sale of the house, agreed that she must have a fair deal. Frances would probably be leaving home soon; she could go anywhere she liked.

The three women climbed the stairs to the top of the house and opened up the little room where their mother had done her writing. The brothers and sisters had gone, gathering up assorted children, with Sue helping herself to a silver Art Deco mirror which she'd had her eye on for years. It was snowing harder now. The garden was quite white and they could see Mary-Lou's pond and, much further away, the scattered lights from farms on the Welsh hillsides.

Helena turned the light on; it was four o' clock and darkening fast.

'I suppose I'll have to clear it out, but it seems sad'.

Jo's dusty typewriter and a sheaf of papers were still on her desk. Con wondered whether, in the last years, she had simply looked out of the window and not written much. All her books in their original bright jackets were on the long shelves which ran round the study, their titles proclaiming the period when they were written. *A Royalist Soldier-Maid*, *Nancy Meets a Nazi* - oh, dear! Con thought, perhaps in time to come somebody would go through her own books and think she must have been mad to write them. But her work on Mary Wollstonecraft was going well; she must concentrate on that. As if she had tuned into her thoughts Margot said, 'They're not all bad'.

'You don't think so?'

'No. I wasn't supposed to read novels while I was a nun, but recently, I picked up one of the early ones to get me to sleep and sat up all night reading it. She had plenty of talent; she just wrote too much and too carelessly'.

Helena said, 'I haven't even looked at what's in the oak chest'.

'Probably piles and piles of rejected manuscripts'.

They were silent till Con said, 'I wonder why people always say "you're living in a dream world" as if that was disgraceful. A dream world is often much more interesting than the real one. That's where I live when I'm writing, I suppose - so does every author. Mother's problem was that she never knew the border between the two'.

The telephone began to ring. Helena ran downstairs and answered it.

It was Johnno, as she had hoped. 'Mum, it's happened! It's a girl, and they're both fine. Katie went into labour a week early and I got back just in time to see her born'.

'Johnno, how wonderful! Have you got a name for her?'

Johnno's words tumbled out; he'd obviously forgotten that this baby was supposed to have been a disaster. 'She's got a lot of dark hair and enormous eyes like a bush baby. I really think she's very intelligent; she looked straight at me. Her name? Oh yes, we settled that, she's called Holly Josephine'.

Helena put the phone down to find Con holding a bottle of good Beaujolais.

'This has been sitting in my car. I brought it into the warm to cheer us up. We'll drink to the baby's health and Mother's health and a peaceful 1989'.

They were all laughing and interrupting each other. Frances was dragged out of her room and the wine was opened, and Con also fetched the last of the mince pies. Outside the windows, it was dark and still snowing. 1988 would be gone in another thirty-two hours; let it go.

Chapter 35

The Triplets' Fiftieth Birthday

Helena continued to live at Plas Gwyn with Frances for the first half of 1989. The other children kept in touch; Richard had Sunday lunch with them, there were frequent letters from Maggs, and Johnno and his family came for the odd weekend. She loved the new baby, Holly, but didn't see as much of her as she would have liked because Katie was keen to be a full-time mother. It was Frances who had to be nursed through her exams, Frances who couldn't be allowed to slip back into depression.

She was still very quiet and spent long hours drawing in her bedroom, but the signs were that she was slowly getting better. Boys and girls would call at the house quite regularly. Con had her in London for a weekend, to explore the galleries and to see if she could stand being away from her mother, and, when this went well, took her to Madrid at Easter. Again, she came back in good shape.

The house had not been sold. Various people looked at it but said it was too big or too far from civilisation. Mike had been wrong about prices; they'd gone so absurdly high that they could only come down and it looked as if they'd have to let it go, in the end, for a smaller sum than had been hoped. Helena was doing what she could to earn a living. She worked on translations when Frances was away, she filled in at various schools as a teacher of French and German and she held a weekly Spanish class in Hereford. The youngest students were teenagers, keen to work abroad; the oldest was Mr Pybus, a widower of seventy who spent each winter on the Costa del Sol. She often felt grateful to her school for turning her out proficient in so many languages, and she had little doubt that, if she was prepared to go anywhere, she'd find a proper job. But nothing could be done about that until the house had been sold.

One evening in July, when she was making supper and listening as usual to the radio (they were talking about the two hundredth anniversary of the French Revolution), Frances burst in.

'Mum, I've got a job!'

'You haven't!' Frances had taken her final exams last week and she and her friends had been going round moaning that they'd probably be unemployed for the rest of their lives. She switched off the radio. 'Tell me all about it'.

Frances was pink and her eyes were shining with excitement; she looked as she had before the disaster. 'Well, Mum, you know Mrs Davies?' Helena didn't actually know her but she nodded. 'She's been talking to me a lot about the future, and she's got this friend called Bryony Crompton'.

'Yes?'

'Bryony something else now. She and Mrs Davies were great friends at art college. She's Welsh, her husband's Catalan and they run a sculpture gallery in Barcelona. Only they come home to see her family every year. She's quite old, I mean old to have babies, but she concentrated on her career till she was thirty-five. They've got a gorgeous little boy called Juan, who's two, and a baby girl'.

Frances choked over her milk shake and her mother patted her on the back.

'Did you meet the children?'

'Yes, I've just been having tea with them. Well, Bryony's going to continue working part-time in this gallery, but her nanny just left and she wants a new one, preferably British. Mrs Davies introduced me to her and we got on brilliantly. She explained that I speak Spanish, and that I used to look after Robin, and she said this is my chance to live in Barcelona for a while and soak myself in the art world. I'll have most evenings free, and two full days a week, and Bryony's seen my portfolio and says it's good and I must go on working. And the little boy liked me very much, which helped. Isn't that amazing?'

Helena was speechless.

'You see, Mum, I've been so worried about going on the dole. Sitting round all day and feeling unwanted, which is why people get depressed. Or serving in a supermarket. I'm twenty-two now, it's high time I left home'.

'Yes', Helena said slowly. Frances was young for her age - when she herself was twenty-two she'd been Johnno's mother - but she couldn't remain a baby. It wasn't a marvellous job, but such jobs were not usually offered to girls from Frances's background. This way she would be living in a family, recommended by her teacher, and she would have time and encouragement to work on her art. If she had stayed at home and got some dead-end job, she might well have broken down again. 'Well, I suppose I should meet Bryony and have a chat'.

'Oh, Mum, you do *fuss*', Frances said.

She did her best to keep smiling as Frances was loaded into the train with her bags and stuck her fair head out of the window to say goodbye. She was going to meet her employers in London and fly with them to Barcelona the same night. It was a morning in early August, cool and sunny, and the station with filled with young people with rucksacks coming and going.

'I'll send you a postcard, Mum. Honestly, I'm thrilled to bits. And I'll be back in a year, at latest'.

It was all she could do not to weep but Frances herself was exalted, radiant. The train moved off and they waved to each other for as long as possible. Then it was out of sight.

As she turned away and began to walk towards the exit she remembered that it was in another station, ten years ago, that she had decided she would not be free to commit suicide until Frances was grown up. Well, there was no danger of that now. But she felt very disoriented, and it seemed impossible to get back into the car and drive home. She walked down the hill, past the Old House and into town.

So that was it. If Frances did not break down, and she prayed she wouldn't, the last of her children would have left home and she would be on her own. All her life she had lived with other people, at home and at school, during her short marriage and the long hard years afterwards. And she had always been needed to look after someone, as the eldest in a family of eleven, or as a prefect, or finally a mother. She wasn't needed now, not even to babysit Holly. It was going to be very hard to get used to a change of that magnitude.

She hadn't even chosen where to live; it had been first with Reg, and then with her mother. Well, when the house was sold she could presumably live where she liked. Hereford, near to Richard, or London near to Johnno, the baby and Con. Or perhaps a completely new place, as she could surely teach languages anywhere in the world. But she clung to the few bits of security she had left; Plas Gwyn, and the part-time jobs she'd slowly built up here. It would be a big decision to move away. Yet she wasn't at all sure that she could settle into an ugly little flat in Hereford and say, this is for life.

Because no one really cares, she thought as she turned up the narrow passage towards Cathedral Green. Plenty of people are fond of me, I'm grateful for that, but they have their own lives which I'm not an essential part of. Well, she was not going to scream her pain to the world or make her children feel guilty. She passed the young couples lying entwined on the grass and went into the cathedral.

She wandered round it for the next half hour. As a girl she had been quite religious, though she hadn't practised for years, and after a while she found herself staring at the high east window and sending up some sort of appeal to whatever was there. Show me the next step, don't let the rest of my life be a long sad postscript to the active useful part, give me something to do.

She found herself in the south transept where there was an effigy, centuries old, of a brightly-painted man and woman lying side by side on a bier. The symbol of marriage, from which she seemed to be for ever excluded. Reg was buried in America and she would lie somewhere on this side of the sea. She kept going back in her mind to that marriage, wondering whether she should have done anything different, always reaching the conclusion that she had tried everything she could.

'You're looking very thoughtful, young woman!'

She turned round. Who on earth still thought she was a young woman? An elderly, but fit-looking gentleman with a deep tan was standing behind her.

'Mr Pybus, how nice to see you'.

'Is your language class starting soon?'

'Yes, in September, and I hope you can come'.

'I'll be there', Mr Pybus said. 'After that, I'm going back to Spain for the winter months. Fine place. Well, won't you come and have a cup of tea with me?'

They went to the little cloister cafe and sat down at an isolated table. A door was open to the bishop's garden and hardly anyone else was around.

'I'm a bit distracted', Helena confessed after they had been talking for a while, 'because I've just waved goodbye to my daughter. She's going to Spain, too. I've no idea when I'll see her again'.

'That's your youngest?'

'Yes, the others are all settled'.

Mr Pybus poured another cup of tea and proffered a home-made cake, which she declined.

'All right if I ask you a personal question?' he enquired.

'Of course'.

'Well, I was just wondering - is there a Mr Maynard?'

'Oh, no. Mr Entwistle actually. I went back to my maiden name after we got divorced. No, that ended a long time ago'.

'Ran away with a younger woman, did he?'

'No, in fact she was a few years older than me'.

'Well, in that case', Mr Pybus said, 'I've got a suggestion. As you know, I spend every winter in a little resort on the Med, they send our pensions out after us. It's a nice life, sun and sea and bingo every night. I'm in good health apart from my corns'.

'Mr Pybus, I'm not sure - '.

'Call me Walter. You're a good-looking woman, Helena - too thin, but we can fatten you up with all the steak and chips they fry out there. As you may have guessed, I'm suggesting you might like to marry me. Take some time to think about it. My late wife never had any serious complaints, and I'm an easy-going chap'.

Helena had been struggling to stop him ever since his intentions had become obvious. She said as gently as she could,

'That's very, very kind, but I don't think so'.

Mr Pybus sighed.

'Too old for you, am I?'

'No, but I've tried being married before and it didn't work. I don't really think I'm much good at that sort of relationship'.

'Well', Mr Pybus said, 'tell me if you change your mind'.

'I will'.

She went home with a completely different set of feelings from when she had waved goodbye to Frances. She was flattered, there was no denying that, but she was also a little disturbed. While the old gentleman was speaking she had had a sudden vivid memory of herself and Reg throwing snowballs at each other after dark on the Gornetz Platz, laughing their heads off and crazily in love. It had been the wrong marriage, and she wished someone had warned her against it, but having experienced a real marriage she did not think she would be able to fall back on playing bingo with Mr Pybus. And she couldn't help noticing that he'd suggested it only after he knew that her last child had left home.

I'm sure I haven't broken his heart, she thought as she unlocked the front door of Plas Gwyn. After all, there are plenty of unattached women in his age-group. He's seventy, isn't he? - old enough to be my father.

Oh, God, Daddy would have been seventy-seven this year.

She closed the door on the empty house and wept.

The next week was very difficult. Frances rang to say that she had arrived safely in Barcelona, but every day around four o' clock she found herself putting the tea things out for two and expecting her to come home. The nights dragged slowly too, in the house which was now much too big for her. She telephoned a local charity and asked if she could give a roof to some young homeless people, but to her surprise they advised strongly against it. And after all, the house didn't belong to her, and might soon be sold. In the end she went to stay for a week with Con.

They had a good time. Con had just finished the life of Mary Wollstonecraft and was working hard in the British Library on Mary Shelley, but they breakfasted together and found something interesting to do every evening. Helena visited Katie and the baby (Johnno was in Germany); she also looked at the prices of flats in London, and was appalled. Towards the end of the visit she made a suggestion.

'Con, I've been thinking. We're neither of us getting any younger, and one day soon I'll have to move out of Plas Gwyn. Why don't we join forces - get a larger place - and I'll do the housekeeping? You don't like it, and I can also look round for a job to pay my way'.

'I must see to the coffee', Con said hastily.

While she was in the kitchen, she thought it over. No two sisters could have got on better than they did; she didn't think they had quarrelled in the whole of their lives and she'd thoroughly enjoyed the last week. It was pleasant to come home from the library and find a hot meal waiting and her clothes ironed, pleasant to chat in the evenings and have someone to go about with. But in the long term, she was happiest on her own. Even when Des had been living here it had sometimes felt cramped, and she liked this flat, she didn't want to live anywhere else. And then there were Helena's children. They'd be ringing all the time, or calling on her or wanting to be put up, and she really didn't think she could stand all those comings and goings. It was the thought of the children that finally decided her.

'Sorry, Len', she said when she returned with the tray, 'but I'm a hermit crab, I don't think it would suit either of us'.

Helena felt an awful sinking of the heart but she said quickly, 'Of course. It was just a thought'.

'But I've got an idea', Con went on as she poured two tiny cups of black coffee, and reached for the chocolate box. 'I got it when Felix told me that he and Felicity are having a big bash this autumn for their fortieth birthday. It's going to be very classy, I believe - a string quartet, readings by well-known actors, the lot. Well, I can't equal that, but has it occurred to you, Len, that we're going to be fifty on Guy Fawkes Day?'

'Oh, dear, Con, I've been trying not to think about it'.

'But I have, and I think that we ought to celebrate. Margot is due back from India on the first of November. We'll have a magnificent party, here in this flat, and we'll ask absolutely everyone we know. Family, and people from the school - I was never as keen on it as you but I'd like the surviving mistresses to see how we've turned out. We can't ask Annersley - she's too old - but we'll ask everyone else and see who comes. I'll arrange it all. I've got some plans for the New Year, too'.

And it was a magnificent party. Con had decorated the flat with golden roses and the caterers had provided a splendid buffet, a huge cake with fifty candles, and champagne. For the first time in nearly thirty years, all eleven Maynards were under the same roof. Phil, looking every inch the successful career woman, had travelled from Brussels, Charles from Durham, Cecil and Hywel from Wales. Felix had brought the young actress who had been at his side on his fortieth birthday; Helena wondered if at last he was going to settle down. She feared that Felicity wouldn't; even here, her eyes were travelling restlessly around the room, hunting for a man. And poor Geoff, who had been one of the victims of the eighties. He hadn't worked for years, and she'd thought of offering him a home, but he was currently shacked up with a tough-looking girl who had three children by various men. Richard was there with his girl friend (he'd still said nothing about marriage), and Johnno, Katie and their baby Holly, who enchanted everyone by trying to pull herself up on the furniture. But it was really a party for the older generation.

The Chalet School was represented. Rosamund Lilley was there with her husband, and Ruey Richardson, now a widow, and a whole contingent from Guernsey. Miss Wilmot and Miss Ferrars turned up, retired years ago but still cheerful, and Grizel Cochrane, who looked as discontented as she always had. Gillian Young had flu but had sent a sheaf of golden chrysanthemums. Frances had also sent flowers from Barcelona.

Margot, only just off the plane, seemed slightly stunned by all this splendour but relaxed when she'd got some good German wine inside her and began to look quite interested. Then the champagne was opened and poured into tulip-shaped glasses, and Johnno stood up.

'Ladies and gentlemen, I'd like to say a few words'. Only his mother knew that he'd probably been up half the night worrying about this speech. 'We've met here to celebrate three remarkable women'. Helena wondered why his eyes kept straying to the door. 'My aunt Con is working on a book which I think, because I've seen it, is going to be one of the great biographies, and my aunt Margot is in the front line of the fight against TB. Both of them helped a lot when we were growing up, Con by giving us presents and treats which we wouldn't otherwise have had and Margot by showing us an example of unselfish service, but I know they won't mind if I say that I'm especially grateful to Mum. It's no secret that my father left home when we were all very young and if she'd also walked away from us, as she must often have been tempted to do, we could so easily have become drop-outs or delinquents. I can speak for my brother and sisters as well as myself when I say that anything we may have achieved, we owe to her'. Richard thumped the table in appreciation. 'So please, remember that the best years are still to come, and raise your glasses to - the Maynard triplets'.

The toast was drunk. There was a great deal of laughter and congratulations. Then the bell rang, and feet could be heard thudding up Con's stairs.

'Ah', Johnno said. 'This is my birthday present'.

The door burst open. Maggs burst in, much browner than when they had last seen her, and behind her, rushing straight at Helena with arms held out, her beloved Robin.

'It was a great secret', Maggs said. She'd been hugged, given champagne, asked a hundred questions. 'Johnno and Con and Spike's parents bought our tickets -'.

'Not me', said Con. 'My surprise is still to come'.

'Well, anyway, they got together behind your back. We're going to be in England for three weeks. They're really nice people, I mean Spike's parents, and you're invited to stay with them whenever you like. And Johnno was having kittens because our plane was delayed and he thought we'd miss the party'.

'Maggs, you look wonderfully well! And Robin's *huge*'. Robin had curled up in Helena's lap, clamped his arms round her neck and immediately gone to sleep. 'But what have you done with Spike?'

'Oh, he'll manage', Maggs said callously. 'He's staying with his parents - says he's glad to have a break from *my* cooking - and he's going to paint the spare room while we're away. The next step is to have another baby. No, I'm not pregnant yet'.

'Maggs, I'm so glad - '.

'So you'll absolutely have to come to Australia', Maggs concluded triumphantly.

Grizel, who was watching the laughing dark-haired girl from the other side of the room, shook her head in disbelief and said - 'the image of Jo'.

There were more toasts. Felix took photographs of his three sisters and Robin and Holly, who looked at each other in bewilderment, were placed together in a big armchair and photographed too. The evening ended with a firework party in the garden and then people began to drift away. Maggs stayed for several hours longer, making plans. They were going to spend a few days in London and then go back to Plas Gwyn with Helena. She couldn't wait to see how much Robin remembered and what his little friends thought of his Australian accent. At last Richard left to catch his train and Maggs and the two sleepy children were driven off by Johnno and Katie; it was impossible to squeeze any more people into Con's flat.

'Right', said Con when the triplets were alone together, 'I'll tell you how we're going to celebrate our birthday'.

'We *have* just celebrated', Margot said.

'There's a second half. Len, I know you're going to be busy while Maggs is here, and did you also say that Frances was coming for Christmas?'

'Yes, she is'. Helena smiled. 'The family is having a week

in England, so she'll be spending it at Plas Gwyn and you must come too. And, what do you think, Frances has a boy friend! He's a Catalan student, called Jorge, and she *says* he's lovely. Only she also says that they're not going to rush into anything. I hope she's taken warning from Maggs'.

'Right. Well, we'll all go for Christmas to Plas Gwyn - the last Christmas, I'm afraid - and then you and I and Margot are flying to Europe. It's my treat; I've no one else to spend my money on. We'll go to the Tyrol, where it all began, and see if the chalet is still standing, and then we'll travel on to the Oberland, see in the New Year at Berne, and find out what's left on the Gornetz Platz. We'll ski, and look up old friends, and have the time of our lives. Just the three of us. What do you think?'

'I can't - ' Margot began.

'Yes, you can, Margot. Let your hair down. And you, Len, you deserve a treat too'.

'It might be interesting', Margot said slowly.

'I think so'. Con got up and began to pour out the last of the champagne. The clocks were striking midnight. 'Drink this; it'll be flat in the morning. You see, as I get older, I begin to feel I'd like to have a look at my roots. Just to see if they're still there. And after all, we have got something to celebrate. Just think, when we were born Hitler was sweeping across Europe and it must have seemed a crazy time to have children. And now Europe is opening up again'.

'Hm'. Margot was thinking of the TB hospital she had left in India. 'Everyone's talking about a new era of peace and freedom, but I think it may all end in tears'.

'Don't be a wet-blanket, Margot. We're going to celebrate the dawn of the 1990s. We'll have a great time'.

That was how they came to be on the ski slopes of the Gornetz Platz, at the beginning of a new decade.

THE END OF THE NINETEEN EIGHTIES

EPILOGUE: JANUARY - MARCH 1990

Chapter 36

New Year's Day

A bitter wind was blowing through the streets and squares, whipping plastic bags and empty coke cans along the pavements, rattling the windows of shops which were all shut for the bank holiday. Nobody about; they must all be recovering from New Year's Eve or in front of their TVs, so there was no one to observe a middle-aged man walking unsteadily through the town centre and obviously crying. He hated himself for his weakness. If he bumped into anyone he knew, or some stranger asked whether he was all right, he could say it was the wind stinging his eyes. But there was no one to bump into; it was four o' clock in the afternoon and it felt like a ghost town.

There'd been an almighty open-air party last night. Broken bottles and containers of cold chips were scattered all over the paving-stones, and it was obvious that more than one person had been sick. The eighties were gone, good riddance, but he himself couldn't join in the general rejoicing. The good years are over, he thought, from now on it's downhill. He felt for his keys, with freezing hands. He was not keen to go home; his children had brought in a crowd of friends and were carrying on with last night's celebrations; his workplace, closed like everywhere else, was the one conceivable place where he could cry in privacy. *Crybaby*, a mocking voice from the past said.

But there was something in a doorway looking like a pile of old clothes; he checked and saw it was an unconscious man of about his own age. Not dead, surely? He tried his pulse, but the man just cursed, opened a bloodshot eye and passed out. He stood irresolute; he'd seen plenty of this in the Third World but it still shocked him when it was in his home city. Eventually he took out a five-pound note and shoved it in the man's pocket. Perhaps he'd have the sense to buy a hot meal, or perhaps he would just drink it. Well, he thought tiredly, if the poor bastard wants to drink himself to death why can't he? I'm not going to wake him up and say it's fun to be alive.

He pushed open the street door. Most of the people who worked here had not been in for several days and there was a stack of mail. He glanced through it, circulars and special offers, crude Star of Bethlehem pictures and last week's free newspaper with a thick black headline:

LOCAL WOMAN HAS TRIPLETS.

That touched a faint chord, a long way back. He climbed the staircase, which was dark and disagreeable, passing several locked doors until he reached the third floor. He'd never worried about setting up shop in a smarter building. He unlocked his door; here there was plenty of light, which was what mattered, and extraordinary views. But the light was fading, the long January night would soon begin and the place was thick with dust. He must do something about it soon, but he was too tired.

Now that he'd shut himself in and couldn't be observed, the tears seemed to have dried up. The symptoms were the same as always, a splitting headache which had now lasted for three days, and he did a quick calculation and decided he could risk some more aspirin. He shook out three pills and then got the bottle of Bristol cream sherry which he kept for visitors and poured a tumbler. The bottle was half-full. He thought, as he sat down at his untidy desk, that he could just go on drinking and swallowing pills for the next few hours to kill the pain.

Sure enough, it was already getting duller. He felt for his cigarettes - he'd been a non-smoker for twenty-five years but taken it up again in the last months of 1988 - and lit one. Breathing tar into his lungs he thought, this is no good, I'd do better if I could talk to someone, or cry it out.

KEEP A STIFF UPPER LIP, BOY, REMEMBER THAT YOU'RE AN ENGLISHMAN.

His father, dead for years but still with the power to terrify.

The voices from the past rushed in and blocked out all others.

YOU LITTLE DEVIL, I'LL HAVE THE SKIN OFF YOUR BACK FOR THIS.

He'd learned to keep that upper lip in place, or be torn to pieces at the conventionally unpleasant boarding school he'd attended. If anybody were to come in now, even a close friend, and ask him how he felt, he would of course smile and say he was fine. Only I'm not, he thought; I'm finished, just a shadow like all the other dead people who walked the streets of Bristol and were snapped in passing by the photographers of the last century.

The sherry and the pills.

He moved his hand but then thought with a spurt of anger, no, I won't drink myself into a stupor, or overdose and be found here dead when someone finally breaks in. It's disgusting and humiliating. I am not going to be like that man down there.

Quite dark now. He threw the aspirin bottle across the room and put his arms on his desk, lowered his head and tried again to cry. Only now that he was free to howl and rage without a witness, the tears wouldn't come. He stayed like that for a long time, with the pain in his head never quite going away, hearing the odd shout or snatch of festive music from the street below.

LOCAL WOMAN HAS TRIPLETS.

He'd known the triplets well since he was - how old? - eight or nine; his parents weren't much interested in having him around in the holidays so he often spent Christmas or the summer staying with or near them, first on the Welsh borders and then in the Bernese Oberland. The family liked young people and always made him feel welcome. Dr Maynard, a nice chap, that had been a tragedy. And Mrs Maynard, who had an unmistakable presence; you might laugh behind her back but once seen she was never forgotten. The babies and toddlers in the background, and those three lovely girls. Two who had been good friends, and one whom he had been in love with, crazily and silently, a besotted teenager. But her life was planned out and had no room for him. They'd gone around in a group, eating apples from the Plas Gwyn orchard, playing board games when the valley was in deep snow, skiing and going for enormous mountain walks in the Oberland.

Could you get back that time? Someone said that the past is another country; perhaps, if you knew the trick, you could get into your time-machine and find them all living as they always had, his parents and childhood friends, and Jack and Jo Maynard, and the triplets with their future looking bright. It was years since he'd seen any of them; he had no idea how to begin to trace them. Perhaps they were all married. He knew that Margot had left the Order, some time ago. Crazy to think of them at all, when he had enough urgent problems; perhaps he should just finish what was in the bottle and blot out the pain.

No. He got up, telling himself that he was probably being extremely stupid, but at least it was something to occupy his mind after two years' continuous suffering. After all, what had he to lose? As he went down the dark stairs, wondering if he was going to slip and break a leg, he kept repeating to himself, it's my only chance, I've got to find the triplets.

Chapter 37

Miss Annersley Turns Ninety

The triplets returned from the Oberland in the second week of January 1990. They'd skied, gone shopping in the towns which had changed out of all recognition since their time, looked up old friends and played the game of 'do you remember?' until they could play no more. It had been the best holiday of their lives but when the time came they were glad to be back in England. Con was anxious to get on with her biography, which was due to be published in autumn 1991. Her sisters had read the first few chapters and agreed that it was good. Margot was not expecting to be called abroad just yet but she had temporary work, with TB patients in London, which would keep her fully stretched. Over lunch in Con's flat, before they all went their separate ways, Helena raised the subject of Miss Annersley.

'Do you know, she's actually going to be ninety on March 31st? I found out quite by accident; the warden answered last time I rang and we got talking. She isn't planning any celebrations. She's got no family at all, not even a nephew or niece, and of course she outlived all her friends. I think we ought to do something'.

'Amazing', said Con. 'We always used to think she was immensely old, but of course she was just an active middle-aged person, like I am now - oh, dear! Tough old bird. So what do you want to do, Len?'

'Well, I thought we could go down to Exeter and arrange a special lunch so she doesn't feel she's been forgotten. It's Saturday, a good day to travel. Could we put it in our diaries now, because it would mean a lot to her to see all three of us?'

'I'll have to go abroad if there's an emergency', Margot said.

'I know, but if there isn't, can you come?'

It was agreed. Then they parted, and Helena caught the train from Paddington, thinking, as she always did when she was at that station, of what she had nearly done. Miss Annersley would have thought her very weak, she reflected. She'd been on a high for more than two months, first the party, then spending Christmas with her daughters, and then the wonderful holiday, but it was now time to get back to normal. Even though for the first time she was not much looking forward to going back to Plas Gwyn.

Two things happened that winter. The old car finally gave up the ghost; a few weeks of travelling to work by bus in the cold weather convinced her that it was high time she moved into town. And they finally got an offer for the house, after more than a year. A centre for disturbed children was to be opened in the countryside and Plas Gwyn, with its many bedrooms and big grounds, seemed ideal. Mike shook his head over the price but conceded that it was probably the best they could get. The purchasers assured her that she could stay on for the next few months until they were ready to start renovation. They wanted to knock down walls, modernise the ancient bathroom, change an awful lot of things.

One Sunday in February she was doing the bedrooms when Margot, who had been staying for the weekend, burst in.

'Have you heard? Nelson Mandela is out; he's going to be on the box in a minute. Come and see'.

Helena came to watch, and thought that her own problems seemed very trivial in comparison. Their meal grew cold as they talked.

Margot's eyes were blazing; she looked at least twenty years younger. 'Doesn't it show that good things can happen *sometimes*? God knows, I never thought the old man would get out alive. This means that I can go back to South Africa'.

Helena's heart sank. 'For good?'

'Oh, no, I like being available to go wherever I'm needed. But I'll certainly stay for a while and check on the TB situation, and look up my friends in Black Sash'.

Both her sisters knew where they were going, Helena thought; each had a job which would keep her content for the rest of her life, only she was still floundering. She'd built her house on shifting sands and would somehow have to come to terms with the aftermath. Perhaps she should systematically have looked for another man after Reg - some women would certainly have done so - but, remembering the awful problems so many children had with stepfathers, she decided it had been for the best. She began to check out full-time teaching jobs, always bearing in mind how far they would be from her family, but she had not made much progress by the eve of Miss Annersley's birthday, when Con and Margot drove down. It would only be a flying visit. Con had a lunch party on Sunday in London, and Margot an AIDS conference in Manchester, but they'd looked up the route and decided they could comfortably get to the home in the suburbs of Exeter where their ex-headmistress now lived.

Although she said nothing to her sisters, Con was thinking seriously. Lately, Kermit had got in the habit of dropping in for drinks and to discuss the launch of *The Two Marys*, and yesterday he'd ended up telling her about his divorce. His wife Lucy, who was much younger, had recently gone off with another man, and now she was expecting a baby so there was no going back. 'She always said she never wanted children', Kermit complained, 'I went along with it, and now she says I'm middle-aged and rather boring and have no paternal instincts. I feel I can't do anything right, though I *am* a bore, probably'. He had then startled her by raising the subject of marriage.

'I mean it, Con. We could run the agency together; I've never met anyone who knew so much about books. And of course you'd still have plenty of time for your own work. I always liked you, you know'.

Con couldn't get it out of her mind; it seemed unthinkable at first but, after that long talk, she'd begun to suspect that Kermit was a nicer and more sensitive man than she had given him credit for. And they would never run out of things to talk about. And it would be quite fun to surprise all those people who thought she was too old to get married. He had a roomy house in Hampstead with a second study overlooking the heath; Lucy wasn't taking anything as she was the one who had walked out. There remained the fact that Kermit didn't make her heart turn over, as a few men had done in the past. But could any woman really expect, in the awful modern phrase, to have it all?

So she had hesitated, and told him that she had to get the visit to Miss Annersley over before she could think about it. The triplets sat up very late talking, and were just about to get in the car after breakfast when the phone rang. Helena went back into the house to answer.

A man's voice, sounding a long way off, with the background noise which indicated a callbox.

'Hello, I'm looking for a family called Maynard, who used to live at Plas Gwyn'.

'Yes, this is Helena Maynard'.

'Sorry, I'm about to be cut off. My name is - '.

The line went dead.

'Do come on, Len', Con said impatiently. 'It's probably someone selling double-glazing, and we're already late'.

They waited for a few more minutes and then left. As they headed towards the motorway, the phone began ringing again.

Miss Annersley's hair was white and thin, and she now wore very strong spectacles. Helena had not seen her for fifteen years, and Con and Margot not for much longer than that, but she knew at once which was which. She also suffered quite badly from arthritis and had trouble getting across the room, but her memory was extraordinary and she could still name a great many of the girls who had passed through her hands. She said that she got great pleasure from listening to her radio, and there were special large-print books which she read omnivorously. They hadn't been able to find any other former Chalet girls to make the long journey with them, but they had alerted those they knew, and several cards had come that day. They had coffee, and then a good lunch, paid for by the triplets, and Miss Annersley was persuaded to take a glass of champagne. Later in the day she'd be entertaining the other occupants of the home to tea.

'It's so kind of you to have come all this way. I hadn't intended to make any fuss about my birthday, because I have no family, you know, who might have wished to remember it. I had only the one brother, Herbert, and he was killed in 1918. But it's made my day to see you three so happy and successful'.

Con felt a sudden awful pang. What would Miss Annersley think, she wondered, about Helena's divorce, or her own affairs with Des and others, or Margot getting arrested at Greenham and walking out of the Church? Not to mention those twenty-seven silly novels. She said impulsively, 'Aunt Hilda, perhaps it was easier for women of your generation - '.

'Not in the least', Miss Annersley said energetically. 'My dear, I'm one of the very few people who still remember the Great War. Women of my age lost their husbands and fiancés in vast numbers and in many cases had to go through life alone, with only work and the friendship of other women to sustain them. Whereas young girls like you' - all the triplets felt a slight pang at being called girls - 'have so many opportunities'.

'But we haven't - '.

She was unable to finish the sentence. She knew both her sisters were thinking that they hadn't done what their mother expected and been happy wives with large families; they hadn't, not one of them, brought a husband along to show off.

'My dear Constance', Miss Annersley said bracingly, 'it's always easy to fret about what we haven't done, but you've all done so well. Helena bringing up all those children to be good citizens, and remaining a nice person in spite of everything. And you writing that splendid biography, which I hope to read if I'm still here. And Margot working so selflessly for the Third World. If your parents could see you today, make no mistake, they would be extremely proud of you'.

They left in mid-afternoon, not to tire the old lady before she got busy with her other guests. They were all glad to have seen her, conscious that they probably wouldn't see her again. Con was still thoughtful as she swung east up the M5.

'I wonder if there was ever a man in Miss Annersley's life'.

'Oh, dear', Helena said, 'it seems almost blasphemous to think like that'.

'Oh, I don't mean a full-blooded affair, but for all we know - her brother might have had a friend and he might have been killed, and they could have been fond of each other without getting formally engaged. I got the impression, from the way she talked about the war, that there was something personal'.

'Why should she have bothered with men?' Margot demanded from the back of the car. 'She rose to a pretty high position without one. I really think the bastards only get between you and your work'.

'Well, one thing's certain', Con said, 'she's never going to tell anyone. That generation was brought up not to talk about feelings, and perhaps that's more dignified than letting it all hang out, as we do now'.

'I hope I'll be half as good a teacher', Helena said soberly.

'Have you decided where to go?'

'Not yet, but there's plenty of time before the autumn. I'll try to get a little two-bedroomed flat and you can stay with me, Margot, when you're in England. And other times I can have the children and grandchildren. In a few months I'm sure it'll all come clear'.

It was still light when they got back to Plas Gwyn. They all felt rather sad when they saw the SOLD notice on the gate, but the garden was full of daffodils and the house still looked attractive, if weatherbeaten. They went inside with relief and Helena started making tea.

They'd just taken their coats off, and settled down in the front room to discuss how long Con and Margot could stay, when the gate clicked. A pleasant-looking middle-aged man with a camera slung round his neck was walking up the short path towards the front door.

Con said, 'I don't believe it', and hurried out.

Her sisters stood up in some surprise. She came back and said, 'I've brought an old friend'.

The man did look familiar, now they could see him properly. His face lit up as he caught sight of the other two women.

'Len! I'm so glad to have found you at home. And Margot'.

'Nobody's called me that for years', Helena smiled, while Margot said in astonishment, 'Tony Barras!'

Chapter 38

Like Hearing the Grass Grow and the Squirrel's Heart Beat

'We've been touring the Black Mountains', Tony said, 'taking photos, and we're staying at the Green Dragon overnight. So I thought I'd stroll over and see if you still lived here. It's been a long time, hasn't it?'

'I don't think I've seen you since Clem's wedding', said Helena, 'and that was in 1979'.

Con was looking at him surreptitiously while the others talked. The years had been kind to Tony; his fair hair was only lightly touched with grey and he hadn't put on weight like most men of his age. Then her eyes strayed to the photograph over the mantel and she reflected that, of the three sisters, she was the one who had worn best. Helena still looked nice, in a subdued fashion, as a young person might wish their mother to look on their graduation day. Margot looked quite battered.

Bits of news were exchanged. He expressed surprise that Miss Annersley was still alive. They had tea, in the blue and yellow china from the Tyrol, and then the talk went back to the photograph.

'It's amazing', Tony said, 'how everything came right for that particular picture. I was only sixteen when I took it, and it's never been exhibited. I suppose we couldn't go back to the same place, and do a retake?'

'Oh, help', Con said, 'the contrast would be too cruel'.

'I'm sure it wouldn't'.

They went out into the back garden and managed to find the identical plum tree. Tony, who had asked their permission to smoke and been doing so continuously for the last quarter hour, got them to pose in the same positions and spent quite a long time getting everything right. When he finally let them go they wandered around a little and looked across the fence to the orchards below Carn Beg; sharp green on the apple trees, patches of white blossom on the sloes and the sun beginning to set.

'Do you remember', Margot said, 'how Mary-Lou crawled

through the hedge while we were all trying to catch tadpoles in that pond, with Anna? That was the first time we met her'.

Tony looked quickly at Helena, but she smiled.

'It's all right. I haven't been angry with Mary-Lou for years'.

'Do you ever see her?' asked Con.

'Well, as you know she and Clem were great friends, but they quarrelled. I bumped into her on the tube the summer before last, and she asked me to get off when she did and come back to her flat for a drink. But Chris - my wife - was very ill at the time, so it wasn't possible. I haven't seen her since'.

They began to walk back towards the house.

'How is Christine?' Con asked politely. 'I hope she's better?'

Tony's face changed.

'Sorry, I thought you knew - well, no reason why you should but there was an announcement in the papers. Christine died'.

They all stopped walking; Con felt particularly shocked. Only a moment ago she'd been feeling quite amused at the thought of Mary-Lou trying to do to Tony's wife what she'd done to Helena, and now this nice woman, whom she had always most unreasonably resented, was dead. Yet Tony didn't look too bad, she thought defensively. Perhaps he had got over it by now; perhaps it had not been a happy marriage.

'I'm so sorry', she said, 'but you did say "we" '.

'I meant myself and my son. He's at the Green Dragon watching TV. Christine died nine months ago. I should have told you before but there's always that awful moment when people are stuck for words'.

Helena was asking him quietly about his children. Tony said his son was at Bristol University and was passionate about photographing animals, and his daughter worked with a housing charity in Newcastle. They went in, and Helena gave them some of the madeira which Johnno had brought back from Portugal and told them to sit down while she prepared supper.

'Let me help', Tony said. 'Nick and I have become quite

efficient cooks'.

They laid the table together. Still talking - they hadn't by any means finished with 'do you remember?' - the four of them shared a light omelette and salad and then Margot, who had been fidgeting for some time, got up.

'Come on, Con; I can't afford to miss my train'.

Con also stood up, more reluctantly.

'Well, Tony, it's been very nice to see you again'.

'I've got a conference in Manchester', Margot explained, 'the links between TB and AIDS. Con's dropping me at Hereford. See you one day'.

Tony said something about staying to help with the washing-up; he seemed in no hurry to go. The two sisters waved, leaving the others standing in the lighted doorway.

'That man likes Len', Con said, as she began to nudge the car down the track.

Margot was thinking of something else and said, 'What?'

'I said that Tony Barras is interested in Len. Probably always has been. And the sickening thing is that he's really attractive. Oh, well, I suppose she's more the wifely type'.

'Do get a move on', Margot said. 'There's a Sunday morning lecture by Daphne Clark; she's the best person in her field and I don't want to miss - '.

'Margot, did you hear what I was saying? Our sister is probably getting a lucky break, for the first time in twenty-five years, and all you can talk about is your conference!'

'Oh, yes, I see. But AIDS is more important, surely?'

Con sighed, and concentrated on driving down the dark and empty road. Kermit was escorting her to the literary lunch tomorrow; she didn't intend to decide anything in a hurry but she would give it a chance.

'That's what I meant. You and I, Margot, are more interested in other things'.

They had been talking for hours. Tony was anxious to catch up on her news and they also talked about Clem, who was living in France, and about his job, which involved taking photographs all over the world. Occasionally he said, 'Am I in the way?', but Helena urged him to stay on; she was sure he wanted to be with someone. Unlike Con, she did not believe that he had got over the death of his wife. He was too thin, he smoked too hard, there were tired lines under his eyes when he stopped smiling; Tony was getting older like everyone else. He needed looking after; so, probably, did his teenage son, and she would have liked to do it. Often in the last few months she'd thought that she would have been happy to share a house with any reasonable person, male or female, just to prop each other up against the loneliness. But she had had a low opinion of herself for years; it did not occur to her that he might have come all this way to see her.

After a while he began to talk about Christine.

'It was ovarian cancer. The worst sort, because it creeps up silently. By the time I persuaded her to see a doctor it was already too late. They tried various things, but I knew and she knew that she was going to die. It went on for almost two years. I watched her waste away; by the end she looked like someone in the last stages of famine. She didn't deserve that'.

'I only met Christine once', Helena said, 'but I could see that she was - '.

'She was like you', Tony said unexpectedly. 'She put us first and herself last. She was so damn worried about the children, after she got too weak to look after them. Kate was away at Bangor University, Nick still at school, and I tried to shield them from what was going on. But they became very withdrawn. I can't talk to them now; at least I can about everyday things but they don't tell me how they're feeling. They seem to have bounced back; I haven't'.

There was hardly any light in the room, only one shaded lamp so that the photograph of the three teenage girls was in darkness, but she was fairly sure that he was fighting back tears. He went on, 'After she died everyone expected me to be relieved. You're allowed to look sad for a few weeks and after that people don't want to know. I went round doing all the normal things - working, answering letters, trying to hold things together for Kate and Nick - and all the time it felt unreal. You know what it's like - well, you've been there. Only I don't know how you came out at the other end. You just pretend everything's fine, pretend you're not suffering - '.

Something obviously had to be done. Helena stood up, crossed the room and sat down next to him. It seemed like the longest walk of her life. She said, 'Tony, it's all right to cry', and then supported him in her arms with his head on her shoulder while he cried and cried.

It felt weird, after all those years. She had never seen a grown man cry, and it obviously didn't come easily; he kept saying he was sorry and she kept repeating that it didn't matter. In the end he let her go and wiped his eyes.

'I haven't done that for about thirty years'.

'Well' Helena said, 'perhaps you should have'.

'It's the British public school tradition, isn't it?' He added with difficulty, 'Len, I didn't know about your little girl. I thought something was wrong, that day we met at Clem's wedding, but I didn't find out until a few weeks ago. I was so sorry'.

Helena's eyes filled with tears and she said pleadingly, 'I can't talk about Tessa. I will tell you some time, but not now'.

Tony moved abruptly and she had a wild idea that he was going to kiss her. She simply didn't know how she would respond. He went on, 'I saw you looking ill and miserable, and it haunted me. I'd always hoped that you were all right. I loved Christine; I would never have - but for months after that, I couldn't get you out of my mind'.

'But why should you care - ?'

'That's a long story', Tony said. 'I suppose it goes back to when we were all teenagers, and I was in love with you'.

'I had no idea', Helena said.

'No, I was very careful to keep it quiet. You see, everyone knew that you were going to marry Reg'.

She thought back to herself as she had been at sixteen. Perhaps it had been obtuse of her not to have noticed. But Tony had been a schoolboy, Reg a confident young professional man.

There had been no contest.

'Reg is dead now, isn't he?'

She came back to the present. 'Yes. But we hadn't spoken for years before that'.

'And were you upset?'

'More than I expected to be, but no, the sad thing is that I wasn't really'.

Another silence.

'Did you ever think of getting married again?'

She could laugh it off, say that she had never thought of it or that it had been against her religion or some other compromise. After a few moments she spoke the exact truth, 'I wasn't against it, but I just thought it was very unlikely to happen'.

'It could, if you wanted me', said Tony.

The Maynards' grandfather clock was ticking through what felt like a long silence. Helena was thinking how, years earlier, she had taken almost no notice of a woman she saw every day, and that woman had died. In the same way, she had known Tony quite well and yet never really noticed him, although if it had occurred to her to compare him with Reg that could have made all the difference to her life. He was hiding behind his camera in those days, revealing nothing. To know what was going on in the mind of all those you met would be like hearing the grass grow or the squirrel's heart beat.

'I couldn't be a substitute for Christine', she said soberly.

'No. I wasn't suggesting that'.

'What are you suggesting?'

'Oh, just that we should get to know each other better. Come and see my studio in Bristol. Meet my children, and I'll meet yours. Or let me take you to France to visit Clem; she was always fond of you. I'll show you the Loire valley'.

Helena tried to laugh.

'Tony, I was *fifty* last year - '.

'So was I'.

'I'm trying to say, you could marry some girl in her twenties, and no one would think anything of it'.

'You mean someone of my daughter's age?' Tony suggested. 'That's all very well, but I wouldn't know how to talk to her, and I could always talk to you'. He put his arm round her and she did not repulse him. 'Helena, you're frightened of something, aren't you?'

'Perhaps', Helena admitted, 'but I won't tell you what it is just yet'. Suddenly it seemed quite amazing to feel his cheek, warm and slightly bristly, against hers. 'If we can take things slowly - '.

'Well, of course we can, my dear girl'.

They wandered out into the garden, holding hands, when it was almost midnight. The spring stars looked brilliant, all this distance from the town, the Plough high overhead. The children's swings and the SOLD notice could just be glimpsed through the darkness.

'You'll still be here in the morning?' Tony asked.

'I expect so'.

'And you won't be sorry to leave this house?'

'No. But, Tony', Helena said, as she held tightly to his arm, 'this has all been very sudden, and if you have second thoughts - '.

'Come over to the pub and meet my son, and tomorrow I'll drive you to Bristol and we'll catch up on the last thirty years', Tony said.

THE END